Cover Image Credit/Copyright Attribution: IIIerlok_Xolms/Shutterstock

Your Post has been Removed

Frederik Stjernfelt
Anne Mette Lauritzen

Your Post has been Removed

Tech Giants and Freedom of Speech

Frederik Stjernfelt
Humanomics Center,
Communication/AAU
Aalborg University
Copenhagen
København SV,
København, Denmark

Anne Mette Lauritzen
Center for Information and
Bubble Studies
University of Copenhagen
København S,
København, Denmark

https://doi.org/10.1007/978-3-030-25968-6

Praise for "Your Post has been Removed"

"From my perspective both as a politician and as private book collector, this is the most important non-fiction book of the twenty-first century. It should be disseminated to all European citizens. The learnings of this book and the use we make of them today are crucial for every man, woman and child on earth. Now and in the future."

Jens Rohde, member of the European Parliament for the Alliance of Liberals and Democrats for Europe

"This timely book compellingly presents an impressive array of

information and analysis about the urgent threats the tech giants pose to the robust freedom of speech and access to information that are essential for individual liberty and democratic self-government. It constructively explores potential strategies for restoring individual control over information flows to and about us. Policymakers worldwide should take heed!"

Nadine Strossen, Professor, New York Law School. Author, HATE: Why We Should Resist It with Free Speech, Not Censorship

The only free cheese is in the mouse trap

Russian proverb[1]

[1] The expression is mostly used in Russian but might originate from an apocryphal statement by Margaret Thatcher on communism.

Preface

This book came about during the Spring and Summer of 2018 after we were connected by our mutual friend Vincent Hendricks. He had an eye for our shared interest in the topic: the new circumstances of free speech in an online world.

We would like to thank not only Vincent but also those who, during our research and writing process, have helped us with their information, inspiration, and critical comments: Finn Collin, Benjamin Rud Elberth, Jens-Martin Eriksen, Rolf Hvidtfeldt, Jacob Mchangama, David Budtz Pedersen, Katrine K. Pedersen, Agnete Stjernfelt, Karoline Stjernfelt, Philip Thinggaard, Mads Vestergaard, and Mikael Vetner.

We have enjoyed challenging discussions of this book project with our research colleagues at *Humanomics Center*, University of Aalborg, supported by the Velux Foundations, and *Center for Information and Bubble Studies*, University of Copenhagen, supported by the Carlsberg Foundation.

Thanks to our translator, Philip Thinggaard, for a quick and meticulous effort, as well as our editors, Peter Christensen, Michael Jannerup, and Ties Nijssen, for their solid and efficient collaboration.

For financial support, our thanks go to the Department of Communication and Psychology, Aalborg University, and to the Center for Information and Bubble Studies, University of Copenhagen.

Copenhagen, Denmark
June 2019

Frederik Stjernfelt
Anne Mette Lauritzen

Introduction

This book sheds a critical light on the Internet, more specifically on the new circumstances it is creating for one of the most important basic principles of modern liberal democracies: freedom of speech. The book has specific focus on the tech giants who, to a still larger extent, set the framework for and define the conditions of communication for most users online—Google, Facebook, Twitter, Pinterest, Amazon, etc.

The book came about during hectic times, not so much due to deadlines but because its subject matter unfolded frantically while the book was being written, with new tumultuous events taking place almost every week. Not long before the plan for the book was drafted, when 2017 became 2018, a new law came into effect in Germany. It made it mandatory for social networks such as Facebook and Twitter to assume the government's job of regulating content in accordance with German law. In March 2018, the Cambridge Analytica scandal broke. It exposed how a shady British company specializing in spin and influencing elections had used the data of millions of Facebook users during the US presidential election and the Brexit referendum, among others. In late March, Google announced its plans to spend 300 million USD on a new initiative which featured a "Disinfo Lab" aimed at removing misinformation from the search engine, the purpose being to make sure serious journalism ranks high among Google's search results. In April and May, Facebook's CEO, Mark Zuckerberg, appeared in hearings with the US Congress and the European Parliament, where he managed to dodge most of the critical questions posed to him during the brief sessions. In late April, for the first time ever, Facebook made public its detailed and previously undisclosed guidelines for the removal of content and blacklisting of users. In the middle of May, a Google internal video from 2016 named "The Selfish Ledger" was leaked, featuring Google's take on the future—a society where information is crucial and each individual demoted to a random container, from generation to generation carrying important information on into the future. In late May, the new EU legislation known as General Data Protection Regulation (GDPR) entered into force. In June, the next Facebook scandal popped up: it turned out the company had given access to the enormous amounts of personal user data to more than 60 technological hardware manufacturers, among them Apple, Amazon, BlackBerry, Microsoft, and Samsung. Furthermore, this had apparently taken place despite the fact that Facebook had discovered, back in 2015, the Cambridge Analytica leaks and tightened its control with how data are handed over to app companies via Facebook. Around the same time, the development of a new law was started in France—with different means than the one in Germany, the French law attempts to make it legal to remove "fake news" from the Internet. In July, the European Commission gave Google (Alphabet) the biggest fine in EU history for activities bordering on monopoly. Later that month, Facebook announced that it had learned of a new political campaign using false Facebook pages, probably set up from Russia. In August, the biggest tech giants blocked access to a conspiracy site named *InfoWars*, all of them on the same day. At the end of that same month, it was discovered that since 2011, Iran has been behind a large misinformation campaign on Facebook targeting hundreds of thousands of users across the planet—the campaign managed to spread to both Instagram, Twitter, and YouTube. In October, an internal Google document was leaked, called "The Good Censor" where a new policy of stricter censorship is developed. That same month, a "troll farm" in Saudi Arabia was discovered. In November, it was revealed that Facebook had, during its many crises, hired a spin company in order to discredit competitors and smearing critics. The same month, the company published new directions for censorship, adding to removal the technique of downgrading access to content not actually removed but merely close to the borderline of removal in some way. Last but not least, in the Spring of 2019, increasing political pressure after the March massacre in Christchurch, New Zealand, prompted several states to sharpen removal policies regarding tech giants.

Writing a critical book in the midst of all these events is sort of like riding a tiger. One is never sure if, once published, new events will already have made some of the book's claims and conclusions obsolete. Still, there seems to be no calm Archimedean vantage point in foreseeable future from which to lean back, observe, and analyze the growing problems with the Internet and the tech giants.

Moreover, these issues are in no way simple. The global, transnational nature of the tech giants, combined with their secrecy and lack of openness when it comes to their internal procedures, creates entirely new conditions for freedom of speech. All of this takes place in times when people are getting used to one particular fact: when it comes to understanding the nature of free speech, the classic scenario of state legislation confronted by citizens expressing themselves in certain ways will no longer suffice. Not if we aim to understand free speech, that is. Rather, the scenario is now supplemented by religious and political threats of violence, which contribute to the drawing of the limits to freedom of speech. As the tech giants are turning into monopolies, and as large parts of younger generations use their platforms, on the platforms' terms and conditions, to access both news and the public sphere, the somewhat clandestine policies of these companies have begun to define what can be uttered and what information is available to ordinary citizens. The tech giants, originally noble endeavors carried out by college students aiming to develop free services to enthusiastic users, have long evaded critical scrutiny.

This book gives a brief overview of how they became powerful and wealthy monopolies; the questionable nature of their business models based on users' more or less involuntary consent to sharing personal data; how personalization of services restricts information and creates filter bubbles, confirmation bias and echo chambers; how community standards restrict what can be expressed based on the principle of the lowest common denominator; all of the problems related to the procedures for the removal of content on these services; the ominous collaborations between tech giants and governments towards forming new, automated censorship bypassing court proceedings; the first digital losers, victims of the giants' lucrative business model; disturbances of the public sphere led by the giants' automated algorithms; and much more.

The tech giants are global, and their influence is felt even in countries that fight them—such as China and a number of Muslim nations. But the giants remain based in California and their activities, policies, the debate on them, and the political forces they deal with are primarily American. Therefore, this book must focus primarily on the American situation—for the simple reason that local decisions, events, and social structures in the United States affect the public sphere and free speech elsewhere—not only in Europe but in large parts of the world.

As mentioned, we do not claim that this is a simple matter, and in no way do we claim that there is one simple solution. Tech giants are companies of a wholly new breed: sprawling, tricky to define, and hard to control. We tend to support emerging ideas of some sort of government regulation of the tech giants; as such, measures would call for openness about their operations and ensure freedom, legal rights, and privacy for people who express themselves and share their data. But regulation would also prevent these companies from acting as if the removal of "fake news" and political extremism by a simple automated control procedure could be done without serious consequences for freedom of speech. At the same time, antitrust regulation and control of monopolies are serious medications that should be handed out in careful doses. Or else, the cure may be worse than the disease. At present, only the United States and the European Union possess sufficient political muscle to arm-wrestle the tech giants from a fundamentally democratic and freedom-oriented stance. In the final section of the book, we attempt to come up with some principles for developing regulation of tech giants in an attempt to ensure more freedom for their users.

Contents

About the Authors

Frederik Stjernfelt is a Full Professor of semiotics, intellectual history, and philosophy of science at Aalborg University Copenhagen. His interests also include Peirce studies, political philosophy, and freedom of expression. He is a member of the Royal Danish Society of Sciences and Letters and has published, inter alia, his habilitation Diagrammatology: An Investigation on the Borderlines of Phenomenology, Ontology, and Semiotics (Springer 2007).

Photo Credit: Morten Holtum

Anne Mette Lauritzen is a researcher at the Center for Information and Bubble Studies (CIBS) at the University of Copenhagen and is finalizing her Master's degree in philosophy. Her research interests include intellectual history, human rights, and the philosophy of technology.

Photo Credit: Trine Kobborg

Chapter 1
What Is Freedom of Speech?

It is a well-known fact that the Internet represents a comprehensive and forceful media revolution. In only a few decades, it has connected billions of people all over the world and given them new access to large quantities of information. At the same time, it has put established media and information formats under pressure: newspapers, journals, CDs, radio and TV outlets, movies, books, etc. Still larger parts of the world's marketing budgets migrate from these media to the online tech giants. To a large extent, the survival of established media now depends on whether they are capable of redefining themselves when faced with the Internet—either as dependent on it, by its terms, or as an alternative to it. This also creates new conditions for freedom of speech.

It seems safe to claim that the spirit of the infancy and youth of the Internet as a mainstream platform, in the 1990s and 2000s, was characterized by an optimistic ecstasy with a clear vision of a promising future ahead. The Internet would enlighten the earth's population, connect it in ways that would soften opposition and even out differences. It would create whole new ways for people to practice their freedom of expression and empower them, even spread democracy and freedom across the globe. "Information wants to be free," rejoiced tech-hippie Stewart Brand back in the 1980s. Another incarnation of the same early optimism appeared in 1996, when Grateful Dead lyricist John Perry Barlow published his moving hippie manifesto entitled *The Declaration of*

F. Stjernfelt, A. M. Lauritzen, *Your Post has been Removed*,
https://doi.org/10.1007/978-3-030-25968-6_1

Independence of Cyberspace.[1] In contrast, the 2010s have been a wake-up call. Skepticists, increasingly vocal during the 2000s, turned out to be right; not everything was hunky dory. As more and more people get access to the Internet, it should be no surprise that tensions, strifes and battles of the real world are played out online as well. Manipulation, crime, cold war—not to mention political and religious extremism—have been given new places to unfold, with a full arsenal of completely new tools at their disposal.

Most likely, the years 2016–2018 will be viewed as a decisive watershed to a new and gloomy way of regarding the Internet:

In 2016, the election of Donald Trump as new President of the US was accompanied by high online activity, in which a Russian "troll factory"—Internet Research Agency in Saint Petersburg, Russia—created false Facebook groups with many different extremist agendas. They sent carefully selected voters messages disguised as Twitter messages from American senders. This was a tremendous effort to affect the US elections and gave rise to heated debate on "fake news" and how to fight them.[2] For obvious reasons, no one can determine to what degree these efforts helped Trump's marginal victory.

In 2017, leading Western nations started seriously discussing regulation of tech giants such as Google, Facebook, Twitter, Amazon, Apple etc. The EU Commission ordered

---

[1] Barlow, J.P. "A Declaration of the Independence of Cyberspace" *Electronic Frontier Foundation*. 02-08-96.

[2] The concept of "fake news" exploded and quickly degenerated into a swearword used by many to insinuate that their opponents are downright liars. At its core, "fake news" referred to commercial websites (such as nationalreport.net and many others) who produce "fake news" to attract user searches in order to sell adverts—but it also refers to more or less elegantly planted "fake news" material by hostile powers. As early as 2017, one of the inventors of the concept, Craig Silverman, distanced himself from this now watered-down concept—C. Silverman "I Helped Popularize The Term "Fake News" And Now I Cringe Every Time I Hear It" *BuzzfeedNews.* 12-31-17.

Google to pay a hefty fine for promoting its own products in its search results, Germany adopted its *Netzwerkdurchsetzungsgesetz*—"Network Implementation Act"—to try to control social media content, high-level representatives of tech giants appeared in hearings in front of the US Congress and France began to draft its regulatory legislation.

And finally, in 2018 came the revelation of the Cambridge Analytica scandal, where it turned out that a private British consultant company specializing in political analysis, spin and campaign support in a number of countries had gained access to the detailed personal data of 50–90 million Facebook users.[3] These data had enabled the company, up until the 2016 US presidential election, to very precisely direct their anonymous or pseudonymous voter influence to target selected, undecided voter groups in the decisive US swing states. It is indeed difficult to determine whether there is any truth to ostentatious claims put forward by Cambridge Analytica that the company was in fact architect of the whole Trump campaign, and that it decided the outcome of the US presidential election. These claims were made by the company's top representatives and caught on hidden camera by *Channel 4*, a British news outlet, whose reporters disguised as Sri Lankan politicians interested in buying similar efforts in order to win their national elections.[4] This affair put new focus on how tech giants collect user data, both openly and candidly, and how they protect these data and the different ways they use them. In the aftermath, Facebook CEO Mark Zuckerberg himself was summoned to hearings in the US Congress in April 2018 and in the EU Parliament the following month. This period in time witnessed growing inter-

---

[3] Strictly speaking, Cambridge Analytica was a subsidiary of British corporation SCL Group, which had its offices in the United States as a way to circumvent the ban on foreign actors intervening financially in US elections. The company was founded by tech investor Robert Mercer and *Breitbart* chief editor and Trump campaign leader Steve Bannon.

[4] "Data, Democracy and Dirty Tricks" *Channel4*. 03-19-18.

est in the political regulation of tech giants, forcing tech giants to take on a more defensive position, launching—to loud fanfare—a series of changes in attempts to anticipate regulatory measures.

The problems with the Internet are manifold. They include a lack of protection of private data; lack of compliance with copyright legislation; extensive transfer of resources from media actually producing content to platforms simply reproducing said content; creation of huge tech companies which solemnly declare transparency and openness while keeping their internal procedures hidden to the public yet retaining control and ownership in the hands of a tight clique of tycoons in Silicon Valley; the same multinational tech giants' sneaky efforts to minimize their tax payments in tax havens; the Internet's increasing opportunities of international crime, fraud, drugs, child pornography, hacking, extortion etc.; the role of the Internet as a way to communicate with and recruit people for political or religious terrorist movements, oftentimes via the hard-to-control Dark Net; the Internet as a platform for systematic disinformation campaigns and the spread of "fake news"; the Internet as a forum for a new cyber Cold War led by military hackers—just to name a few.

This book does not set out to discuss all these downsides to the brave new online world. We choose one specific area: *freedom of expression*. This does not mean that we will ignore these other issues—they are all connected. But it does indeed mean that we will embark on an analysis of what the Internet has opened up for in terms of new conditions, possibilities and problems related to free speech.

"Freedom of speech" is itself a hotly debated topic—especially after the heavy debates following the Muhammad cartoon crisis, which began in Denmark in 2006 and put Islamic threats to free speech on the agenda. As a concept, freedom of speech often refers to freedom of speech guaranteed by law, as central parts of the democratic constitutions of many western countries, following the French *Declaration of the Rights of Man and of the Citizen* of 1789 and the American *Bill of Rights* of 1791. Both documents acknowledged freedom of speech as one of the basic principles on which to base modern constitutions. This point does not mean, however, that such constitutional protections are absolute. Most countries have exceptions regarding for instance threats, personal defamation, the right to privacy, false product claims—not to mention that certain public officials can renounce their freedom of speech on certain topics. Others have exceptions regarding blasphemy, pornography, "hate speech"[5], etc. But those are nothing more than exceptions, which means that in modern democracies freedom of speech is seen as a fundamental ideal to strive for in legal and political terms and should only be limited by explicit and specifically motivated legislation on specific exceptions.

When it comes to freedom of speech guaranteed by law, a distinction is made between *formal* and *material* freedom of speech, according to Danish legal philosopher Alf Ross. The former is concerned with whether a system of censorship is in place—in the absence of censorship before or after the fact, we have formal freedom of speech.[6] The latter concerns the presence of statements with a particular content, which—once put forward in the public sphere—can be ruled on *post hoc* or in some other way treated as crimes. In this sense, no countries can claim to have full freedom of speech—even though a significant decrease is observed in what types of statements are criminalized. As an example, many countries decriminalized blasphemy and pornography during the twentieth century.

This basic understanding of freedom of speech focuses on the government—on how and to what extent it defends the rights of each individual citizen to express him- or herself as he or she wishes. This does not, however, fully cover what one might call "actual" freedom of speech. There are also borderline cases, such as pressure from *another* state or a terrorist

[5] In this book we put "hate speech" in quotation marks to signal that in our opinion it is a vague category which does not refer to any well-defined group of utterances, cf. the review of "hate speech" legislation in Strossen (2018).

[6] Cf. Mchangama & Stjernfelt (2005) pp. 756ff, 774ff.

group against people who express themselves, be it in the form of violence or threats, for political or religious reasons. Strictly speaking, Iran's 1989 fatwa against author Salman Rushdie, which is still active, is a successful attempt to extend the Iranian jurisdiction to apply to citizens of other nations. It is successful insofar as Iranian agents and sympathizer activists outside Iran have taken it upon themselves to persecute Rushdie in an attempt to carry out the Iranian death sentence which serves, simultaneously, as an instant warning to others who might consider following his footsteps. An example from Denmark is international pressure originating from both Muslim states and Islamist activists. This pressure has indirectly but efficiently forced Danish media to refrain from publishing caricature drawings of the Prophet Muhammad since 2010. This constitutes an actual restriction of Danish freedom of speech, with no regard to the Danish state monopoly on violence or the country's legislation. In a multicultural world, times could lie ahead where jurisdictions of different countries and groups may overlap or collide, resulting in lack of clarity or even conflict as to the limits on freedom of speech.

A third usage of the concept freedom of speech relates to whether there are even media available to spread certain content. During the later years of the absolute monarchy in Denmark, for a long time a few specific publications had the privilege of disseminating political news. For a while *Statstidende*, the official government journal, even had monopoly on the publication of such news. It meant that no media were allowed to communicate political news or political discussion not acknowledged by the regime. This was government policy—but also other circumstances can cause such restrictions. If for instance all media in a given country, spontaneously or coordinated, agreed to keep out certain content, then there would in fact be no freedom of speech regarding this content, despite the absence of explicit bans on it. If certain media gain in-practice monopoly control on communicating the news, then the editorial policies of said media would define the limits of the freedom of speech practiced.

Freedom of speech can also refer to topics broader than the opportunity of individuals or organizations to express themselves freely. It can refer to the right to search for information freely and obtain it freely. In this usage of the concept, the rights holder is not the active and expressing party, but the passive and receiving party. If the media of a given country are strictly controlled—be it control of the formal, material or actual freedom of speech—then the audiences who use these media do not enjoy freedom of speech in this broader understanding of the term (even though these users themselves do not necessarily attempt to practice that expression and are hindered). Thus, the UN's Declaration of Human Rights includes this information search aspect in its article on freedom of expression: "Everyone has the right to freedom of opinion and expression; this right includes freedom to hold opinions without interference and to seek, receive and impart information and ideas through any media and regardless of frontiers."[7] A similar choice of words can be found in the European Convention on Human Rights. This broader understanding of free speech includes anything which might impede the free exchange of information for citizens and civil organizations.

A number of classical freedoms— often referred to as "first generation" human rights—are closely connected to freedom of speech. This goes especially for the freedom of religion or belief, which is the right of individuals to define their faith and affiliation to a religious community. Sometimes this is confounded with *libertas ecclesiae*, which is when churches call for exemption from certain legislations, but that is an entirely different matter (and possibly in opposition to freedom of speech). The freedom to believe was among the principal motivations behind the fight for freedom of expression in Europe between the seventeenth to nineteenth

---

[7]"UN Universal Declaration of Human Rights (1948)" *Amnesty International.*

centuries, and it is still a disputed and restricted right in many countries, for instance in China and the Muslim world. Freedom of the press and freedom of thought are closely related to free speech, and both are often used synonymously with freedom of speech. The same goes for the freedom of assembly and association, which underpin the citizens' right to gather physically and in organizations to share information and points of view.

In the following chapters, we will examine all these aspects of freedom of speech online—and we will do our best to make it clear which forms of this concept we are discussing and when.

Chapter 2
The Free Networks of the Enlightenment

In the seventeenth and eighteenth centuries, freedom of expression emerged as a central theme of the dawning Age of Enlightenment. This was caused not least by churches and princes maintaining strict political control of expressions of divergent opinions. The new Protestant state churches, Lutheran as well as Calvinist, turned out not to offer more freedom than the Catholic church. In fact, it was often less, which meant that religious, philosophical and political dissidents regularly ran into serious problems when expressing their ideas publicly. Thus, ideas of freedom of expression began to surface. One of the first urgent calls for freedom of expression came from Dutch-Jewish philosopher Baruch Spinoza, who in his "Tractatus Theologico-Politicus" (1670) called for *libertas philosophandi*—freedom of thought. As stated by British historian Jonathan Israel, Spinoza was the first major philosopher who was also a democrat. Spinoza believed it important to distinguish politically between people's actions and their views and expressions. Whereas the former should be governed by legislators, the latter should not. This would create a more free and peaceful society—and if people had the possibility to influence the laws they were subject to, they might be more inclined to respect them.

Similar thoughts would gradually propagate in the "learned republic" of associated philosophers, journalists, publishers, bookstores, collectors, encyclopedists, writers, editors and others that emerged in the seventeenth and eighteenth

F. Stjernfelt, A. M. Lauritzen, *Your Post has been Removed*,
https://doi.org/10.1007/978-3-030-25968-6_2

century. Compared to our day's focus on digital networks, it is thought-provoking that this "Republic of Letters" was in fact a self-organized "grassroots" network that challenged the ecclesiastical and absolutist hierarchies of the times. Historian Niall Fergusson (2017) gives a detailed mapping of historical periods in which networks have been able to threaten, upset or recalibrate established political hierarchies. This was made possible by new media, among them cheap printing of books and quicker transport of mail, but also by intensifying traditional procedures such as transcription, book loans and travel. These networks held the germ of many characteristics which are intensified in today's much larger and faster networks. They constituted a crucial historical sanctuary outside the reach of states and churches, a precursor of civil society. This naturally led states and churches to try to restrict and pursue these networks. In turn, the networks could react by organizing themselves in closed cliques, lodges, secret societies—focused gatherings where expression was freer, but which also subjected people to the dangers of echo chambers and information bias. In these networks, freedom of expression was increasingly practiced and expounded, to foster enlightenment based on the first-hand experience of believing, thinking or expressing oneself freely. Well-known names from the Enlightenment tradition include encyclopedists Pierre Bayle and Denis Diderot, English freethinkers like Anthony Collins and Matthew Tindal and German dissidents like Lorenz Schmidt or Theodor Ludwig Lau. But Christian dissidents also saw the need for free speech—an example is radical pietist Johann Konrad Dippel, alchemist, freethinker and a good candidate for a real-life Dr. Frankenstein. In 1706, he published *Ein Hirt und eine Heerde*, demanding full freedom of religion and expression as the only path to true faith. His writings were burned by the Danish government, and he was even sent to prison on the island of Bornholm for his outspokenness.[1]

During the 1700s, freedom of expression became one of the key issues for this emerging international network, which

---

[1] See Mchangama and Stjernfelt (2016) p. 135ff.

eventually spread to large parts of Europe and to its American colonies. The ideas of the Enlightenment Age were at the heart of the most important political upheavals of the late 1700s, such as the American and French revolutions in 1776 and 1789, respectively. They both resulted in influential articulations of freedom of speech: the French Human Rights Declaration of August 1789 and the American Bill of Rights from 1791. The former pronounced: "The free communication of thoughts and of opinions is one of the most precious rights of man: any citizen thus may speak, write, print freely, except to respond to the abuse of this liberty, in the cases determined by the law."[2] The latter and more radical one, not containing the French restrictions regarding abuse, reads as follows: "Congress shall make no law respecting an establishment of religion, or prohibiting the free exercise thereof; or abridging the freedom of speech, or of the press; or the right of the people peaceably to assemble, and to petition the government for a redress of grievances."[3] This is the famous First Amendment. The emerging networks of the Enlightenment Age had managed to anchor freedom of expression in the constitutions of two large Western countries. These laws are fundamentally formulated in the negative, that is, in contrast to the absolutist and ecclesiastically dominated states of the time, these new states influenced by the Enlightenment *refrained* from preventing their citizens from expressing themselves freely. In his influential article "What is Enlightenment?", German philosopher Immanuel Kant gave a more positive definition of the importance of freedom of expression in the Enlightenment movement.

In this article from 1784, Kant suggests that enlightenment is man's "emerging from his self-imposed immaturity"[4], that

---

[2] Our translation of "Déclaration des Droits de l'Homme et du Citoyen de 1789" Conseil Constitutionnel. Last visited 08-04-18: conseil-constitutionnel.fr/—Translations in the book are our own, except when citing already translated works.

[3] "First Amendment" *Legal Information Institute*.

[4] "Immaturity" translates German "Unmündigkeit", literally referring to the nonage state of underage citizens without full autonomy and citizen rights.

enlightenment consists of the *public* use of reason, in which the individual as an intellectual being may express what he cannot do in his official capacity: "[...] the public use of one's reason must be free at all times, and this alone can bring enlightenment to mankind. On the other hand, the private use of reason may frequently be narrowly restricted without especially hindering the progress of enlightenment. By 'public use of one's reason', I mean that use which a man, as *scholar*, makes of it before the reading public."[5] Private use of reason refers not only to private life but especially to those appointments and offices that may impose restrictions upon the individual concerning what may be said—something less common today, but which we recognize from the professional confidentiality upheld by doctors and social workers, among others. Kant argues that, contrary to such restrictions on one's office, when addressing a general public, anyone should be able to make public use of their faculty of reason in front of an audience—thus making such a freely addressed public sphere the framework of an enlightened society.

Historically, the "general public" Kant refers to had emerged from the learned networks of the Enlightenment Age as a self-organized communications forum with its own media, outside of and across the narrow public spheres maintained and controlled by churches and courts. In principle, this general public, beyond the control of governments and religions, now lends legitimacy to the new democratic states. The general public, as in the civil society and their networks, organizations and the media which thrive off them, enables enlightenment to take place. Mistaken ideas are corrected; arguments are developed and contradicted; new ideas and science are formed; viewpoints clash; criticism of and protests against policies are articulated; political agreement and disagreement can be formulated, and last but not least: informed elections can take place. It is well known that the realization of this ideal public sphere has shown its disadvantages, as mapped by disciplines such as mass psychology and cultural criticism: fads, seduction of the masses led by charismatic

---

[5] Kant (1784) pp. 484–85.

figures, the public impact of culture and pop industries, not to mention what we today refer to as echo chambers and filter bubbles. However, despite these built-in disadvantages, most theories of democracy agree that free debate is a fundamental condition for modern liberal democracies.

The Kantian argument for freedom of expression is closely linked to his idea of the autonomy of the individual: Human beings possess a particular dignity because they have the ability to take a step back and morally judge their own opinions and actions. This autonomy may only be expressed fully if political circumstances allow everyone to think and express themselves freely. In this sense, freedom of expression has a central place among the natural rights of humans—in the tradition of natural justice going back to the seventeenth century and all the way back to the Stoic view of humans as creatures of reason and political equality.[6]

At the beginning of the nineteenth century, Jeremy Bentham criticized this very idea of natural rights as "nonsense upon stilts"—to him the only legitimate rights were those guaranteed by a political authority. This led to an alternative, utilitarian justification of free speech that found its classic articulation in John Stuart Mill's *On Liberty* from 1859. To him the *utility* of freedom of expression is the measuring stick and the central argument is that if a given society lacks freedom of expression, not all possible suggestions for the solution of a given problem will be expressed, and it will then not be possible to reach the best solution. Obviously, this basic reason for having freedom of expression is completely different from the one found in Kantian thought—but this should not block our understanding that the two reasons are oftentimes in agreement with each other, and that in most concrete cases, they work well together. As it is notoriously difficult to measure utility, at the end of the day the utilitarian argument is hardly less speculative than the Kantian one. Is it useful for a democratic society to accept anti-democratic statements from Nazis, Communists and Islamists? At first

---

[6] See the chapter on "Homo humanitatis" in Budtz Pedersen et al. (2018).

glance, probably not. But the counter-argument goes: Such acceptance might be useful after all, since the knowledge of anti-democratic views may help immunize the public against those very views. It is generally useful to have an uncensored public sphere that assures people that others mean what they say and are not forced to pretend or lie because of legislation. Unlike the Kantian definition, the utilitarian one emphasizes the pragmatic, social benefits of free expression. In a sense, this dimension complements a rights- and individual-based definition so important for this book, which has as its core topic the tech giants' transformation of the public sphere. However, the emphasis on benefit to the public must always be counterbalanced by freedom of expression as an individual right. In cases where the two definitions clash, in our opinion the latter should outweigh the former.

Both theories are compatible with the idea of freedom of expression as a means of testing authorities and established legislation—and ultimately breaking with them. Two of the many examples from modern times are the decline of slavery around 1800 and women's right to vote around 1900—both changes became possible through extensive public debate prior to their realization. In this sense, a free public sphere enables the articulation and breakthrough of new political views and movements in a democracy.

The abolition of censorship in most modern democratic states took place from the 18th to the twentieth centuries and has, as a tendency, gone hand in hand with a greater tolerance of divergent views and opinions—be they religious, political, ethnic, etc. As mentioned earlier, this does not mean that freedom of expression is absolute. In a certain way, the ongoing negotiation of its boundaries is a central theme in modern democratic politics, due to the idea of freedom of expression as a fundamental right, which should only be limited in cases where very convincing counter-arguments to do so are present. Threats, explicit incitement or planning of violence and false personal defamation belong in this category. More debated examples include "hate speech", which is not a crime in the US, but which has been criminalized in many European countries in various ways. Other controversial examples are criticism of religion and blasphemy, which are no longer prohibited in most modern democracies since the Enlightenment. This is not the case in many Muslim countries, which are working on enacting such laws internationally through the UN and by formally or informally pressuring public opinion in countries without such prohibitions.

In a certain sense, freedom of expression is counterintuitive—why not just silence abhorrent statements? The tolerance that freedom of expression implies is not easily achieved. It includes the duty, both of the government and of the individual, to tolerate views, statements, pictures and books which may be considered abominable and grotesque, but which also have a right to reach the public. As has so often been said, tolerating views one agrees with is the easy part. But the fact that also Nazis, Islamic extremists or Communists should have the right to express their views on reality and the future is something that many people need a certain degree of self-reflection to accept. Something similar applies in the case of "hate speech", which is why some argue that it should be tolerated and not banned. "Hate speech" is a notoriously ill-defined category, and in the laws of many countries, it is only described by simply listing a number of somewhat randomly selected groups of people—labelled for example religious, ethnic, sexual, racial, etc. These groups cannot be criticized beyond a certain limit, but it is a difficult limit to define accurately—"insult", "mockery", "degradation", etc. are imprecise terms often used. Compared to threats, which are usually covered in a separate clause, "hate speech" is less clearly defined. "Hate speech" legislation is not just a collective libel clause either. Most often, the definition of "hate speech" differs from that of libel in that it does not involve any assessment of the veracity of the statement (in the case of libel, charges may be dropped if the allegations are proven to be true, which is usually not the case with "hate speech"). Very often, "hate speech" legislation and verdicts end up applying also to the political criticism of the behavior of such groups. Such criticism is not necessarily untrue or politically illegitimate; most political activity naturally includes the discussion and changes of the general conditions of different groups in society (rich, poor, public employees, entrepreneurs, refugees, retirees, etc.) who are therefore addressed in general terms. It is therefore difficult and maybe even impossible to maintain "hate speech" legislation and at the same time avoiding its misuse to silence legitimate political standpoints and even true statements about problems concerning different groups in society. As Professor at Law Nadine Strossen remarks, the introduction of "hate speech" legislation very often results in its use against those marshaling it, because different governments may use it to try to silence their opponents, once a "hate speech" law is accepted.

However, it is a defining feature of modern, liberal democracies that the very discussion *itself* of such boundaries must take place in full public view. Such discussion makes use of freedom of expression, which guarantees people the ability to *cite* examples of prohibited content or of what others would like to see prohibited. This is unlike what happens in dictatorships or absolutist states. Here, both the general boundaries of statements and their translation into individual decisions and decrees may be decided secretly in the government apparatus without legal trial or public insight or discussion. In this sense, the limits of freedom of expression are and should be the subject of ongoing, public and free debate.

Chapter 3
A New Golden Age of Enlightenment?

For a long time during the 1990s and 2000s, positive stories about the Internet prevailed. A growing number of people with online access, first in the Western world, then gradually across the globe, would start a new era of Enlightenment with freedom of information and freedom of expression in a new radical sense. An unprecedented number of individuals would gain easy access to the large amounts of information uploaded by many different players, from individuals to media outlets, to organizations and government authorities. As a growing number of free search engines came about, it became easier to seek out information. There is no doubt that much of the elementary optimism was actually correct: the world has become a significantly more enlightened place thanks to the Internet, in the basic sense of "enlightenment" as the increased dissemination of information and knowledge—but also in the sense of Enlightenment as empowerment of the individual.

However, it was almost as if the Internet called upon people's science fiction fantasies, both dystopian ones of a dark future characterized by over-technification, surveillance and control, and utopian ones seeing the network as a solution to almost all key human problems. In 1997, Danish science journalist Tor Nørretranders prophesized about "the radical information democracy"[1]—editors, publishers,

[1] Nørretranders (1997) p.141.

F. Stjernfelt, A. M. Lauritzen, *Your Post has been Removed*,
https://doi.org/10.1007/978-3-030-25968-6_3

broadcasters of all kinds became the emblem of evil, whom he accused of doing nothing more than manipulate, streamline and even suppress the flow of information. Now, with the internet, they could be phased out and made redundant, as online individuals would be able to put together their own newspaper, journal, book or TV show based on information searched for, found and combined by—themselves. The fact that there might still be need for organizations to sift, fact-check and synthesize the steadily growing amount of online information did not seem to worry promoters of such radical optimism, who saw a whole new, utopian, collaborative and responsive community emerge on the Internet. It would even replace the cumbersome electoral procedures of representative democracy, because ongoing, maybe even daily, online referenda would represent a more sensitive mapping of the people's will. In this view, there was no room for doubt that the will of the people would always be democratic and could never turn into terrifying spontaneous decisions. Today, supporters of "disruption" argue that, since the Internet can very accurately map the actual preferences of voters based on their "likes" and other search behavior, one could just draft policy according to such knowledge: "What if ... local authorities did not need the opinions of citizens but instead measured their behavior and got to know their preferences that way?" Then this could be supplied by online polls as "a good way to wrap up something which sometimes becomes endless debate", to quote the anti-parliamentary choice of words laid out in "Five Technological Themes", a report from Danish consultant DareDisrupt.[2] Others—for instance American

[2] DareDisrupt: "Fem teknologiske temaer" (Five Technological Themes), p. 70 and 135, 2018. The report was made on behalf of Local Government Denmark in 2018 and can be found on www.kl.dk (Danish version only). Most recent visit 08-04-18: http://www.kl.dk/ImageVaultFiles/id_85157/cf_202/Kommunernes_Teknologiske_Fremtid_-fuld_version-.PDF. It is indeed unsettling to realize that an association such as Local Government Denmark is considering bypassing local elections. However, DareDisrupt and Local Government Denmark miss the fact that people do not vote based on preferences only but also based on ideals and ideologies.

innovation consultant Lewis Perelman—thought that schools would become superfluous once everyone had a computer in their home to search and get the information they needed. If everyone were connected in one and the same open and transparent network, eternal problems of humanity such as ignorance, conflict, crime and war would simply disappear.

Other hopeful voices spoke about how the Internet would foster people's generous drive towards collaboration, that is, they saw the Internet as a gift economy in the sense of Marcel Mauss and other anthropologists. CEO of Facebook, Mark Zuckerberg, has applauded this idea of giving your information and services away for free and in return receiving equally free information and services from others.[3] It seems that the gift economists of the online world did not study Mauss' ideas in full, namely the part where exchanging gifts becomes a competition, obliging people to give a gift in return, in an attempt not to lose face. The reciprocal gift overbidding of the Kwakiutl indigenous tribes could result in aggressive "destruction feasts", the so-called "potlatch". In extreme cases, a chief could publicly destroy all of his property, including his food supplies, weapons, holy copper objects, canoes, even slaves, in order to ultimately put his opponent in a checkmate position, by giving him a gift that was impossible to reciprocate—and if the other could not reciprocate, that chief and his tribe would be enslaved to the opponent.

Other early Internet enthusiasts imagined that the growing collaboration among users within the network might form a whole new shared global brain where the many users connected via the Internet would become the brain cells of a whole new higher-order consciousness at a planetary level that would surpass human consciousness when it comes to both intelligence and sensitivity. Few people discussed whether such a sensitive superintelligence would be morally good or politically open in any known sense, let alone adopt a kind stance toward the people who constituted it—or if it

[3] Kirkpatrick (2010) p. 287.

might pursue completely other goals, goals incomprehensible and not necessarily pleasant to us as individuals.

In the 2000s, when social media such as MySpace, Friendster, Facebook, YouTube, Twitter, Instagram and others emerged and grew, they were regarded as "power tools to the people" with radical social benefits. They would inaugurate not only a democratic redistribution of knowledge, but also new and intensified connections between people who would soon share most or all of their data with a growing circle of contacts and "friends", ultimately with anybody. The big tech companies seem to have started as playful experiments, imagining themselves as charitable initiatives to make the world a better place, rather than actual firms. In any case, it is safe to say that they became able to spread highly optimistic, generous and beneficial tales about themselves, about how they would supply the world with information under the motto "Don't be evil" (Google), or about how the real goal was to make the world a more open and transparent place by connecting as many people as possible under the motto "Don't be lame" (Facebook)—rather than monetizing these services, which was almost regarded as a slightly annoying side effect to take into consideration.[4] Even during the April 2018 hearings before Congress, Mark Zuckerberg displayed that attitude. This is as believable as if big oil companies tried to convince us that their primary task is really to help people transport themselves comfortably to visit their friends and make the world a more connected place—and that any profits derived from that were merely a secondary detail. However, the fact that Zuckerberg has also hailed the motto "Move fast and break things" is indicative of tolls and downsides to the fast growth of users and free services. After ten years of growth and becoming the world's biggest corporations, the big tech companies now find themselves in need of taking not one but two basic considerations into account: One, they have

[4] At least according to Kirkpatrick's (2010) biography on Zuckerberg. Martínez' (2016) critical insider account of Facebook supports the claim that the company's ads department had low priority and low prestige within the organization all the way up until the 2010s.

to consider their users, of course, who need an enjoyable and useful free service to compensate for the time, attention, uploaded data and digital traces they put at the companies' disposal, all free of charge; two, they must increasingly serve shareholders and the tech giants' clients, that is, the advertising companies who pay for the whole party by buying an ever-increasing amount of banner advertisements of ever-increasing types and kinds.

Chapter 4
The Digital Enlightenment Project Facing Challenges

As early as the 1990s, there were critical voices with a skeptical and even gloomy view of the beneficial effects of the Internet. Cultural critic and media theorist Neil Postman was generally skeptical towards technological solutions to political problems. He understood technology through Goethe's classical metaphor of the Faustian pact with the Devil. He believed the Internet would only add to the information congestion that he already saw as one of the most important issues of modern society, and which makes it increasingly difficult to distinguish important from unimportant information. In hindsight, it is obvious that critics like Postman developed a highly limited and erroneous view on the possibilities of the Internet: "To put it plainly, I think the Internet is something like power steering or cruise control in cars. I mean, not that it's not useful, but once you invent the basic car, you've got it. Now these things are useful, and the automobile companies add them on to the cars and then they convince consumers that they absolutely have to have them. I'm not saying that they're completely useless—of course, they're not. But the Internet doesn't help us address the problems that we need to address."[1] Postman went as far as to dismiss the entire computer and Internet revolution as a mere diversion from the real problems of society. "The Internet and computer tech-

[1] Clark, N. "Home Alone With Technology: An Interview With Neil Postman" *Iowa Journal of Cultural Studies* (1996): pp. 151–159.

F. Stjernfelt, A. M. Lauritzen, *Your Post has been Removed*,
https://doi.org/10.1007/978-3-030-25968-6_4

nology are just distractions."[2] He basically considered it a new form of commercial entertainment technology with very limited utility; cf. his famous diagnosis: "We're amusing ourselves to death." It is obvious that this kind of neo-Luddism completely missed its target and did not acknowledge the Internet's already then burgeoning potential for education, dissemination of information, intellectual empowerment and cooperation.

Even so, Postman had glimpsed some critical issues that would prove very real. One was the commercialization of the Internet. Another was the difficulty of controlling a phenomenon of such extensive international scope, as long as the control was only exercised on a national level: "... it's too international to be controlled."[3] Postman was asked about the potential advantages conveyed when a user's computer collects only information and knowledge that in fact suit the user's individual interests, and he gloomily replied, in what turned out to be a foreshadowing of Google's personalization strategy fifteen years later: "I can see your point, except in itself it does tend to increase fragmentation."[4] This is another important point, today captured in terms such as echo chambers, confirmation bias, and filter bubbles. It is not a given fact that increased connectivity online in itself entail transparency, agreement, gift economy and cooperation, as tech giant leaders are repeatedly chanting. Increased connectivity may just as well lead to disagreement, tunnel vision, fragmentation, tribalism, shitstorms, online bullying and violence. Where these matters are concerned, Postman clearly foresaw the contours of problems that today appear abundantly clear.

As early as the mid-1990s, Postman was opposed by radical tech optimist Nicholas Negroponte,[5] and in fact, an entire history dissertation could be written on the back and forth between pessimists and optimists during the 2000s and 2010s.

---

[2] Clark, N. "Home Alone With Technology: An Interview With Neil Postman" *Iowa Journal of Cultural Studies* (1996): p. 154.

[3] Ibid., p. 156.

[4] Ibid., p. 155.

[5] Negroponte (1996).

We shall not elaborate on that but instead draw attention to the fact that even though most tech pessimists radically underestimated the possibilities of the Internet and overestimated its shortcomings, they often had a better understanding of the nature of its concrete problematic issues. This was in stark opposition to the intoxicated apologists who tended to believe that the good side of the Internet would automatically win out and marginalize or eradicate the bad. Our recommendation is, therefore, to be optimistic but to listen carefully to the pessimists.

There is some irony to the fact that many of the fantastic possibilities the Internet holds for public enlightenment, free speech and intellectual empowerment have run into still more problems. First, these problems have to do with a process of commercialization that is changing the Internet. What once was a decentralized, anarchistic and relatively transparent platform for the interaction of many parallel, individual, small actors became a place where most interaction occurs via the opaque commercial platforms of a few gigantic companies. Second, the problems have to do with the fact that the Internet is increasingly becoming a forum for already existing powers and power struggles between commercial, religious, political and state actors. As a result, freedom of expression is under pressure. The first issue implies that freedom of expression may be suspended the moment it is convenient to commercial interests. Tech giants like Facebook, Twitter and Google have gained a powerful position that increasingly allows them to adapt and restrict access to information and to the rules of public conversation based on various political and commercial considerations.[6] In other words, they are monetizing freedom of expression. The second issue implies

[6]Throughout the book, we address the western tech giants, especially Google and Facebook, but also Twitter, Amazon, etc. Government-run Chinese alternatives such as the social media WeChat and Weibo, search engine Baidu and internet retailer Alibaba (which interestingly enough means "thief" in Arab) have even more free speech issues than their western counterparts, but they—still?—have little muscle outside of China.

that the very same incentives to suppress an adversary's voice in "real life" now repeat themselves online, only with a great number of new technological possibilities at hand. In addition to traditional repressive censorship that attempts to suppress, prohibit or cleanse the public space from unwanted opinions and statements, new forms of censorship have been created aiming to prevent statements and opinions from spreading. These forms also include harassing, threatening and "doxxing" senders or destroying their credibility. The idea of the Internet as the tool that would bring about a new Golden Age of Enlightenment has been turned on its head.

This distortion is closely linked to the fact that the Internet is increasingly dominated by huge companies like Google, Facebook and Twitter. Google was founded in 1998 by two PhD students at Stanford, Larry Page and Sergey Brin. The company name was inspired by the word "googol", which means the number 10 to the 100th power. The company's many activities are centered around the search engine Google Search, which eventually outcompeted the Internet's many early search engines with its feature PageRank, which ranks search results according to how often the website is linked and the importance of the links. The company's stated goal was "to organize the world's information and make it universally accessible and useful". Google went public in 2004, and they have gradually developed or acquired a wide range of free services that facilitate collaboration (Google Docs), file storage (Google Drive), social networking (Google +), video sharing (YouTube), access to books (Google Books, Ngrams), email (Gmail), topographic maps (Google Maps), mobile telephony (Android), browsing (Google Chrome) and others. The company's growing research department explores a plethora of things from flying cars to advanced AI and to conquering death. In 2015, all the company's activities were gathered in the parent company Alphabet (which is, however, still often referred to as Google). In 2000, the company started showing ads based on the search history of users, which swiftly became its main source of income. From 2005, Google started generating tremendous revenue, and in recent years, the company has ranked as the world's second largest after Apple. The company is among the most ingenious tax avoiders and channels its money out of the US via Ireland, the Netherlands and Bermuda.

Facebook was founded in 2004 by Mark Zuckerberg and a handful of fellow students at Harvard, initially just as a digital version of the University's yearbook, showing photos and information about new students, called *TheFacebook*. The idea was to give students a free tool to keep in touch with their friends and different interest groups as defined on the platform.

The first serious investment came the same year from Silicon Valley legend Peter Thiel. The concept spread, first to other universities, then to regular users in the United States and later to a growing number of other countries. In 2006 came the addition of news feed, which showed news, first from the user's circle of friends, later from different media and advertisers. In 2008, after settling a lawsuit filed by other Harvard students who claimed Zuckerberg had stolen their idea, Facebook was free to expand and develop the product. They now became able to add news, a messenger service, acquisition of photo sharing service Instagram, chat service WhatsApp and much more. The first many years, the focus was on scaling, increasing the number of users, which was indeed skyrocketing. This number is today estimated around 2 billion worldwide. It was not until recruiting Sheryl Sandberg from Google in 2008 that the company began aiming to run ads as its source of revenue. This method took form in 2010 using the extensive collection of data on users obtained from their behavior on Facebook and from other sources—a business model which rapidly turned the company into one of the largest in the world. Facebook went public in 2012. In the years following the 2016 US presidential election, Facebook was accused of being one of the main sources of "fake news". And after the revelation in 2018 that the propaganda company Cambridge Analytica had had access to the data of more than 50 million users, Facebook has initiated a highly publicized restructuring of the platform. This naturally also aims to preempt regulations threatened by a number of political forces.

Twitter was founded in 2006 by programmer Jack Dorsey and a handful of his friends. It offers quick and free dialogue through short statements —tweets—with a maximum length of 140 characters (increased, in 2017, to 280 characters). The service quickly came to serve as a conduit for the exchange of breaking news and opinion, and increasingly for brief public statements made by politicians, celebrities and others. Twitter's success led Facebook to integrate similar features on its platform, but Twitter withstood the competition, and though they are not nearly as big as Google or Facebook, they remain a strong social network, carrying great influence in the world of politics. We thus see heads of state around the world launching political initiatives through a tweet. Twitter, too, generates revenue through advertising.

With their effective free service, these tech giants and their relatives such as Pinterest, Tumblr, Yahoo, Snapchat and many others have attracted huge numbers of users who make it possible to generate growing revenues through advertising. The changing commercial and political focus of these companies is, however, radically changing the public sphere and has gradually challenged the digital Enlightenment project of the Internet.

Chapter 5
The Internet 3.0

On September 11, 2001, Internet users searched Google for information on the unfathomable events taking place in Manhattan. But the search "New York Twin Towers" came up with no hits. A full month had passed since the words "twin towers" had last been indexed. This meant that at this crucial moment, the term as a search object had not been updated. All the search results Google came up with were frustratingly irrelevant for the acute needs of the users. As an emergency solution, Google created a breaking news page featuring "News and Information on the US Attacks", which was placed on top of the search list. The page featured links to the websites of news outlets and other news organizations as well as useful links to aid organizations, emergency aid, phone numbers of airlines and hospitals. This episode made Google, during the following year, develop a news filter as part of its search algorithm. This meant that current headlines now came up on top of the search list when a user entered the relevant search words.[1]

A lot has happened since. For a long time now, as a company Google has gained an indispensable position as a public utility. The company offers everyone free information. Equipped with a smartphone or an Internet connection, any-

[1] Lafrance, A. "The Power of Personalization" *Nieman Reports*. 10-18-17.

F. Stjernfelt, A. M. Lauritzen, *Your Post has been Removed*,
https://doi.org/10.1007/978-3-030-25968-6_5

one can get an immediate answer to any lexical question. But the information met by the user is no longer the same. It is now ordered according to radically different principles than what we have seen previously. Somewhat unwittingly, people all over the world have invited Google and the other tech giants in on the most private spheres of their lives. These giants see this development as a data race for relevance—relevance for the individual user and for the voracious advertisers.

The growing integration of digital experiences into everyday life is not the result of one isolated shift. It is the consequence of gradual changes. The Internet of today is often described as the third wave. First came the Web 1.0 of the 1990s, which was merely built around websites, email and simple search engines. Then came the Web 2.0 of the early 2000s with its expansion of blogs, wikis and social networks and where Google started to sell ads associated with search words.[2] Starting around 2010, the Smart Web 3.0 has taken over—this third wave is driven by big data and smartphones.[3] Big data refers to three overlapping ways of using data. It simply refers to the massive and increasingly available amounts of data. It also covers the analytical techniques used to extract useful information from data. And finally, it is associated with companies such as Facebook, Twitter and Google, who use extensive data analyses on user behavior as a core part of their business model.[4]

Meanwhile, the algorithms on which tech giants base their businesses have become more and more complex. An algorithm is simply a rule-governed procedure aimed at solving a class of problems—parallel to a recipe where one keeps adding ingredients in the form of data. The term dates back to ancient Greek mathematics, the name derived from al-

[2] "Web 2.0" was the title of a conference hosted by e-book publisher Tim O'Reilly in 2004.

[3] Lynch (2016) p. 7.

[4] Lynch (2016) p. 8.

Kwarizmi, an Arab mathematician from the ninth century. Computer software became a readily available way to formalize, develop and further automatize algorithms for many different purposes. In the context of tech giants, the word refers to central complexes of computer software which govern searches and rankings of search results (Google) or networks of "friends" and followers and what information flows through a given network (Facebook, Twitter) etc.—all while gathering user data for advertising purposes.

Algorithms function on the basis of data inputs and require those inputs to be sorted in specific data categories. Just like a cake recipe requires rule-bound input of e.g. flour, eggs, yeast, sugar, etc. in a certain sequence, algorithms presuppose certain types of data, which it is able to recognize: An algorithm for the determination of prime numbers accepts integers as input only; an algorithm for birthday wishes requires dates as input; an algorithm for image comparison uses pixel sequences, etc. This implies that an algorithm requires a world categorized in specific data categories. If those categories are insufficient for the purpose at hand, there may be certain things wished for, which the algorithm may not be able to accept or express – or, conversely, there may be things unwished for, which it produces as output.

The algorithms are continuously updated by software engineers, and their ability to recognize, identify and categorize data is constantly trained through machine learning in which humans present the algorithms with a series of examples of a given category (e.g. pornography) for the algorithms to recognize. Part of such an "ability to learn" can also be automatized through so-called deep learning, where data are filtered through self-adjusting networks. For instance, it is possible to create several varieties of a given procedure (e.g. the same ad in different colors), which are then launched simultaneously in order to choose the one that turns out the most effective. During this process, big tech algorithms become ever more comprehensive and complex and it is unlikely that any one programmer can get an overview of them in their entirety. The tech giants have been criticized for only giving very few and specially skilled people—programmers—access to these algorithms, without seeking input from other types of experts.[5] Algorithms are manmade and thus not necessarily fair, objective or neutral—their categorizations may contain many different kinds of biases, intended or unintended, e.g. of race, gender, politics and many others. Cathy O'Neil has famously called such harmful kinds of models for "Weapons of Math Destruction". The models are opinions embedded in mathematics and technology.[6]

December 4, 2009 was a decisive day for the third wave of the Internet, as it marked a radical shift in how information is consumed. That day, Google launched a fundamental modification of its search function, "Personalized Search for Everyone".[7] Up until then, the key to Google's success had been the famous algorithm PageRank, named after one of Google's founders, Larry Page. It ranked key word search results based on the number and popularity of connections a given website had to other websites. It was inspired by the ranking of scientific articles based on how many times they had been quoted. The most well-connected websites came up at the top of the search list—no matter who entered the search word. But from that day on, in 2009, the objective criterion was supplemented by subjective ones, tied to the individual user. That made the platform personalized, and since then, two users no longer get the same results from the same search. Now Google tracks user behavior to generate and store massive amounts of data based on geographic location, search history and other demographic information. Furthermore, personalization provides insight into user behavior based on the dizzying 3.5 billion searches entered

---

[5] A deeper characterization of artificial intelligence and algorithms can be found in a guide published by *Wired* magazine: Simonite, T. "The Wired Guide to Artificial Intelligence" *Wired*. 02-01-18.

[6] O'Neil (2016).

[7] Google "Personalized Search for everyone" *Google Blog*. 12-04-09.

every day.[8] New algorithms enable Google to come up with ever more sophisticated guesstimates about who the user is and what information is personally relevant to that individual. There are two fundamental purposes to this data collection. First, these data are supposed to bring to the top of the search list the news and search results that are most relevant to the individual user. But at the same time, these data help advertisers find people likely to buy their products. The latter is the key to understanding the tech giants' business model. Ads targeted according to this information are bought by marketers, enabling them to present, on the Google list of pages found, ads which are adapted to the detailed personal preferences of users. In practice, this means that each user is presented with different, personalized versions of the Internet. Many people might still assume that when a word is googled, the results will be objective and the same for everyone—that they are simply the most authoritative results. That was indeed the case in the early days of search algorithm PageRank, but that standard version of Google is long since outdated.[9]

Personalization, and the data collection that goes with it, has not only become the main strategy for Google but also for other tech companies such as Facebook, Twitter and many others. That same year, in 2009, Facebook introduced its *like* button, which made it possible for users to express a simple accept of some presented content or other. It also made it possible for the people who had posted the content to use the number of likes as a measuring stick of their individual popularity. Facebook and Twitter record an extremely detailed portrait of each individual user based on things like clicks, likes, words, movements and networks of "friends".[10] Facebook COO, Sheryl Sandberg, explains the idea behind the strategy in this way: "People don't want something targeted to the whole world—they want something that reflects what they

[8] Galloway (2017) p. 5.

[9] Pariser (2011) p. 2.

[10] Galloway (2017) p. 99.

want to see and know".[11] This is smart and not least very convenient for the user. It enables you to dive directly into specialized news and stories about exactly the topics that are especially important to *you*—more easily than ever before.

Gradually, personalization has moved closer to many parts of an individual user's life.[12] To begin with, only ads were tailor-made, then came news and then the entire flow of information: essentially, large chunks of the user's online life. The business formula is simple: The more personally relevant information the tech giants can offer, the more personally targeted ads they can sell, and the higher the probability of the user buying the product offered.

From the moment news was adapted to the user, suddenly it was possible to get news in real time, customized to the individual user. Many people still get their news through TV, radio, newspapers or digital news sources other than social media. But the figures from "Reuters Digital News Report 2017", mapping out news consumption in more than 36 countries, among them Denmark and the US, show that more than half of users—54% to be exact—get news via social media, with an even higher percentage among younger generations. In all countries involved, 33% of youth between the ages of 18 and 24 now *primarily* get their news from social media, and in many countries, news consumption via messengers such as WhatsApp are growing fast. In these statistics, Facebook is by far the most important source of news.[13] As early as 2007, founder Mark Zuckerberg boasted that Facebook might be the biggest news source in the world: "We're actually producing more news in a single day for our 19 million users than every other media outlet has in their entire existence."[14] Since then the number of users has increased a hundredfold.

---

[11] Kirkpatrick, M. "Facebook Exec: All Media Will Be Personalized in 3 to 5 Years" *ReadWriteWeb*. 09-29-10.

[12] Pariser (2011) p. 8–9.

[13] "Digital News Report 2017" *Reuters Institute for the Study of Journalism, Oxford University.*

[14] McGirt, E. "Hacker. Dropout. CEO". *Fast Company*. 01-05-07.

However, the word "producing" is overstating things quite a bit, given the fact that Facebook does not produce researched, investigative, fact-checked journalism. The company does not produce news in any standard public sense but limits itself to passing on news produced by and financed by other organizations—not to mention tidings of the more private kind about cats, food, love and hate, which users exchange among themselves. But even this softer news category is not produced by Facebook, but by its users. Even in its section Trending Topics, Facebook does nothing but forward news coming from others—some of which are important, some less so.

Personalizing the entire flow of information means that the tech giants' algorithms have come to orchestrate large parts of the user's life. The user consumes gossip alongside status updates, news alongside entertainment and ads. The idea is for the user to live and move inside the current: adding, consuming and redirecting information. In an interview with *Wall Street Journal* on the future outlook of the company, Google CEO Eric Schmidt notes: "I actually think most people don't want Google to answer their questions [...] They want Google to tell them what they should be doing next."[15] It may sound bizarre, but Schmidt elaborates by using a leap of imagination. Picture yourself walking down the street. With the information Google has gathered about you, the company knows more or less who you are, what your interests are and who your friends are. Within only a few meters, Google also knows your exact location. Now imagine you need milk and there is a place nearby where milk is sold. This is the moment Google will remind you that you need milk. Moreover, Google will let you know if you're also near a shop that sells precisely those horse track betting posters you recently searched for online. Or it will let you know if it turns out that the nineteenth century assassination you just read about took place across the street. In short: the objective is

---

[15] Jenkins, H.W. Jr. "The Weekend Interview with Eric Schmidt: Google and the Search for the Future" *The Wall Street Journal*. 08-14-10.

that the user will live in a world where personally relevant information is presented everywhere.

It is nothing new that information and news are adapted to the user. For instance, traditional media are often shaped according to opinions and interests of the individual reader, who belongs to a specific segment. Consider a phenomenon such as the sometimes heavily lauded Danish "four newspaper system" from the early twentieth century. It made sure that everyone read a newspaper published by the party they voted for—with news and opinions tailored to each party's electorate. Today the difference is that it is possible to specify all the way down to the individual level. Secondly, the sender's intention is profit, which is connected to the market, and not political orientation, which is connected to society. Naturally, the result of this adjustment is that the remaining media landscape may be ignored. Tech giants help you handle the infinite amount of information available online. They give you an individual news diet. The problem is that this individual tailoring of information automatically creates filter bubbles.[16] Filtering out all things with no direct immediate personalizable relevance creates a bubble of what one already knows, is already interested in, already likes. Generally speaking, a filter bubble has three characteristics: it causes isolation, it is invisible, and it is imposed.[17] The user may thus be left alone, placed in a sort of intellectual isolation. With search results and news feeds completely tailored to each user, we all see radically different versions of the Internet. Furthermore, the factors that determine the ranking of search results change constantly. This also happens with the algo-

---

[16] The existence of filter bubbles is disputed because it may ascribe technology too much power, as long as people believe that such bubbles are an automatic consequence of algorithms. It can be viewed as three levels: filter bubbles are the result of personalized algorithms, which again are the result of programmers, their decisions and more or less conscious principles and values. In this light we see no reason to dismiss the existence of filter bubbles – with the addition that their existence is not unconditional but may be mitigated by an active effort of users.

[17] Pariser (2011) p. 9.

rithms themselves, many of which are programmed to automatically generate variations of themselves in order to get even better results in the form of attention and clicks. It is, therefore, impossible to know exactly how one user's search results differ from those of others.[18] Because the filter bubble is invisible—in the sense that the tech giants avoid drawing attention to the filtering process—one may easily be fooled to believe that it is objective, neutral and true. That is not the case. As tech giants keep the black box of their algorithms a secret, it is difficult or even impossible to notice biases in it, that is, whether it leaves out crucial information. Who does the algorithm believe the individual to be? And why does it show the results it ends up showing?

Lastly, whether the user wants to live in a filter bubble or not is not up for discussion. The filter bubble is imposed—albeit to a lesser extent on Twitter. Neither Facebook nor Google allows for the user to make an active choice about how their world is filtered. Twitter is more open about the fact that it goes through the "profile and activity" of users in order to find out their interests and about the fact that they sell ads based on these interests. As opposed to the two other companies, Twitter allows to opt in or out. It is even possible to see how many advertisers are tracking the user. But even though it is possible to opt out of the "interest-based advertisements" in personalization and data settings, it is not possible to remove oneself entirely from the advertisers' target audience. For instance, Twitter tracks which apps, apart from Twitter, are on the device and which websites (with Twitter integration) the user visits.[19] In the default settings this feature is enabled, which could be a sign that Twitter has already shared the information with potential advertisers. But at least Twitter has allowed for an opt-out. It should not be underestimated, however, that deciding default settings beforehand

---

[18] Lafrance, A. "The Power of Personalization" *Nieman Reports*. 10-18-17.

[19] Fox-Brewster, T. "Creepy Or Cool? Twitter Is Tracking Where You've Been, What You Like And Is Telling Advertisers". *Forbes*. 05-18-17.

gives a certain power to the tech companies—a strategy many online companies use based on the observation that very few users consider their settings, not to speak of changing them. Rather, the users rush past the dire and complicated legal text they must accept in order to even get started. The users are busy, they have only so much attention available to make decisions, and in general they trust everything to be okay when no one else seems to take a deeper look at the settings. More often than not, the standard settings give the companies very deep access to data and digital traces left by the user. Such trust in the companies seems misplaced.

But why are filter bubbles such a big problem if it has the convenience of tailoring the information flow to one's own preferences? Because the user risks being misinformed. It may lead people to believe that factually false beliefs are in fact true. Inside the filter bubble, users risk getting trapped—or trapping themselves—in a closed chamber of conspiracy theories, lies and "fake news", designed especially for the individual user. For example, if you join an anti-vaccine group on Facebook, the algorithms will redirect you to many other groups which also flirt with conspiracies: Why not join an anti-GMO group as well? Or what about the Flat Earth Society (yes, it does exist)? Or how about a group that has the recipe for healing cancer naturally? The recommendations can drag the user into isolating communities, which see their own realities through their own "facts." The system of algorithms may calculate that a given user is the anxious type, finding solace in conspiracies. This is likely to have dangerous consequences. In 2016, many Brazilians believed that the authorities lied when they said the dangerous zika virus could lead to damaged fetuses. Rumors were all over the social media, and no one was sure if the true cause of the damage was vaccines, pesticides or mosquitoes.[20] In Europe and the US, between 2014 and 2017, Russian bots and trolls spread misinformation about vaccines via Twitter. The campaign was

---

[20]Worth, K. "As Brazil Confronts Zika, Vaccine Rumors Shape Perceptions" *Public Broadcasting Service*. 02-16-16.

an attempt to weaken public confidence in vaccination and expose users to contagious diseases. In August 2018, the World Health Organization announced that a record high number of people were affected by the measles in Europe. According to experts, this wave of infections is the result of a decline in the number of people being vaccinated. In the US, the number of parents refusing to vaccinate is also on the rise.[21] On Twitter, one might get the impression that this otherwise safe and efficient vaccine is extremely disputed. Theories and ideas found online lead both highly and less highly educated people to believe that they are capable of seeing through the pharmaceutical industry and professional health recommendations.

Inside the filter bubble, the users find confirmation in their already existing points of view, or at least in the un-activated ones rooted in exactly *their* particular personality type. This tendency is called confirmation bias, and today this is boosted by algorithms automatically sorting aside information that might challenge the user's existing views of the world.

The filter bubble not only traps users inside a confine of already established interests and positions, but it also keeps them *out* of the other bubbles. Here, a person is no longer presented with alternative world views, let alone enabled to see how the bubbles of others actually look. You may not meet the worlds, ideas and arguments of opponents, be they political, religious or other. You may lose the beneficial habit of attempting to understand why others have the opinions they have and fall back on assuming that other viewpoints are simply crazy, stupid, pathological or evil. Sometimes, when outside bubbles, we may realize that an opponent is right, other times it's necessary to know the details of the opponent's position to be able to find compromise. The filter bubble does not support such crucial social options—quite the contrary.

[21] BBC News "Russia trolls 'spreading vaccination misinformation' to create discord" *BBC News.* 08-24-18.

The years 2015–16 saw a vicious example of filter bubbles at work. Google-owned video sharing service YouTube became a key place for the Alt-right movement to organize their extreme rightist views, of white supremacy, malicious racism and the like. This went unnoticed by many users, because it was happening in a growing bubble of enthusiastic users whose activity most other users did not discover—unless they actively searched for those kinds of videos. The YouTube algorithm sent viewers of the extremist material still more videos of the same kind, oftentimes even more extreme ones (more on this later). Some users with many followers were even paid a cut of the on-screen ad revenues their videos would generate. Selected super-users were even paid to produce more videos featuring their political extremism and upload them to their "preferred" YouTube-channel.[22] In the spring of 2017, this was revealed by traditional media, leaving YouTube with almost as much explaining to do as Facebook would have in 2018. Quickly, a number of patchwork solutions were introduced to reassure the public and advertisers, but even though YouTube probably no longer decidedly pays fascists for their views, the structural problem is here to stay: big, problematic, crazy movements can germinate in the shadows of tech giants without the general public finding out. The media ought to hire investigative journalists to continuously check a variety of dissuasive keywords on the different platforms in order to identify such filter bubbles.

Nevertheless, empirical studies of polarization show that the aforementioned problems caused by filter bubbles will be developed in full only in a future where the vast majority of news coverage takes place online. During the 2016 presidential elections in the US, the most important news sources were still television networks such as CNN and Fox News

---

[22] Moser, B. "How YouTube Became the Worldwide Leader in White Supremacy. When Google promises to "curb" extremism on its lucrative video platform, it means nothing more than keeping advertisers happy" *New Republic.* 08-21-17.

(which can also cause bubble effects, to be sure, if a person sticks to one single channel only). According to a 2017 survey, the groups of people in the US who spent the *least* amount of time online were also the groups who had seen the highest increase in political polarization from 1996–2012. Such a result is a compelling reason not to conclude that the full effects of filter bubbles are already here.[23] This does not exclude, however, the existence of bubbles related to knowledge, news, etc. Maybe the result tells us that people with less online experience are more prone to wind up in a filter bubble, whereas people who spend more time online have become more capable of withstanding the effects of bubbles? Despite these important findings, the general diagnosis of filter bubbles is presumably a forecast, admonishing a possible future trend.

Generally speaking, personalization has given the tech giants a very powerful position—they have indeed become a camera lens between user and reality. The user may live inside the filter bubble, where freedom of choice has been replaced by free selection between items on a highly personalized menu only. The filter bubble controls what we see and what we do not see. It is indeed convenient that Google comes up with exactly the right recommendation and presents ads for things the user is actually interested in. But it happens at the expense of the user's freedom. In order for people to act freely, the future must be open and information freely available. In the data race for relevance, tech giants have in fact turned into predictability machines. To a large extent, the giants' harvest of big data makes it possible to predict human behavior, and this means that the future can be calculated and controlled. In the third wave of the Internet,

[23] Cf. Oremus, W. "The Filter Bubble Revisited" *Slate*. 04-05-17; Boxell, L; Gentzkow, M; Shapiro, J.M. "Is the internet causing political polarization? Evidence from demographics", Working Paper, Brown University. Last visited 12-19-18: https://www.brown.edu/Research/Shapiro/pdfs/age-polars.pdf.

users risk having to give up their freedom in order to achieve convenience. This presents a big danger for freedom of expression, understood in the accompanying sense: freedom of information. This is not so much a matter of censorship and removal of certain topics—that happens as well, more on this later—but the fact that the user is led to believe that the individual's bubble makes up the whole relevant world.

Chapter 6
Attention and Dopamine Hits

In January 2017, George Orwell's futuristic dystopian novel *1984* was brought back to life. The reason this 70-year-old classic all of a sudden became a no. 1 bestseller on Amazon is likely to be found in the White House. But in focusing too much on the dangers forecast in *1984*, we should not forget an older and less famous vision, Aldous Huxley's *Brave New World* (1932). It is at least as relevant as the Orwellian dystopia. Its content easily translates to today's criticisms of technology, as it describes how people will love the very same technology that deprives them of their ability to think clearly and critically. Both visions of the future have been put face-to-face by cultural and media critic Neil Postman: "What Orwell feared were those who would ban books. What Huxley feared was that there would be no reason to ban a book, for there would be no one who wanted to read one. Orwell feared those who would deprive us of information. Huxley feared those who would give us so much that we would be reduced to passivity and egoism. Orwell feared that the truth would be concealed from us. Huxley feared the truth would be drowned in a sea of irrelevance. Orwell feared we would become a captive culture. Huxley feared we would become a trivial culture, preoccupied with some equivalent of the feelies, the orgy porgy, and the centrifugal bumble puppy."[1] Postman's presumption, that Huxley's future vision

[1] Postman, N (1989) p. 11–12.

F. Stjernfelt, A. M. Lauritzen, *Your Post has been Removed*,
https://doi.org/10.1007/978-3-030-25968-6_6

was not the least relevant of the two, rings truer today than ever before. In the Information Age, there is an abundance of information and competition over our attention. This has created an attention economy in which tech giants compete for harvesting the most attention and reselling it to third party advertisers.[2] But this war over attention has its victims. First, it has led tech giants to develop still smarter designs whose purpose it is to create dependence. The idea is for users to spend as much time as possible on the platforms and click, like, share as often as possible—to engage. Second, companies add targeted, usually secret, ingredients to their algorithms, which then reward the content that attracts the most attention and traffic. This has led to a knowledge deficit in an online world dominated by emotions. We have long been blind to the negative consequences of this attention-based infrastructure and have come to love a technology that gobbles up our ability to think reflectively.

Information has never been as easily available and all-embracing in its offerings as it is today. As IT guru Mitchell Kapor once put it: "Getting information off the Internet is like taking a drink from a fire hydrant."[3] Such an overwhelming amount of available information has caused a deficit of attention. All the way back in 1971, a Nobel Prize winner in Economics, Herbert Simon, warned of this: "[I]n an information-rich world, the wealth of information means a dearth of something else: a scarcity of whatever it is that information consumes. What information consumes is rather obvious: it consumes the attention of its recipients."[4]

Today, attention should be considered a limited resource. The Internet has become a chaotic marketplace, where the price of information is not paid with dollars and cents, but with attention. Unlike financial means, however, attention is

[2] "Attention economy" became a widespread concept after Davenport and Beck cam out with their book *The Attention Economy* in 2001.

[3] Hansen and Hendricks (2011) p. 13.

[4] Simon (1971) p. 40–41.

distributed more evenly among people.[5] Furthermore, attention cannot be accumulated like money. We are constantly more or less attentive to something. But the common denominator between attention and money is that if the resource is used on one thing, it is at the expense of something else.[6] Philosopher and psychologist William James pointed to this back in 1890, with his well-known definition of attention: "[Attention] is the taking possession by the mind, in clear and vivid form, of one out of what seem several simultaneously possible objects or trains of thought. [...] It implies withdrawal from some things in order to deal effectively with others."[7] The brain, of course, has a limited capacity to handle information. Many perceptions are eliminated, if they take place outside one's field of attention. The phenomenon is called 'inattentional blindness' and has been exposed by Daniel Simons and Christopher Chabris in a famous psychological experiment, "The Invisible Gorilla".[8] The participants watched a video where some basketball players threw two balls around among each other. Participants were asked to count how many times the balls were thrown by one team and at the same time say if they discovered anything unusual. The interesting thing was that while they were busy focusing their attention on the ball and on the players, about one in

---

[5] An important measure of attention is of course *time*—how much time does a user spend on a website and how many ads can the user deal with in that period of time? Attention as a resource, however, is not entirely evenly distributed, as different people can process different amounts of content in the same amount of time, and experienced and intelligent Internet users can visit a lot more websites in a given period of time than less skilled users. Tech giants take this into account by sometimes using other measuring sticks than time, especially the number of sites visited and the number of clicks made; thus, ads can be paid for according to number of visitors and number of clicks.

[6] Wu, T. "Attention Brokers" *NYU Law*. 10-10-15.

[7] James, W. (1890) The Principles of Psychology. Chapter 11: Attention. Classics in the History of Psychology, Green, C.D. (ed.) Last visited: 05-08-18: http://psychclassics.yorku.ca/James/Principles/prin11.htm.

[8] Simons, D. J. & Chabris, C. F. "Gorillas in our midst: sustained inattention blindness for dynamic events" *Perception*, vol. 28. 05-09-99.

two test subjects completely overlooked something: a person in a gorilla costume walked straight through the middle of the group of players, stopped in the middle, beat his chest and wandered off. The experiment shows spectacularly how attention is a scarce resource. There is a lot we sense but do not actually see.

On tech platforms there is high demand for attention. To advertisers, attention is a valuable resource because it is necessary in order to nurture demand for a product, raise awareness about a certain news story or gain political influence.[9] The advertisers' high interest in this scarce resource has led to fierce competition between the tech giants over who can harvest the most attention. Facebook, Twitter, Google and other tech companies can be seen as middle men locked in rivalry, wedged in between the attention economy and the monetary economy, because what they resell is user attention. In a way, the attention economy is no new thing. Studies from as early as the 1970s saw ad-driven American TV networks through a similar lens: their business concept is selling their clients' attention to advertisers. A parallel to this are free newspapers: they also lure clients to give away their attention free of charge, only for it to be capitalized in the form of ad sales. But on the Internet, the attention economy is taken much further, with the help of new means such as addiction and personalization.

Google started this game early, in 2000, by applying the rather obvious idea of offering ads associated with keywords entered by users. Facebook seems to have had significantly more trouble finding out how their accumulated data about users, their likes, their posts and their networks could be used for advertising purposes. According to Facebook insider Antonio García Martínez, it was only in 2013 that the company really cracked the code by opening up a user's news feed to ads that could be targeted to that individual user.[10] That was the result of a combination of ideas. These included:

---

[9] Wu, T. "Attention Brokers" *NYU Law*. 10-10-15.

[10] Martínez (2016) p. 292, 384–88, 394.

extracting user behavior in many general categories (e.g. "hip hop music" instead of the more specific "Eminem"); supplying Facebook's own data with massive amounts of external personal data purchased from data brokers, who had—since the 1960s—built a large industry of targeted print ads via the postal system in the US; identifying the user across indicators such as name, address, phone number, email and IP-address; and retargeting, i.e. continuously following browser and shopping behaviors in real time and registering not only whether they clicked on or merely looked at the ads, but also whether they actually acted upon them.

In this race for attention, the winner is the tech giant who is able to exploit a user's time and attention to the maximum. Therefore, the giants fight to keep the user glued to the screen. Google's former product manager, Tristan Harris, has become a strong critic of the methods his former employer and others deploy to keep user attention. In his opinion, the giants' computer engineering designs have become so sophisticated that they actually hijack the users' brains.[11] Or to put it less dramatically, the systems have become better at exploiting the users' instincts than the users themselves are at controlling them.

Consumers have always been convinced and persuaded by a variety of sellers, town criers or advertisers. But what is new about the attention economy is that the tech platforms are designed to cause outright dependence. That way they harvest the maximum amount of the users' attention in what turns out to be a very unequal struggle because the individual user is up against corporate programmers and psychologists using advanced personalized data, all of whom work hard to predict how the individual user is likely to respond to different temptations. Take for example YouTube's auto-play feature. It is designed to make users spend as much time as possible on the platform by placing—immediately after the end of the video chosen by the user—a related video not

---

[11]Thompson, N. "Our Minds have been Hijacked by Our Phones. Tristan Harris Wants to Rescue Them" *Wired*. 07-06-17.

chosen by the user. It is undoubtedly entertaining when YouTube sucks the user into a current of *lol cats*, finding ever funnier and crazier versions. But YouTube is not preoccupied with the fact that this can divert users not only from attending to their personal wellbeing in the form of sleep, family time and work, but also from serious news, debates and public life. In similar fashion, the teaser clickbaits work by holding back interesting information in order to make users click through more ads in order to reach the wanted information.

In line with Tristan Harris, Facebook co-founder Sean Parker has revealed that Facebook was developed from the idea of maximum exploitation of users' time and attention. Parker explains how the Facebook *like* button is designed to give the user "a little dopamine hit", which motivates the user to upload more content and spend more time on the website. The same hit is released by comments to posts and images. Parker elaborates: "It's a social-validation feedback loop … exactly the kind of thing that a hacker like myself would come up with, because you're exploiting a vulnerability in human psychology."[12] This makes "liking" the fundamental connection made between "friends": it is all about social acceptance. But what if the button instead said "important" and referred to something a person found important for his "friends" to see?

There is an interesting myth about the *like* feature — that it supposedly can be traced back to French philosopher René Girard, who is even referred to as the "Godfather of the like button". The element of truth to this myth has to do with Peter Thiel, Facebook's first big investor, board member and one of the most prominent opinion leaders of Silicon Valley. Thiel is famous for his libertarian critique of government in all its forms and for his vision of stateless societies forming on independent islands, ships and the like. Thiel is claimed to have based his early investment in Facebook on an analysis of the

[12] Solon, O. "Ex-Facebook president Sean Parker: site made to exploit human 'vulnerability'" *The Guardian*. 11-09-17.

business concept's opportunities built on René Girard's theory of "mimetic desire".[13]

The idea is that unlike human needs, human desires are not spontaneous or given but mediated through other people, as they are largely directed at what the person observes *others* to desire. People want what others have. Facebook is designed to do exactly that, mediate between people's desires: you continuously update your knowledge of what others "like" and respond to it by hitting "like" yourself — and exposing to your "friends" an image of yourself as someone who has attained the coveted objects of desire. Thiel himself took Girard's classes when Girard was a professor at Stanford University. Thiel saw Facebook as a technology that was based on the mimetic nature of humanity and which gave mimetic desire new ways to flourish and spread.

In the year Facebook was founded, 2004, Thiel sponsored a symposium with and about Girard, entitled *Politics and Apocalypse*. It was held at Stanford near Silicon Valley, and Thiel himself participated with his talk "The Straussian Moment", referring to the German-American political thinker Leo Strauss.[14] That talk showed Thiel's awareness of the multiple components of Girard's theory. The mimetic desire implies that everybody wants what others have. That of course leads to infinite strife and conflict between people — occasionally culminating in a "mimetic crisis", gang battles, rebellion, persecution, civil war, revolution, war, etc. Girard now claims that the traditional way of overcoming such a crisis and re-establishing peace is to designate a scapegoat who is then obliged to bear all responsibility for the crisis and who is consequently imprisoned, exorcised, killed or otherwise sacrificed and pacified, so peace can prevail. But, of course, peace does not last because the war was never really the scapegoat's fault, and the constant crises require a

[13] Shullenberger, G. "Mimesis and Violence Part I: Peter Thiel's French Connection" *Cybergology*. 08-02-16.

[14] The symposium was later published as a book, cf. Hamerton-Kelly (2007).

constant supply of scapegoats. Girard, who was a Catholic, claimed that Christianity, in its right interpretation, is the only cure against ongoing strife and exorcism of scapegoats, since the Crucifixion of Jesus is the last and definitive sacrifice, which is why Christians must turn the other cheek. This is where Thiel strays away from his master. In his essay, combining Girard with Carl Schmitt, Thiel rages against Enlightenment ideas which he accuses of hiding the true, violent nature of humanity—and which, nevertheless, are in the process of being exposed in a disclosure that will once and for all overthrow modernity itself. In this view, the Enlightenment project is mistaken in that "... the whole issue of human violence has been whitewashed away by the Enlightenment."[15] Enlightenment, according to Thiel, caused a shutdown of all discussion of human nature (which is actually pretty inaccurate, seen from the point of view of intellectual history).[16] He also blames the Enlightenment movement for the vulnerability of the West when up against terrorist violence, because Western principles stand in the way of a hard and efficient response from the West. We therefore need "...to awaken from that very long and profitable period of intellectual slumber and amnesia, that is so misleadingly called the Enlightenment."[17]

Thiel then considers what a Christian prince or statesman is supposed to do, once the Enlightenment project runs dry. But he comes up with no clear answer other than that leaders must be prepared to bravely lead a world completely different from the Enlightenment version of the modern world, with its peaceful but entirely elusive and ineffective discussions which Thiel so adamantly mocks the Enlightenment project for having promoted. With his martial preference for Schmitt and his insistence on a society that can only be politically united if it singles out a common enemy, Thiel does not

---

[15]Thiel (2007) p. 209.

[16]The eight conceptions of humanity currently at odds with each other, as mapped out in David Budtz et al. (2018) are all to varying degrees rooted in Enlightenment ideas.

[17]Thiel (2007) p. 198.

seem to share Girard's pacifism. They do share, however, the drive to expose humanity's true nature. Thiel compares Leo Strauss to Girard, pointing to *time* as what separates the two. While Strauss is hesitant to reveal the dark side of humanity, Girard is more impatient as to how quickly modernity should be overthrown by the disastrous revelation of humanity's violent nature. On this matter, Thiel is on Girard's side: as soon as possible!

A month after Thiel's symposium on Girard, he went on to invest the decisive 500,000 dollars in Facebook. Why this investment? Empirically, it is true that the existence of Facebook actuates the next steps of Girard's theory: battle and strife are coming thick and fast, tribalization is increasing, not least because the attention economy naturally focuses on the most striking and click-amassing aspects: fear, anger, hatred, rage, balkanization, violence, etc. It is also evident that the scapegoat logic thrives on the platform, in the form of more or less organized social media shitstorms directed at select victims. As noted by writer Geoff Shullenberger, these somewhat violent Facebook phenomena might be more than simply unexpected side effects; they may in fact be Facebook's key defining "features".

Did Thiel consider Facebook an opportunity to start an enormous mimetic crisis, so that the Enlightenment project could end as soon as possible? In the essay he references Girard: "However, the new science of humanity must thrive the idea of imitation, or mimesis, much further than it has in the past."[18] In Thiel's short 2014 manifesto, *Zero to One*, Girard's name is absent — but not his theory. In the final chapter, the heroes and idols of different cultures are analyzed through Girard's theory—inherent in these persons are

[18]Thiel (2007) p. 209. It is a thought-provoking fact that several of the tech giants' principles seem to be traceable to more or less well-understood humanistic and philosophical doctrines, e.g. political communitarianism, Mauss' gift economy and Girard's theory of desire. Although the effects of humanists on the Internet might come off more as "grimpact" than impact, they can hardly be held responsible for the use of half-baked versions of their doctrines.

both potential gods and scapegoats. The heroes of our times are the founders of technological start-up companies, notes Thiel with little modesty. At the same time, he warns against "The Founder's Paradox": the fact that the heroic status of the founders may quickly be reversed and turned against them, resulting in scapegoat persecution.[19] In Shullenberger's eyes, Thiel thinks of Facebook—in the absence of effective authorities—as an effective way to channel mimetic violence. This gives Facebook a powerful arsenal of violent means in its battle against the authorities, which would also protect the heroic tech entrepreneurs like himself from being singled out as scapegoats.[20] Such a perception of Facebook is, needless to say, in some contrast to his friend Zuckerberg's rosy ideas of "a global community".[21]

Regardless of how well the tech giants have or have not understood the basic nature of human beings, they have indeed obtained large, data-driven psychological powers. Dan Ariely, a Professor of Psychology and Behavioral Economics, believes that irregular reward systems such as likes, tweets and comments can be seen as an updated version of American behavioral psychologist B.F. Skinner's work from the 1930s.[22] Skinner placed rats in specially built boxes, where they

---

[19] Thiel (2014) p. 173ff.

[20] Schullenberger, G. "Mimesis and Facebook Part 2: Harnessing Violence" *Cyborgology*. 08-09-16.

[21] Thiel's connection to people like Steve Bannon has aggravated Facebook's current image problems. Cambridge Analytica whistle-blower Christopher Wylie claims that top men from Thiel's intelligence tech giant Palantir took active part in processing the leaked Facebook data at Cambridge Analytica, without any official contract between the two companies. Thiel has publicly declared his support for Trump, but Palantir denies having had any collaboration with Cambridge Analytica—cf. Karpal, A. "Palantir worked with Cambridge Analytica on the Facebook data it acquired, whistleblower alleges" *CNBC.com*. 03-27-18. Palantir does, however, admit that their company's analyst Alfredas Chmieliauskas collaborated with Cambridge Analytica, allegedly as a private individual, cf. Lomas, N. "Palantir confirms a staff link with Cambridge Analytica" *TechCrunch*. 03-28-18.

[22] Ariely, D. "Apple should use the iPhone to stop distracting us" *Wired*. 04-17-18.

learned to press buttons to get food as a reward. Skinner discovered that the most effective way of maintaining a particular behavior is by giving out the rewards randomly. One might think that the rat in Skinner's box would press the button less if reward was not certain. But in the experiment, it turned out that the rat pressed harder and longer than when the reward followed automatically. Even when the reward disappeared, the rat would continue to press. Today, users hammer the keyboard or drum on the touch screen hoping for virtual reward in the form of recognition through new emails, retweets and likes. Similarly, the rat would hammer the button on the Skinner Box hoping for food. The information that ticks in on a phone may often be uninteresting—and only rarely is it indispensable. But suddenly something important or useful *could* pop up. Therefore, the phone must be checked 100 to 150 times a day. Deducting six to seven hours of sleep, that equals six to eight times an hour.[23] The same technique is known from the classic slot machines, or one-armed bandits: the player never knows if the next move will trigger nothing, pennies, or maybe the big jackpot. There is still no clear definition of smartphone addiction. But some countries have begun, little by little, to recognize the problem: In France, a total ban on smartphones in schools has been introduced, citing public health as an argument. The United States now has rehabilitation centers for children who cannot let go of the screen. Spain recently recognized the phenomenon as disorder requiring treatment on par with ludomania and alcoholism—that is, a pathological condition that restricts the users' freedom and prevents them from acting and expressing themselves freely.

It is tempting to believe that the huge amounts of freely available information have made the world a wiser place. After all, information may be a source of learning. In 2007, Clive Thompson from tech magazine *Wired* even blessed the new opportunities that Silicon Valley memory equipped the very act of thinking with: "[...] the cyborg future is here.

[23] Guldager, D.H. "Du tjekker den 150 gange i døgnet – sådan slipper du af med afhængighed" *TV2 Nyheder*. 01-11-18.

Almost without noticing it, we've outsourced important peripheral brain functions to the silicon around us. And frankly, I kind of like it. I feel much smarter when I'm using the Internet as a mental plug-in during my daily chitchat."[24] But in the Information Age, it is more important than ever to differentiate between knowledge and information. Tech giants do not take into account that these two concepts are different. Knowledge implies information, but information does not necessarily imply knowledge. First, the difference is that knowledge is accompanied by a truth requirement. Facts must be respected. As a requirement, this cannot be satisfied only by being informed about what others like, think, believe, hope or feel. Second, there is a difference in the way information is processed. Pure information is obtained easily, quickly and cheaply. But knowledge cannot simply be collected, it is a systematic practice with a given purpose. It is based on organizing, processing and formatting information. And it requires tools, will, judgment and audacity. Users may be fooled by information, but it is harder to be fooled when they have knowledge.[25]

In its abundance, the Age of Information has led to a form of knowledge collapse: To the tech giants there is no difference between content elements. There is nothing but content. It's all about attention and traffic, aimed at *something*, no matter what. But this happens at the expense of truth and facts. The user is flooded with information and opinions—easily produced, sometimes even completely free of charge, and they do not have to deal with facts and truths. No distinction is made between cute cat videos, ISIS propaganda, ads, conspiracy theories, scientific insights or breaking news. It turns out that since it is only about attention and traffic, producing and distributing disinformation has become easier than ever before. A well-known example is the by-far most virally active piece of online news during the 2016 US presidential campaign: *The Pope Supports Trump*. It generated

[24]Thompson, C. "Your outboard brain knows all" *Wired*. 08-25-07.

[25]Hansen and Hendricks (2011) p. 11–14.

960,000 shares, reactions and comments on Facebook. But the news was fake, fabricated and produced in Macedonia for the purpose of generating ad profits.[26] By comparison, the most popular piece of mainstream news got 849,000 reactions. It came from *The Washington Post* and was about Trump's history of corruption charges: "Trump's history of corruption is mind-boggling. So why is Clinton supposedly the corrupt one?"[27] As early as 2013, the World Economic Forum announced that disinformation is the new global challenge. Citizens, politicians, academics, and reporters can all be misled. When misinformed, people believe that factually false convictions are in fact true. Disinformation may be distortions of facts, fact-denying conspiracy theories, lies or false news stories.[28] Obviously, the challenge of navigating through this maze has always been there. But on the Internet, it happens on a new scale and at a new pace.

American professors Jonah Berger and Katherine Milkman set out to investigate what types of ads, videos, news stories, etc. go viral in the infinite offerings of online information. What does it take to win jackpot in this advanced algorithm system? By studying data from all the *New York Times* articles published over a three-month period, they found that feelings are what makes content go viral.[29] More specifically, content driven by activity-mobilizing emotions wins, by eliciting both negative ones like anger and fear and positive ones such as awe and fascination. The reason is that they incite action in the form of likes, retweets, shares, debates, counter-

---

[26] Craig Silverman has done a great deal of work mapping out websites that fabricate "fake news" in order to attract advertisement traffic; at the time of writing his list is comprised of 169 such websites, see "BuzzFeedNews/2017-12-fake-news-top-50". Last visited 07-30-18: https://github.com/BuzzFeedNews/2017-12-fake-news-top-50/blob/master/data/sites_2017.csv

[27] Silverman, C. "This Analysis Shows How Viral Fake Election News Stories Outperformed Real News On Facebook" *BuzzFeed.* 11-16-16.

[28] Hendricks and Vestergaard (2017) p. 98.

[29] Berger, J. & Milkman, K. L. (2012) "What Makes Online Content Viral?" *Journal of Marketing Research*, vol 49: pp. 192–205.

arguments, etc. They make an effective fuel to activate the algorithm system and set an agenda. This explains President Trump's unstoppable viral success: People get excited when he tweets that Mexicans are rapists and killers or proposes to ban all Muslims from entering the United States. Both supporters and opponents contribute to spreading this on the web. On the tech platforms, emotions set the pace. Apart from emotions, in his book *Contagious: Why Things Catch On* (2013), Berger points to five other ingredients which help accelerate social transmission: A story must give users who share it *social currency*; it must be able to *trigger*, such as when the word "beer" causes one to think of salted peanuts; it must be of *public interest* to the general public; it must have *practical value,* e.g. by saving time or offering something; and finally, it must be a good *story* that is easy to reproduce.[30] It is worth noting the complete absence of concepts such as true and false.

Information has been commercialized to such an extent that all expressions have become a sort of commodity where the user must supply the right elements. Dry and complex problems, no matter how important, rarely find an audience. The users' audience can easily press the *like* button, but no one has developed a *challenging but really important story* button and given it the same opportunities for exposure in the algorithms' scoring system. Incited by the company's adversity, Facebook started to offer more expression possibilities. In 2015, a change was made, so the user—in addition to *liking* a post—was also able to hand out a heart, a surprised emoji or a sad face. But overall, all is about making the story *trend*—regardless of whether it is true or false, difficult or easy, new or old, relevant or irrelevant.

A consequence of the algorithm systems of the tech giants is that your ability to stand out and reach an audience is limited to your ability to reap and spread attention. Expressions with the most attention get the highest degree of exposure and thus the most advertising payments, while expressions

[30] Berger (2013) pp. 21–24.

with less drown in the noise. The limelight-stealing stories are short-lived and characterized by fleeting emotions with high entertainment value, conflict and sensation. The story of 35-year-old Twitter user Eric Tucker is a spot-on example. On November 9, 2016, he tweeted to his mere 40 followers that paid protesters were taken by bus to protest rallies against newly elected Donald Trump: "Anti-Trump protestors in Austin today are not as organic as they seem. Here are the busses they came in. #fakeprotests #trump2016 #austin." The tweet quickly went viral, adding lots of fuel to the national conspiratorial fire. It was shared 16,000 times on Twitter and more than 350,000 times on Facebook. The dubious origin of this piece of "news" was smoothed out little by little. At first, Reddit was referenced as a source of this breaking news. Then, suddenly the source was conservative debate forum Free Republic. Soon after, there were various Facebook pages such as the hardliner conservative publisher Robertson Family Values with more than a million followers and it was eventually promoted in a confirming tweet from the White House itself: "Just had a very open and successful presidential election. Now professional protesters, incited by the media, are protesting. Very unfair!" There was just one small problem: These buses with paid protesters did not exist. The story was simply not true. After two days, when Tucker had realized the effects of his provocation, he deleted the original tweet and posted a picture of the very same tweet with FALSE stamped in red on top of it. But not surprisingly, the correction notice got minimal attention—only 29 retweets and 27 likes within the following week, to be exact.[31] The truth is simply not as entertaining and stimulating as red-hot rumors. This is also well known from traditional print media, where the correction notice pertaining to a front-page story is usually written in fine print somewhere deep inside the paper. But on the web, the possibilities for the penetration of misinformation are multiplied.

---

[31] Maheshwari, S. "How Fake News Goes Viral: A Case Study" *New York Times*. 11-20-16.

Sociologist Danah Boyd has also noted how certain feelings achieve viral success. She explains how people consume content that simply stimulates their minds and senses. That is the reason why users are drawn to content that excites, activates, entertains or otherwise elicits emotional response. This content is not always the "best" content – in the sense of acquiring knowledge. But in the same way that the body is programmed to crave fat and sugar because they are energy boosts and are rarely found in nature, humans are also programmed to pay attention to things that stimulate and awaken passions: Obnoxious, violent or sexual content; humiliating, embarrassing or offensive gossip.[32] The tech platforms have, in other words, become the dictatorships of emotions—especially negative ones. The algorithm system rewards what is fleeting and short-lived. As a consequence, content that does not match such uncurbed emotional release simply risks drowning in the noise. Again, an infringement upon freedom of speech takes place—both in the sense of freedom of information and the right to freely express one's point of view.

---

[32] Boyd, D. "Streams of Content, Limited Attention: The Flow of Information through Social Media". *Conference: Web 2.0 Expo*. 11-17-09.

Chapter 7
Tech Giants as Ad Brokers

In 2017, *The Australian* published a confidential document leaked from Facebook. It revealed how the company had offered advertisers the opportunity to target ads to 6.4 million Facebook users as young as 14 who were going through psychologically vulnerable phases of their lives. In these phases, the teenagers felt "worthless", "insecure", "stressed" or "anxious", among other things. To track these emotional downturns, Facebook had monitored the messages, images, interactions and activity of their users on the Internet.[1]

Using big data harvested from user behavior and analyzed by sophisticated algorithms, Facebook, Twitter, Google and other tech companies can predict large parts of people's preferences and behaviors. This is tremendously valuable for advertisers who want to control and manipulate consumer behavior. Internet guru Jaron Lanier, who in his recent book recommends for people to shut down their accounts on social media, calls the real objective of the attention economy "behavioral modification". The tech giants quite simply strive to change people's behavior.[2] Generally speaking, advertising is not necessarily manipulative. But when very specific parts of the personal information of the consumers are used against them to lure them to buy products that they would

[1]Tiku, N. "Get Ready for the Next Big Privacy Backlash Against Facebook" *Wired*. 05-21-17.

[2]Lanier (2018).

F. Stjernfelt, A. M. Lauritzen, *Your Post has been Removed*,
https://doi.org/10.1007/978-3-030-25968-6_7

not otherwise buy, then it is. When an ad for slimming tea targets teens right at the moment they feel the most down, or when ads for liquor brands can be directed at easy-to-tempt alcoholics, then it is. The concerns of today not only revolve around how much information the tech giants have on us. The question is also to what extent this information can be used as a weapon against the users without us having—or getting—a chance to even find out.

Facebook, Twitter and Google have different and, to various degrees, idealistic points of departure. Google's mission is to organize the world's information and make it universally available and useful. Twitter wants to give all people the possibility to create and share ideas and information—at any time and without any hindrance. The third giant, Facebook, wants to give people the possibility to engage in friendships, create communities and make the world more open and connected. But the bottom line for all three tech giants depends on the same elementary business model: targeted, relevant advertising.

Google's main source of income is the ads placed at the top of search results, next to the search results and on the searched websites. At the congressional hearing in April 2018, in front of a rather slow-witted Senator, Mark Zuckerberg made it clear: "Yes, Congresswoman, we run ads. That's the business model [...]."[3] That was not how things were to begin with, but in 2008, Facebook recruited Sheryl Sandberg from Google as second in command. In hiring her, Facebook got a hard-working ad broker who finally managed to crack the code and radically expand the company's advertisement foundation. According to international media agency GroupM, Facebook and Google together now control 84% of the digital ad revenue in the US, giving them a de facto duopoly on the advertising market.[4] And at Twitter, ad reve-

---

[3]Transcript courtesy of Bloomberg Government. "Transcript of Zuckerberg's appearance before House committee". *The Washington Post*. 04-11-18.

[4]Garrahan, M. "Google and Facebook dominance forecast to rise" *Financial Times*. 12-04-17.

nue makes up roughly 86% of the total income of the company.[5]

The core of the three companies' business models makes them ad brokers rather than the IT companies of their origin. Their main task is to monetize their services by the use of very detailed user profiles to capitalize on the opportunity to accurately target advertising to highly specific and selected user groups—characterized by anything from age, race, gender, housing, income, looks, religion, health, location, psychology, problems, hobbies, detailed music preferences, literature, movies, food, make-up, anything. The advertisers are the real clients of the tech giants, and the user is but the product. With this massive monitoring of user behavior, both online and offline, companies can make accurate and automated predictions about what ads, news and political messages users are most susceptible to, and about what content will make them click, like, share and scroll down the endless feed. Whether or not tech giants in fact sell data is a matter of semantics. If you claim that they do, they furiously refer to the fact that they do not hand over user data to advertisers and they might file a court case against you for libel. But they do sell data in the sense that they give advertisers data-based access to hyper-accurately target their advertising.

In an academic article written for Stanford University back in 1998, Google founders Larry Page and Sergey Brin explain the problems involved when combining search engines and advertising: "The goals of the advertising business model do not always correspond to providing quality search to users. [...] we expect that advertising funded search engines will be inherently biased towards the advertisers and away from the needs of the consumers."[6] It was meant as a criticism of the advertising setup of the day, which—lacking targeted focus—would bombard users with as many ads as possible. Instead, Page and Brin wanted to target their efforts

---

[5] Beers, B. "How does Twitter Make Money?" *Investopedia*. 04-25-18.

[6] Brin, S. & Page, L. "The Anatomy of Large-Scale Hypertextual Web Search Engine". Last visited 04-26-18: http://infolab.stanford.edu/~backrub/google.html.

at specific users with fewer and increasingly customized ads.[7] No doubt, it was a significant improvement for users, not to mention advertisers. Combined with new algorithms that quickly sorted through what was and was not useful online, the search engine became a success. But the two partners did not pay attention to their own criticism as they suddenly faced the choice between what was good for the users versus what was good for the company. The popular and highly admired PageRank algorithm was modified and instead, from 2009, personalized searches became the core strategy, resulting in more opportunities and skyrocketing interest from advertisers. Today, Google together with Apple, Microsoft, Amazon and Facebook are the top five biggest corporations in the world.[8]

When Facebook, Twitter, Google and others offer free services for users, there are two sides to this. From a user point of view, it is obviously attractive to have a good and well-organized service for information and friend contacts, and not to mention free. Speechifying in flowery terms, the CEOs of these companies boast that their real purpose is to assist users and improve the world. However, from an economic point of view, the primary motive is to entice potential users into a digital panopticon, one which is incredibly skilled at harvesting data.

Users do not really sense they are being watched. They may be surprised once in a while, when they find a remarkably relevant ad on their screen. The platforms present themselves as networks of unlimited freedom and communication, offering nothing more than posts, search results, tweets and comments. But let us for a moment zoom in on the example of Facebook. The company registers every single click, every

---

[7] Blumenthal, P. "Facebook And Google's Surveillance Capitalism Model Is In Trouble" *Huffington Post*. 01-27-18.

[8] In 2006, the five biggest were Exxon Mobil, General Electric, Microsoft, Citigroup, Bank of America; in 2016 only Microsoft remains in the top five: Apple, Alphabet (Google), Microsoft, Amazon, Facebook. The source is S&P Dow Jones Indices, quoted from Taplin, J. "Is It Time to Break Up Google?" *New York Times*. 04-22-17.

"like" and every comment. However, the collection of data is not limited to content the users explicitly choose to upload (and which they recently, after numerous protests, have the opportunity to remove). It also collects browser history, what the user has been doing on Facebook and outside Facebook, and achieves external personal data such as geographic, financial, medical and other information about the user by purchasing large amounts of data from lesser-known but huge data broker companies, e.g. Acxiom, DataLogix, Epsilon and Experian (European countries have laws to partly block data brokers, especially since May 25, 2018, when GDPR came into force). These are large but not very publicly-known companies, which, ever since the 1960s, have provided detailed personal data to an already extensive industry of targeted traditional paper advertisements by mail. These players now gained new digital customers. After the Cambridge Analytica scandal of early 2018, Facebook declared that the company would stop brokering such personal data, but not that the company would eliminate already brokered data.[9] The company even creates so-called shadow profiles of people not yet on Facebook, if all they have done is contact someone who is indeed on Facebook, or if they visit a website featuring a *like* and *share* button.[10] At the congressional hearing, Zuckerberg was forced to admit that the company follows user movements around the Internet, even when they are logged out of their Facebook accounts.[11] With this massive surveillance, tech giants have the opportunity to gather large amounts of raw data on users and translate the data into personal information. At the congressional hearing, Zuckerberg was unable to give an estimated average amount of data per user, but it is estimated that Facebook has developed more than 52,000 categories

---

[9] Following this, several of these companies took a stock dive, which indicated how they had largely acted as data collectors for Facebook.

[10] Tufekci, Z. "Facebook's Surveillance Machine" *New York Times*. 03-19-18.

[11] Plougsgaard, H. "Facebook samler også data fra personer, der ikke bruger Facebook" *Jyllands-Posten*. 04-11-18.

for organizing these data.[12] The data broker Acxiom, one of Facebook's biggest business partners, is said to have 1500 data points on each and every one of more than 500 million individuals across the globe, most of them in the US.

These data are categorized and converted into information and thus become a valuable asset for advertisers trying to predict, direct and manipulate consumer behavior. In the digital panopticon, the user becomes a commodity—in the form of a data package—to be processed and negotiated for financial use. Big Brother and Big Business have formed an unholy alliance. The detailed personal data are not forwarded to the advertiser, but it is the *access* to users by way of these data that is being sold. In that way tech giants can claim that they do not sell data—and even sue anyone who claims that they do.

An interesting aspect to the digital panopticon is that it comes off as a *friendly* kind of power. No explicit threat, command, prohibition, or physical punishment is involved. On the contrary, the panopticon is based on positive benefits and convenience: free communication, information, community, knowledge sharing and searching. The worst sanction a user can meet is exclusion: without accepting the terms of service (that is, without surrendering data or complying with the community standards), access is denied. This is a very subtle form of coercion, based on the user's fear of missing out. This seeming kindness has turned out to be an incredibly effective strategy for harvesting data. In the eyes of the tech giants, it is a question of connecting with people's psyches. This kind power motivates the user to constantly disclose, share and participate, to communicate points of view, wishes and preferences. According to German cultural philosopher Byung-Chul Han, this "friendly" power is to blame for the user's crisis of freedom: this is not freedom repressed, but freedom

[12]The list of person categories offered to advertisers for targeting their ads has 29.000 categories (2016 numbers); Angwin, J. & Mattu, S. & Parris, T. "Facebook Doesn't Tell Users Everything It Really Knows About Them" *ProPublica*. 12-27-16.

exploited.[13] In order to gain convenience, users subject themselves to a form of *self*-surveillance, because they willingly hand over their information to the platforms and thus also indirectly to the hungry eyes of the advertisers. In 2019, professor Shoshanna Zuboff developed an analytical conception of the business model – "surveillance capitalism".[14]

Usually, involuntary surveillance is seen as a problematic or even criminal invasion of privacy. But in the digital panopticon, the surveillance takes place voluntarily because it is considered a mutual advantage – a partnership. This is what makes this form of surveillance so effective and relatively uncontroversial. But in a sense, this partnership is an illusion. The users take part without real informed consent. They may have accepted the terms of service, but they never know how they are categorized and measured when profiled and resold to advertisers. The users participate without knowing exactly what they are participating in. Once consent is given, the tech giants are free to continuously modify the terms of service—for instance they can change the algorithms without having to ask the user to acknowledge such modified conditions.

---

[13] Han (2017) p. 15.

[14] See Zuboff (2019).

Chapter 8
Improving the World or Capitalizing on It?

One thing is difficult to decipher: to what degree do tech giants *actually* see themselves as saving the world, and to what degree do they see themselves as capitalizing on it? Obviously, one does not exclude the other, but how do the two sides balance and what is the actual improvement the tech giants bring? In an interesting interview, Mark Zuckerberg defended the company's treatment of user data by framing it as a historical philosophical trend where people are becoming more open and more willing to share data about themselves with friends, with companies, ultimately with anybody. But the trend is also a normative one: according to Zuckerberg, people must be brought to realize that *they only have one identity.*[1] Not only does Zuckerberg here exalt himself as a philosopher but he apparently feels compelled to accept highly normative consequences of his own ideas—and to claim that these consequences should be acceptable to his users, imposing this philosophy on them. *Everyone should know everything about everyone*—this is the moral imperative Zuckerberg uses to legitimize his business model. Such an idea would erase the distinction between public and private, which has played an important role in

[1] "You have one identity (…) The days of you having a different image for your work friends or co-workers and for the other people you know are probably coming to an end pretty quickly (…) Having two identities for yourself is an example of a lack of integrity". Kirkpatrick (2010) p.199.

F. Stjernfelt, A. M. Lauritzen, *Your Post has been Removed*,
https://doi.org/10.1007/978-3-030-25968-6_8

modern societies where privacy has been considered a fundamental political good, and where the elementary freedoms of expression, of thought, of beliefs have been articulated to protect individuals and their sphere of privacy against government abuse and regimentation. The moral consequence of Zuckerberg's dictum—beyond the very handy legitimization of his business model's unlimited data collection—is that people should not behave differently in different contexts. You cannot be one person to your friends, then another to your family, and a third to your colleagues, etc. You cannot run away from your past, either, if suddenly something more preferable comes up. And neither can you evolve and develop your personality, put past mistakes behind you. In Zuckerberg's line of thought, people bring their detailed digital identity with them everywhere and, what is more, that identity should be fully available to anyone. It is curious that he does not see how this would cause a tremendous loss of personal freedom—the freedom to evolve, change, apply different skills in different contexts. During the congressional hearings in April 2018, one Senator took a shrewd look at this data gathering and innocently asked Zuckerberg what hotel he was staying in while in Washington. Zuckerberg preferred not to disclose that information. Perhaps he did not want fans, journalists or assassins lurking around. But that would indeed be the collateral damage if he took his own medicine.

Mark Zuckerberg's philosophical considerations may appear amateurish, but we must take them seriously, coming from a man who controls the conditions framing the online activities of billions of people. It is no wonder that his reflections have shifted, looking at the enormous growth and change Facebook has seen over the past fifteen years since Zuckerberg started out from his college dorm room in 2004. As *New York Magazine* editor Max Read points out, it is doubtful whether Zuckerberg—or anyone at all—even knows what Facebook really is anymore.[2] Read elaborates by noting that it is the very same company that sends birthday reminders while at the same time striving to ensure the integrity of

---

[2] Read, M. "Does even Mark Zuckerberg know what Facebook is?" *New York Magazine*. 09-01-17.

the German elections. Zuckerberg's initial goal was for information to flow as freely as possible, captured by the slogan "Information wants to be free"—in Facebook, this developed into the slogan "making the world more open and connected". In Facebook's onboarding information for new employees, their "Little Red Book", it is described in this way: "Facebook was not originally created to be a company. It was built to accomplish a mission—to make the world more open and connected."[3] In the 1990s, "Connecting People" was the slogan of then mobile phone giant Nokia. But in the spring of 2018, the phrase became associated with Facebook. It turned out that in a 2016 internal memo entitled "The Ugly", Facebook deputy director Andrew Bosworth had presented the company's strategy for growth at any price, including death victims, by concluding, in mantra-like fashion: "We connect people. Period."[4]

As British historian Niall Ferguson states, in his book *The Square and the Tower,* it is naive to believe that new technologies connecting people with each other outside of existing power structures will automatically and seamlessly lead to peace and agreement. His counterexample is when the modern printing press was invented around 1450, leading to a media revolution even greater than the Internet and proba-

---

[3] Quoted from Ferguson (2017) p. 354.

[4] R. Mac, C. Warzel & A. Kantrowitz: "Top Facebook Executive Defended Data Collection In 2016 Memo—And Warned That Facebook Could Get People Killed" *BuzzFeed*. 03-29-18—here, Bosworth's memo is quoted in extenso. Bosworth's memo documented a surprising awareness inside Facebook of the dangerous sides to the growth strategy: "So we connect more people", he wrote in another section of the memo, "That can be bad if they make it negative. Maybe it costs someone a life by exposing someone to bullies. Maybe someone dies in a terrorist attack coordinated on our tools. And still we connect people. The ugly truth is that we believe in connecting people so deeply that anything that allows us to connect more people more often is ∗de facto∗ good". Bosworth thus found that terrorism and death were consequences that one had to accept to realize the growth strategy: "In almost all of our work, we have to answer hard questions about what we believe", he wrote in his memo. "We have to justify the metrics and make sure they aren't losing out on a bigger picture. But connecting people. That's our imperative. Because that's what we do. We connect people".

bly one of the most important facilitators of the Reformation of the following century. It made deviant theologians and other dissidents capable of quickly publishing their new thoughts without having to get permission from neither Church nor King. As an example, Martin Luther is believed to have published a new text around every two weeks throughout his adult life.[5] This led to a large clash with the church authorities—but in and of itself it did not lead to freer, more democratic or even peaceful conditions, quite the contrary. Many of the new protestant theologies were even more authoritarian and belligerent than the Catholic Church, and the many competing churches often found themselves in conflict with each other, all of which led to the vast religious wars of sixteenth and seventeenth century Europe, culminating in the Thirty Years' War. *Connecting people.*

After the discovery that Facebook had been used as a key tool to spread false news and manipulate democratic elections, Zuckerberg is now in a process of changing this philosophy. On February 17, 2017, he issued a creed entitled "Building Global Community". Here, the concept of "community" replaces that of free information and of connecting ideas as key elements of Facebook philosophy. It is the largest public manifestation of Facebook principles thus far. It seems as if Zuckerberg has now realized that connecting people is not enough. The manifesto keeps to positive feel-good terms, but the backdrop is "fake news", Russian bots and cyber warfare. People do not automatically become friendly and peaceful by being more connected. More likely, the many links between people open new paths for misinformation, outgrouping, balkanization, hostility, crime and war. Apparently, this needs to be solved through moral sermons with a call for values. Now Zuckerberg says: "... the most important thing we at Facebook can do is develop the social infrastructure to give people the power to build a global community that works for all of us."[6] This is then elaborated into five aspects of "community": sup-

[5] For more on the not so peaceful sides of Luther's workings, see Stjernfelt (2017).

[6] Zuckerberg, M. "Building Global Community" *Facebook*. 02-16-17.

port, security, information, civil society and inclusion.[7] "Global community" comes off as if everyone is connected to everyone, resonant of McLuhan's idea of "global village"—but there is quite a gap between an average user's circle of "friends" and any kind of global connectedness. In the US, almost 80% of Facebook users have fewer than 500 "friends".[8]

This quaint philosophy of a global community is based on a repeated reference to *values;* to ideas of "our values", "collective values" and "our common values". It appears to be a redundant argument, insofar as it presupposes the very global community of values that should first need building. But the whole problem is that large groups of people *do not* agree to share common values. The vocabulary of "community" and "values" is derived from the American political philosophy known as communitarianism with its emphasis on self-organized communities sharing values. Conveniently enough, those ideas enjoy support from both the right and left (the Republicans love to pit local communities against the Washington elite; Democrats love self-organized protest groups). It builds on the idea of local communities whose

---

[7] Zuckerberg, M. "Building Global Community" *Facebook*. 02-16-17.

"1. How do we help people build **supportive communities** that strengthen traditional institutions in a world where membership in these institutions is declining?
2. How do we help people build a **safe community** that prevents harm, helps during crises and rebuilds afterwards in a world where anyone across the world can affect us?
3. How do we help people build an **informed community** that exposes us to new ideas and builds common understanding in a world where every person has a voice?
4. How do we help people build a **civically-engaged community** in a world where participation in voting sometimes includes less than half our population?
5. How do we help people build an **inclusive community** that reflects our collective values and common humanity from local to global levels, spanning cultures, nations and regions in a world with few examples of global communities?"

[8] The statistic is from 2016: "Average number of Facebook friends of users in the United States in 2016" *Statista*. Most recent visit 06-25-18: https://www.statista.com/statistics/398532/us-facebook-user-network-size/

possibility to pursue politics is based on sharing pre-political values. But Zuckerberg overlooks the fact that communitarianism, with the village as its political ideal, easily inherits the downsides to the village: social incestuousness, strait-lacedness, xenophobia, gossip, conformity, hate towards other villages.[9] As is well known, you can't be friends with everyone; maybe you can't even be "friends" with everyone. Significantly enough, as a political philosophy communitarianism is not kindly disposed towards political liberalism, universal rights, free speech and the idea that even if people do not share values, they may share principles for the coexistence of different values. Nor are Facebook's principles—termed community standards—kind to freedom of speech, see below. There are thus local versions of the "global community" in which a person can easily get trapped. Zuckerberg continues: "What is your limit when it comes to nudity? To violence? To rough content? To profanity? Whatever you decide, those will be your personal settings. We will regularly ask you these questions to increase participation and so you do not need to go dig for them yourself. For those who choose not to decide anything, the default settings will be what the majority of people in your region have chosen, just like in a poll."[10] Knowing how difficult it is to change personal settings online, the vast majority of users will simply decide to accept the local default settings. This effectively indoctrinates them to have the same opinions as the majority of people in their local region (it remains unknown if by "region" Zuckerberg means village, city, county, country or continent). But the communitarian aspect is clear: people should share values with their local society, with their "community".

Just below the surface of the community ideals, the gears of the capitalist machinery keep turning. Tech giants have complicated algorithm-based advertising systems where advertisers quickly and automatically buy access to highly specific user groups. Advertisements are traded in an online

---

[9] As argued by Jett Heer in "Facebook's Promise of Community is a Lie" *The New Republic*. 09-07-17.

[10] Zuckerberg, M. "Building Global Community" *Facebook*. 02-16-17.

auction, where the price is automatically calculated, after which the ads immediately appear tailor-made to the platform profiles of the meticulously selected users. Users themselves enjoy the targeted content, but often they are not aware of the principle of how the tech giants' handle their data. Tech platforms generally do not involve the users or the public in how data are handled: what the data are used for, how one is profiled as a user and how that profiling is associated with third parties. Algorithms are like the Coca-Cola recipes of the big tech companies. But when pious preachers of transparency, openness, mutuality and community keep the very core of their own business models hidden from public inspection, investigation and critique, it rings hollow.

Most of us know the simple recommendations on the platforms. People who have bought *The Matrix* will probably also buy *The Matrix 2*. If you are interested in yoga books, you may also be interested in buying yoga gear. These are examples of recommendations that focus on the product. Consumption patterns are analyzed, and the information is used to calculate what the next potential purchase might be. This is relatively harmless and follows a classic and well-known logic of marketing. But it's only the tip of the marketing iceberg. Today, not only the product can be personalized, but also the very type of argument that makes the user choose one product over another. The strategy behind this is called *persuasion profiling*.[11]

Two PhD students from Stanford University, Maurits Kaptein and Dean Eckles (the latter was also a researcher at Facebook from 2012 to 2015), made an experiment where they started an online bookstore and encouraged customers to browse through titles and mark the books they would be most likely to buy.[12] They experimented with different sales strategies and found that it is possible to track what kind of argumentation seems the most convincing to a given person. Some consumers prefer expert reviews, others fall for promotional

---

[11] Pariser (2011) p. 120.

[12] Pariser "Welcome to the Brave New World of Persuasion Profiling." *Wired*. 04-26-11.

offers and others react to recommendations of friends. They also found that certain pitches are counterproductive. One consumer hurries to buy a product on discount, while another believes that discounts are a sign that the very same product has lost value. Eckles and Kaptein themselves claim that they can increase the impact of recommendations by 30–40% by eliminating the types of arguments that are counterproductive to the individual consumer. These are very big numbers. But more importantly: The experiment also shows that one and the same person responds to the same type of argument in widely different contexts. A consumer's persuasion profile can be relatively easily transferred from one commodity group to another. This means that these profiles are worth a lot of money because they are extremely attractive to advertisers.

Also, new methods within *sentiment analysis* are employed.[13] Data analysis tools are now so advanced that they can generate highly detailed data and even measure what mood a user is in. By analyzing text messages, Facebook updates and emails, it is possible to distinguish between good days and bad, or sober messages from drunken ones. The latter is based, among other things, on the number of spelling mistakes. Facebook is familiar with the methods: In 2015, "Danmarks Radio", a public service media outlet, broke the following news: "Facebook updates featuring suicidal thoughts are being studied closely by Facebook."[14] The idea was that Facebook would help the potentially suicidal person find appropriate treatment online in order to avoid self-harm. It is indeed commendable that Facebook suggests that kind of help. But it is also unsettling: A company can now measure, on a relatively detailed level, what state of mind a given user is in—including hard times and even clinical depression. Strangely enough, this news was not followed by any noticeable pushback over the massive amounts of surveillance enabled by big data.

---

[13] Pariser (2011) p. 121.

[14] Villarreal, K. "Facebook-opdateringer med selvmordstanker bliver nærlæst af Facebook" *DR indland*. 02-26-15.

Undoubtedly, extremely customized and relevant content is quite convenient. A good example is DirectLife, a Philips device featuring a fitness tracker and a virtual trainer.[15] It can figure out which argument makes a person eat healthier and exercise more regularly. For example, if the user is the kind who responds to positive feedback, the virtual trainer will say: *Nice work!* This is brilliant, but can we expect all companies trading these profiles to have good or even relatively unproblematic intentions, such as improving the health of users or trying to prevent them from suicide? Potential buyers of such profile information are not necessarily limited to commercial companies, but could also include religious, political and other movements with intentions of a rather different nature. Whether they celebrate a good cause is one question, another is the methods behind the cause. In the wrong hands, persuasion profiling enables the buyers to manipulate individuals and take advantage of the psychological traits of a person through sentiment analysis.

Within the algorithm-based advertising system, examples abound of the abuse of big tech tools. In 2017, US nonprofit organization ProPublica revealed that Facebook allowed landlords to discriminate against tenants based on ethnicity, disability, gender, and other characteristics when listing their properties for rent.[16] The algorithms automatically generated the categories based on data from user profiles. It became a scandal. Nine months later, nothing had changed. ProPublica tested Facebook's new advertising rules and tools, freshly updated and explicitly declared "diversity-enhancing", but they found that it was still possible to buy rental housing ads and place them outside the view of certain categories of people: African Americans, people in need of wheelchair ramps, Jews, Hispanics, people interested in Islam, and so on.[17]

[15] Pariser (2011) p. 121.

[16] Angwin, J. & Tobin, A. "Fair Housing Groups Sue Facebook for Allowing Discrimination in Housing Ads" *ProPublica*. 03-27-17.

[17] Angwin, J. & Tobin, M. & Varner, M. "Facebook (still) Letting Housing Advertisers Exclude Users by Race" *ProPublica*. 11-21-17.

In some sense this is a natural consequence of targeted marketing—when targeting ads to certain selected groups, other groups do *not* see them and are not informed about the offer. In March 2019, Facebook accepted to overhaul their advertising system to attempt to rule out discriminatory ads in job, housing and loan ads.[18]

This can be exploited in numerous unsympathetic ways. Google has sold ads associated with racist and highly prejudiced keywords, and the service has even automatically and unintentionally recommended several bizarre words during the process, as revealed by *BuzzFeed*, an online media outlet. Advertisers could target ads based on keywords such as "black people ruin neighborhoods", "Jewish parasites" and "Jews control the media"—keyword combinations targeting racists and anti-Semites. Google responded that they would work hard to stop these offensive ads which violate their policy of abusive speech. This happened right around the time when Facebook was struggling to customize their ads platform, which allowed advertisers to target messages to "Jew haters".[19] From a free speech perspective, one could argue: Nazis have a horrific worldview, but they also buy stuff, so should an advertiser be forbidden to address them specifically? The above-mentioned case of rental housing ads is downright illegal, as these groups of people are protected under the US Federal Fair Housing Act. However, ads associated with racist content are not illegal in and of themselves. They are unsympathetic to the bone, but not criminal. The problem is rather that the companies themselves have an advertising policy which they believe has been violated. Both cases show that abuse of information is not unique to one company. These issues are tightly interwoven the complex and automated advertising system that has made Facebook and Google two of the world's most valuable companies. The

---

[18] Jan, T. & Dworskin, E. "Facebook agrees to overhaul targeted advertising system for job, housing and loan ads after discrimination complaints" *Washington Post*. 03-19-19.

[19] Kantrowitz, A. "Google Allowed Advertisers To Target People Searching Racist Phrases" *BuzzFeed*. 09-15-17.

problem is also found on Twitter. Also here, it has been revealed that advertisers were able to target ads based on users' racist and patronizing comments.[20] Google and Facebook get most of the criticism because of their dominant position in the advertising market. However, the extent of the problem is more difficult to determine in Google's advertising system, where advertisers target users by associating ads with keywords that they expect the user to search. On Facebook, however, advertisers can choose criteria for targeting people and their characteristics from a large catalog of information. In 2016 alone, Google removed 1.7 billion ads that violated the company's ad policy.[21]

In July 2018, Danish public radio show *P1 Orientering* reported on a particularly controversial categorization based on sensitive personal information within the Facebook ad system. Facebook had categorized 65,000 Russians as interested in "treason" and 130,000 Nigerians as interested in homosexuality. It may seem innocent to allow ads targeted to such groups and their particular interests. However, this meant that both groups could easily be identified by the authorities of those countries via their Facebook profiles, which could put people in danger. In most countries, treason is illegal. Russian authorities in particular take a strong interest in the category, and in Nigeria, homosexuality is penalized by up to 14 years in prison.[22] With no intention of it whatsoever, Facebook's categorization has given intelligence agencies in all countries a golden opportunity to comb the population in much more detail than what is allowed under most democratic constitutions. If a user is categorized on Facebook with a behavior showing an interest in "treason", then the Russian authorities can quite easily identify that user. It only requires the following bait: In Facebook's adver-

[20] Maheshwari, S. & Stevenson, A. "Google and Facebook Face Criticism for Ads Targeting Racist Sentiments" *New York Times*. 09-15-17.

[21] Kantrowitz, A. "Google Allowed Advertisers To Target People Searching Racist Phrases" *BuzzFeed*. 09-15-17.

[22] Ledegaard, F. H. & Pedersen, R. M. "Facebook har stemplet 65.000 russere som interesserede i 'landsforræderi'" *DR Udland*. 07-11-18.

tising system, they pretend to be advertisers wanting to target every user who lives in Russia and whom Facebook has registered as interested in 'treason'. In the ads, users must be lured to click a link that sends them to a specially designed website owned by the advertiser. The ad needs not have the slightest thing to do with treason. It could be for something as innocent as a discount on new gardening tools. But it allows the advertiser to learn that the user clicking on the link lives in Russia and is interested in "treason". The link sends the user to a website where a traceable IP address is automatically left, which makes it easy to identify the person. The process is a special variety of *phishing*, a method to con Internet users to reveal their name, bank account, phone number, email, post address, etc.[23] In a place like Russia, the consequence is that the Russian intelligence agencies may, in principle, systematically monitor users and record those they consider as potential traitors. This advertising trick not only enables government agencies to identify potential victims; the trick also lies open to other forces wishing to shame or harass specific groups.

Facebook has explained that "treason" was thought of as an ad category because of its historical significance. But since it is also an illegal act, the company has acknowledged that the category is problematic. The criticism raised by *P1 Orientering* made Facebook remove "treason" from its category system worldwide. On previous occasions, Facebook has felt it necessary to remove "communism", "shia Muslim" and "Islam" because religious beliefs and political inclinations are seen as sensitive information subject to special protection. At the same time, however, it is still possible to target ads to people who are interested in "Christianity", "homosexuality" and "anxiety".[24] Facebook's advertising policy is far from consistent, and the giant should consider whether health information or sexual orientation ought to be considered as sensitive personal information, only to be made publicly available after getting the user's consent.

---

[23] Ledegaard, F. H. & Pedersen, R. M. "Facebook har stemplet 65.000 russere som interesserede i 'landsforræderi'" *DR Udland.* 07-11-18.

[24] Ledegaard, F. H. & Pedersen, R. M. "Efter DR-afsløringer: Facebook fjerner "islam", men ikke "kristendom"" *DR Indland.* 05-22-18.

The consequence of this categorization is that Facebook users will need to be very acutely aware of how they express themselves so as not to get labeled as something they might not like. The users must be extremely aware of what they like, comment or click on, share, etc. It is a consideration that may naturally lead to self-censorship. But even cautious users never have complete control over, let alone access to, the categories Facebook foists upon them. This restriction of free expression is not censorship in the sense of rules-based content removal. Rather, it is a kind that thrives because the users have no access to which categorizations their behavior leads to. As a consequence, they may have good reason to hesitate to speak out digitally, even in front of close friends or "friends". Facebook's own website states: "Your interests are based on your Facebook activity and on other actions." *Other actions* are exactly what constitutes the business secret, but it probably includes click behavior, browser history plus additional data acquired from data brokers. Facebook itself emphasizes that advertising interests and sympathies are not the same. The 65,000 Russians were thus not categorized as "traitors" but as *interested* in "treason", for example, as a topic of historical research interest. A distinction should be made between the user's online activity and the user's personal characteristics. According to Facebook, the company only has information about the former, not the latter. On a conceptual level, this distinction is clear, but it seems very likely and indeed very possible to reason from one to the other. Research in the field shows that it is possible to guess, with up to 88% certainty, the sexuality of a user based on the individual's likes on Facebook—similar possibilities hold for the user's ethnicity, religious beliefs, political attitude, personality traits, intelligence, mood, consumption of addictive substances, parents' separation, age and gender.[25] There is an increasing number of revelations of how the tools of tech giants are used in many ways where

---

[25] Kosinski, M. & Stillwell, D. & Graepel, T. "Private traits and attributes are predictable from digital records of human behavior" *PNAS*. 04-09-13.

the line between use and abuse is extremely difficult to draw. Big data enable quick and targeted access to the weak spots of each individual user.

Marketing strategies used on the giants' platforms are generally difficult to decipher. They operate at their best when invisible to the user. Consider for a moment the virtual personal trainer DirectLife yelling out: "You're doing a great job! I'm telling you this because you respond well to positive feedback!" It would probably not have quite the same effect.[26] And the problem gets still worse: Marketing strategies, of course, work in the same way when promoting ideas as they do with products. The 2016 US presidential campaign bears witness to this. The Cambridge Analytica scandal would later, in March 2018, clear the front pages. Through the workings of Cambridge Analytica, the Trump campaign had gained unique insight into the lives of voters. Huge amounts of data were collected, as part of a psychological research project at Cambridge University, and resold by researcher Aleksandr Kogan to the UK consultant company Cambridge Analytica. The consultant was able, by using for instance the just-quoted Kosinski article, to map how users made decisions and subsequently figure out how their efforts could affect a decision-making process. The results were very precise voter profiles divided into 500 different psychological categories. The profiles were then used to target anonymous or pseudonymous campaign messages—shaped in accordance with these categories—at selected swing voters in the few but crucial US swing states. It was not necessarily obvious to these people that they were exposed to election propaganda. And it was certainly not clear to them that they were the subjects of targeted campaigns. After all, they have no access to information about which other users receive the same information and which do not. These voters do not, in principle, enjoy freedom of expression in the sense of freedom of information, in which they can choose freely from a given quantity of available information.

---

[26] Pariser, E. "Welcome to the Brave New World of Persuasion Profiling." *Wired*. 04-26-11.

According to Cambridge Analytica's own top management—and as captured on hidden camera by British network *Channel4*—what made the difference and what wound up deciding the 2016 US elections was the company's micro-targeting ads directed at only 40,000 wavering US voters in the decisive swing states. Of course, we do not know how accurate the campaign's boasts are, or whether this was just a sales pitch made to *Channel4*'s journalists posing as potentially interested clients. But it is, however, thought-provoking that Facebook, in a piece of research from before the scandal broke, boasted about the company's ability to influence voter turnout.[27] Speaking of Facebook's much mentioned transparency and openness—when *The Guardian* began to unveil the scandal in March 2018, Facebook's first reaction was to file a lawsuit against the British newspaper and shut down the profile of Christopher Wylie, the central whistleblower and former research director at Cambridge Analytica. Not exactly a role model for transparency and freedom of expression. In 2011, the US Federal Trade Commission made an agreement with Facebook regarding privacy practices and is expected, in 2019, to charge Facebook with a 5 billion dollars fine for violations of the agreement.[28]

However, not only the Trump team has used micro-targeting. It happens across the board and has been going on for many years. The first political campaign that used massive data from Facebook was the 2012 Obama campaign. In the Trump campaign, Cambridge Analytica was able to collect user data from as many as 87 million Facebook accounts via Aleksandr Kogan, who had 300,000 users actively sign up for and give their consent to a psychological test, which made

---

[27] Corbyn, Z. "Facebook experiment boosts US voter turnout: Mass social-network study shows that influence of close friends raises participation" *Nature*. 09-12-12. If you are able to influence the voter turnout in a positive way, you can probably also do the opposite. The latter is what Trump's campaign manager and vice president of Cambridge Analytica, Steve Bannon, was explicitly interested in, according to whistleblower Christopher Wylie.

[28] Wong, J. C. "Facebook expects FTC fine up to $5bn in privacy investigation" *Guardian*. 04-24-19.

him able to harvest data not only from themselves, but also from all their "friends". To this day, it remains unknown whether Kogan, who also has ties to the University of St. Petersburg, Russia, passed on this data to Russian authorities. In 2012, the Obama campaign had about a million of their Facebook supporters provide access to data from all their "friends". According to one of the campaign leaders, this allowed the campaign to reconstruct *the entire Facebook social graph* (i.e. the chart displaying all connection relationships between the users). This was significantly more users than what Cambridge Analytica got access to in 2016. But contrary to the Cambridge Analytica campaign, the Obama campaign had its one million active supporters mold their "friends", who were then influenced politically by people they at least already knew. In the other campaign the 300,000 intermediaries knew nothing, and the campaign messages appeared in people's news feeds out of nowhere. In that sense, the Obama campaign's use of large amounts of Facebook data was more honest—but still it highlights another problem. The day after the Cambridge Analytica revelations on March 18th, 2018, Obama campaign leader Carol Davidson made the following statement: "They [Facebook] came to office in the days following election recruiting & were very candid that they allowed us to do things they wouldn't have allowed someone else to do because they were on our side."[29] The Obama campaign was allowed to use massive amounts of Facebook data because the company sided with one of the candidates against the other (Republican candidate Mitt Romney). Thus, access to this scarily effective political micro-targeting based on big data can both be based on economics (who can afford to buy the relevant ads?), on fraud (who manages to trick data out of gullible tech giants?) and on the companies' own departure from their expressed neutrality ("Facebook is a platform for all ideas," as Zuckerberg repeatedly, but not very convinc-

[29] Quoted from Rogers, J. "Obama 2012 campaign 'sucked' data from Facebook, former official says" *Fox News*. 03-20-18.

ingly, chanted during the congressional hearings). It all depends on what the political situation requires. Other options for obtaining access to such data include legislation, persuasion, hacking, espionage, pressure, bribery, etc. However, if only one political party out of several has access to such powerful instruments in their campaign, it constitutes a break with the fundamental norm of political equality and fairness in the electoral process. Voters affected lose their freedom of expression, understood as their freedom to seek out and compare information independently and for the purpose of forming their opinions.

As already mentioned, Cambridge Analytica had used Facebook data to categorize users into 500 different specified psychological profiles on which to base the targeted affecting. Through micro-targeting, politicians can access the voters' private lives and psyches, thus affecting carefully selected segments of voters. German philosopher Byung-Chul Han calls this phenomenon *data-driven psychopolitics*.[30] Micro-targeted messages to voters are hardly much different from micro-targeted ads. In both cases, sophisticated algorithms make it possible to predict people's behavior very precisely and optimize a candidate or product profile. Today we see, according to Han, an increasing amalgamation of the citizen and consumer, of the state and market, of the vote and the purchase.[31]

Orientation towards market demands increasingly seem to pull tech giants away from what might be left of their early idealism, prompting them to behave like the more seedy examples of greedy companies employing dirty tricks. In November 2018, *New York Times* published a long piece of investigative journalism[32] on the tactics of crisis management

---

[30] Han (2017) pp. 62–63.

[31] In the book "Democracy Hacked", Martin Moore describes three types of hackers who successfully distorted the 2016 US election: individuals, plutocrats and foreign states. See Moore (2018).

[32] Frenkel, S., Confessore, N., Kang, C., Rosenberg, M. and Nicas, J. "Delay, Deny and Deflect: How Facebook's Leader Fought Through Crisis" *New York Times*.11-14-18.

chosen by the Facebook leadership—particularly Mark Zuckerberg and Sheryl Sandberg. Under the headline "Delay, Deny and Deflect", the article showed how the company had used denial and smear campaigns to conceal the extent of the problems with data privacy and political disinformation. In October 2017, Facebook hired the political spin company Definers, which has a history of making aggressive political campaigns for Republican candidates, but increasingly expanding into business spin. This company had disseminated rumors about Facebook competitors like Google and Apple in order to "muddy the waters" (in the words of a Definers leader) and divert critical focus away from Facebook. Simultaneously, Definers had spread articles trying to portray protesters as anti-Semites because of a protest poster showing Zuckerberg and Sandberg as a world-embracing octopus at the congressional hearings. This was a reference to the antitrust case against Standard Oil in the 1900s, but Definers claimed that singling out the two Jewish top Facebook persons was anti-Semitic. In an incredible show of hypocrisy, Definers simultaneously published papers attacking Facebook critics for being paid marionettes for the liberal Hungarian-Jewish philantropist billionaire George Soros, a staple target for right-wing, anti-Semitic conspiracy attacks. All this activity, of course, appeared in public with no direct connection to Facebook's name and was only revealed through the *New York Times* article. Facebook immediately cut its ties to Definers, and the Facebook top claimed not to have been informed about the Definers contract. Simultaneously, Facebook defended itself in the following way: Definers was "[...] useful to help respond to unfair claims where Facebook has been singled out for criticism, and to positively distinguish us from competitors."[33]—in the words of Elliot Schrage, former head of communications and policy, who went on to take the blame.

[33] Facebook: "Elliot Schrage on Definers" *Facebook newsroom.* 11-21-18.

The growing number of issues springing from the advertising system make it seem like the tech giants are unable to handle the problems themselves. In connection with the Cambridge Analytica scandal, Facebook actually discovered the leak as early as 2015, long before the US elections. The company responded by asking Kogan specifically to delete the data in question (which he did not) and more generally by blocking all apps active on Facebook from gaining access to the data of their users' "friends". As was revealed in June 2018, however, the sharing of massive volumes of user data with hardware developers like Apple, Samsung, and BlackBerry continued even until after the Cambridge Analytica scandal broke in March 2018. The trick was to get *like* buttons and automatic Facebook connectivity integrated into their devices.[34] A new scandal, in July-August 2018, was less intentional. Here, Facebook publicly admitted that the company was aware of new infiltration attempts up to the US midterm election in November 2016. It included 32 fake Facebook accounts that reached nearly 300,000 users with ads, posts and organized political events, rallies, protests, all on topics such as race, feminism, mindfulness, and resistance to Trump. What they all had in common was that they were efforts to create division and disagreement. It is believed that the pages may once again have been created by Russian activists from the Internet Research Agency, but this time in a way that may be more difficult to detect.[35] New cases of data misuse continue to surface. In December 2018, a British parliamentary committee on online misinformation confiscated a batch of Facebook documents, which was in the possession of an employee of software company Six4Three during a visit to London. Here, it appeared that Facebook from 2012 to 2015 gave privileged access to user data to companies such as

---

[34] Dance, G. & Confessore, N. & LaForgia, M. "Facebook Gave Device Makers Deep Access to Data on Users and Friends" *New York Times*. 03-06-18.

[35] Dwoskin, E. & Romm, T. "Facebook says it has uncovered a coordinated disinformation operation ahead of the 2018 midterm elections" *Washington Post*. 07-31-18.

Netflix and Airbnb in order to boost traffic and engagement on Facebook.[36]

Just like the relationship between code-makers and code breakers, data collection vs. data protection is a case of dog-eat-dog. On the horizon we are seeing the contours of a fundamental and interminable war between the owners of growing data masses on the one hand, and on the other many different stakeholders who use various means (hacking, espionage, trade, pressure, persuasion, partnerships ...) to seek to get their hands on data that can be used for political turnover. Through their massive surveillance structure, tech giants possess extremely personally sensitive data. That does not mean, however, that they automatically possess the relevant and increasingly demanding mechanisms to protect those data. It does not seem difficult to invent ever new abuses of the system, as long as it makes use of an automated ad system that allows for the aggressive, detailed and targeted marketing we have seen in recent years.

---

[36] Satariano, A. & Isaac, M. "Facebook Used People's Data to Favor Certain Partners and Punish Rivals, Documents Show" *New York Times.* 12-05-18.

Chapter 9
Free Speech Under Pressure

As mentioned above, the UN Declaration of Human Right states that "everyone has the right to freedom of opinion and expression; this right includes freedom to hold opinions without interference and to seek, receive and impart information and ideas through any media and regardless of frontiers." This is freedom of expression in a broad sense, as the wording contains both individuals' and organizations' freedom to express themselves and their right to seek out information freely and search for information freely.

In today's online world, freedom of speech is under pressure, because the tech giants have been given a position where they can lay down the rules of public conversation and access to information. This is a consequence of freedom of expression having been capitalized by tech giants. The right to express one's opinion and seek out information is no longer exercised without interference, because the tech companies adapt and limit the *free* information exchange of individuals and organizations, based on commercial interests as well as supercilious, paternalistic ideas. First of all, and as discussed in previous chapters, interference takes place, and it takes place automatically and opaquely through the platforms' algorithm systems. But there is also a manual, censoring interference taking place, based on policies formulated by the

F. Stjernfelt, A. M. Lauritzen, *Your Post has been Removed*,
https://doi.org/10.1007/978-3-030-25968-6_9

giants in order to create an information environment which aims to reflect their own ideals. These policies are vaguely and hazily worded. The phrasings reduce complex legal decision making, which we will elaborate on in the following chapters. This interference means that who and what is gaining ears today is increasingly determined by large private technological players.

There is no doubt that the creation and spread of the Internet initially caused a landslide towards increased real freedom of expression. Any user could now create their own website or blog from which to preach their incontestable opinions about nothing and everything and participate in many different debate forums and commentary threads and make serious or less serious comments about other people's statements, positions and personalities. If you were smart or lucky, you could get in touch and debate with a brand new and broad readership—and moreover, you were exempt from the objections of opinions editors. In the classic media setup, the opinion editor was responsible for combing through written pieces submitted "to the editor" by ordinary people in order to decide which ones to promote and expose. Of course, one was still subject to the laws of one's country and its partial restrictions on freedom of expression—although it has taken most states a long time to adjust, not only to monitoring the printed word but also the digitally communicated word.

The advent of the Internet also meant highly increased freedom of speech in the broader sense, the one about seeking out information: the ever-increasing data volumes available on the web allow the user to access news, search information, gain knowledge, get informed about debates, positions and controversies, all at an incredibly fast pace. The top tech representatives never fail to mention, in manifestos and speeches, how much they believe their companies contribute to this increased freedom of expression. In November 2010, at the doorsteps of the "Arab Spring," Eric Schmidt and

Jared Cohen from Google rejoicingly described how dedicated they were to "promote freedom of expression on the Internet and protect privacy."[1] They even envisioned rebels equipped with cell phones able to summon "flash mobs" and "... shake repressive governments, building new tools to skirt firewalls and censors, reporting and tweeting the new online journalism, and writing a bill of human rights for the Internet age."[2] It sounds like a Diderot or a Tom Paine of the twenty-first century—eloquent and ecstatic declarations of Enlightenment, hard not to be moved by.

But are these giants really defenders of freedom? As early as 2010, significant slippage was already well underway. The anarchist utopia of the early Internet, with its many individual players and their self-organized structure, had proven just as illusory as the free liberal market of classic liberalism with its multiple parties with equal status. Both phenomena share one and the same reason; in an open market, the best providers can invest profits to become even better and, in many cases, they can eradicate enough of their competitors to approach monopoly. Tech giants such as Amazon (founded in 1994), Google (founded in 1998), Facebook (founded in 2004) and Twitter (founded in 2006) became some of the world's largest companies during the 2000s and 2010s. Not only did they thrive on the Matthew Effect—"for whoever has, to him more shall be given"—but also on the even more important network effect; the sheer size of the network is in itself part of its attractiveness, so that the largest networks naturally attract new clients who are eager to get in touch with as many other users as possible. At the same time, the marginal cost of adding new users is incredibly small. A new user, however, continues to be just as valuable to the company as when they boarded, because advertisers are willing to pay in proportion

[1] Quoted from Ferguson (2017) p. 372.

[2] Ibid. p. 366.

to the number of users reached, the number of times viewed and the number of clicks.

An important aspect to this attention economy is, of course, maintaining the users once they sign up. This is done by offering them useful, convenient and free services—but also by not scaring them away. Among other things, this means not showing them content they might find offensive. This basic trait means that from early on, the big tech companies formulated policies for content removal as part of their "user policies," "terms of service" or "community standards," on how the user was expected to behave on the platforms. If users did not comply with these rules, their posts could be deleted and their access blocked—temporarily or permanently. More often than not, these rules were only described scantily and in generic or hazy terms—but in all cases they were significantly tougher and more narrow than the legal restrictions on freedom of expression in most democratic countries.

This uncertainty is multiplied by the fact that individual tech companies have different versions of these rules. Oftentimes they will begin with a general version, the "terms of service," which is the legally binding description of the mutual obligations of both service provider and user.[3] Secondly, a more detailed version is outlined in the community standards. And thirdly, a considerably more detailed version in the form of the internal staff guidelines, a document

---

[3]The American "Safe Harbor Act" (see below) to a large extent exempts Internet companies from responsibility for the utterances of their users—at the same time the act guarantees that even if an Internet company *in fact*, by its own initiative, monitors and controls the utterances of users, that will not take away their protection of the "Safe Harbor Act." Controlling users does not mean that you are required to report them for offenses. Most other Western countries of the Western world have *conditional liability*, which means that the companies are not responsible for user behavior, as long as they do not have any current knowledge of it; while countries such as China and many Middle Eastern countries maintain *strong liability*, which makes it the responsibility of the companies to prevent circulation of illegal material, cf. Gillespie (2018) p. 33.

not available to the public and which is usually only known if leaked by a whistle blower.[4] For a long time, such control of what can be expressed on the tech giants' platforms could seem completely unproblematic. They are private companies. In a sense, they run a new kind of media in mutual competition with each other. Their community standards then correspond to the editorial policies of newspapers. Thus, they correspond to the fact that—as a mere matter of course—we expect a difference between what can be published in *The New York Times* and in *The New York Post*. In a competitive market, private companies have the full right to set their course as they wish and exclude points of view they do not like to bring. No one's freedom of speech is violated, if a newspaper turns down, removes or ignores a letter or op-ed, because people can always take their statements elsewhere—on the Internet, people even have abundant ways of making their own websites, deciding on the editorial line themselves.

The problem with such an analysis of tech giants as mutually competing media is that their enormous success of recent years has in fact rid them of real competition—they are increasingly bordering on de facto monopoly. In practice, Microsoft and Apple have a duopoly in the field of software, while Google and Facebook are on their way to becoming a duopoly when it comes to their core business: selling ads based on free digital services. As mentioned above, together the two have more than 80% of the American online advertising market and are only threatened by Amazon. But they are also monopolies seen from a user point of view: As of April 2018, Google had 90,61% of the world's search activity—distant followers are Bing (3,24%), Yahoo! (2,09%) and the search engine of the Chinese government, Baidu (2,04%);

[4] Gillespie (2018) ch. 3 goes over the "community guidelines" of a number of social media and finds a confusing affirmation of a mixture of freedom of expression, respect, community and policies—most often without reflecting on the inherent contradictions of such an affirmation, and instead presented in facetious and inaccurate jargon.

all other search engines have less than 1%.[5] Google is estimated to have more than 2 trillion searches per year, which corresponds to 2.5 million searches per second. By 2016, Google's parent company Alphabet had six other platforms, each with more than a billion users: Gmail, Android, Google Chrome, Google Maps, YouTube and Google Play Store. For some years now, Facebook has had between 65% and 85% of the social media market share; as of January 2017, it was 87,3%, dropping to less than 70% in the spring of 2018, possibly due to the Cambridge Analytica scandal of March 2018. Competitor numbers are substantially lower: Twitter and YouTube (owned by Google) have around 7% and 8% respectively, while Pinterest, who specializes in photo sharing, now has 15%.[6]

Companies which have a de facto monopoly can easily overcome pressure from the competition. Getting new users is cheap for them; they can name prices themselves (in this case for advertisers), because no other players can offer such extensive market penetration; and they can continuously buy out hundreds of emerging competitors. In that way Google, among many other deals, have purchased Android (2005), Measure Map (2006) YouTube (2006), DoubleClick (2007), Ebook (2011) and Motorola (2011); their most recent larger acquisition is GIF search engine Tenor (2018). As part of a long list of other acquisitions, Facebook took over FriendFeed (2009), Friendster's patents (2010), Instagram (2012) and WhatsApp (2014); the most recent large acquisition is Confirm (2018), an identification verifier.[7] Facebook has even

---

[5] "Search Engine Market Share Worldwide – May 2017-May 2018" *Statcounter*. Most recent visit 06-25-18: http://gs.statcounter.com/search-engine-market-share

[6] "Social Media Stats Worldwide – May 2017-May 2018" *Statcounter*. Most recent visit 06-25-18: http://gs.statcounter.com/social-media-stats.

[7] How an acquisition procedure tends to proceed is vividly described by Martínez (2016), who personally sold the startup AdGrok to both Twitter and Facebook.

developed a tool by the name of Onavo Protect, which is marketed as a service to protect user data but which in fact maps the online behavior of users; that makes it possible to monitor whether new apps or services are becoming popular among Facebook users. If that is the case, Facebook will simply acquire the new company, which is what, most famously, happened with WhatsApp.[8] In August 2018, however, the Onavo app was excluded from the App Store, because it did not comply with Apple's policy for data collection and privacy. On previous occasions, Apple CEO Tim Cook has criticized Facebook's approach to privacy, but this was the first time Apple actually acted upon it by excluding a Facebook app.[9] Later we shall discuss the possibility of subjecting tech giants to anti-monopoly regulation.

When companies such as Google and Facebook are approaching de facto monopoly status, it is no longer such an innocent matter what statements are prohibited, marginalized and removed from their sites, as a breach of their community standards. Especially for younger generations, services such as these have become the main source, for many the only source, of news and public debate. But regardless of how much their top managers say so, eloquently phrased when glasses are raised, the community standards no longer reflect an ambition of free debate, in the sense of inclusion of all points of view and protection of the freedom to also tolerate provocative, strange, and unpopular expressions. Rather, the community standards reflect an ambition of not scaring off users. And an ambition not to offend advertisers by showing their ads anywhere near controversial content. This puts them right between two opposing considerations: on the one hand

---

[8] Bloomberg editorial board "Don't Break Up Facebook" *Bloomberg Opinion.* 07-16-18. Most recent visit 07-30-18: https://www.bloomberg.com/view/articles/2018-07-16/don-t-break-up-facebook).

[9] Tsukayama, H. "Facebook's Onavo app booted from Apple's App Store over privacy" *Washington Post.* 08-23-18.

the freedom of expression, which is often praised in odes to openness, transparency and access for all persons and points of views. And, on the other hand, a detailed policy for the removal of content, a policy which, however, does not enjoy the same openness but which generally is kept hidden, both when it comes to detailed guidelines and what motivates the practical interpretation of them.

Chapter 10
Nipples and the Digital Community

In a Danish context, the first time the public was exposed to these flaws was in 2012. It was the seemingly banal case of documentary writer Peter Øvig Knudsen, who published the two-volume book *Hippie* about the Danish hippie movement and their so-called Thy Camp in 1970. The photo documentation of these books included photos from the camp, where hippies walked around naked, swam undressed and the like. It was, of course, a central part of the hippie movement. These seemingly innocent documentary photos, however, turned out to violate several standards of several tech giants.

On November 1, 2012, it became apparent that Apple refused to market Øvig's *Hippie 2*—referring to the fact that the book contained photos of naked people, making it an act of indecent exposure. Øvig stated about Apple's iBookstore: "If Apple becomes the most dominant book store in Denmark, we have a situation where censors located in the US, across the Atlantic, decide what books can be bought in the biggest book store in Denmark." He then added: "This makes for a very unsettling future outlook. We have no influence over Apple, and our attempts at dialog with them reveals that they have no interest whatsoever in discussing this with us."[1] Subsequently, the only reason the book could be purchased through Apple's bookstore was that the publisher Gyldendal

[1] Ritzau "Peter Øvig: Apple-censur er grotesk" *Ekstra Bladet*. 11-01-12.

F. Stjernfelt, A. M. Lauritzen, *Your Post has been Removed*,
https://doi.org/10.1007/978-3-030-25968-6_10

prepared a censored version, covering the more sensitive parts of the images. As an ironic reference to Apple, tiny red apples were placed across genitals and breasts on the photos. Danish Minister of Culture, Uffe Elbæk, declined to do anything about the matter, referencing Apple as a private player who is free to set its own guidelines.

In the spring of 2013, the case spread to Facebook, where several of Øvig's posts were deleted and he was suspended from the platform, again citing indecent exposure present on some of the photos posted on his Facebook page. When he subsequently linked from the Facebook page to a website far outside of Facebook, describing and discussing what he perceived as a censorship, his Facebook page was blocked again. Facebook would not even allow critical discussion of the case outside the reach of their own service. Television network TV2 asked Facebook's Danish representative, Thomas Myrup Kristensen, what was wrong with nudity: "In and of itself, there is nothing wrong with nudity. Here in the Nordic countries, we are quite relaxed about nudity. But other cultures see things differently. At Facebook we have to protect a set of guidelines that covers our whole community of 1.1 billion people," said Thomas Myrup Kristensen, adding: "There are rules as to how we define them. I cannot get into exactly how we do it. It is a matter of nude nipples not being allowed. They are not — that is what this is about."[2] Author Peter Øvig's problems would return in 2016 when he published a book on the Danish squatter BZ-Movement of the early 1980s. Once again, his Facebook was suspended — this time because it contained a link to Øvig's own website which featured a photo from a nude protest organized by the BZ-movement in from of the Copenhagen Town Hall in 1983. This constitutes a detailed regulation that not only affects content posted on social media but also content for sale in bookstores, as well as content on private web pages entirely

[2] "Facebook til Øvig: Derfor sletter vi dit nøgenfoto" *TV2 Nyheder*. 06-13-13.

outside the realm of Facebook, as long as these pages are linked to from the person's Facebook page. Or in Øvig's own words: "Not being able to decide what to put on your own website is simply bizarre."[3]

It may seem a peripheral and harmless matter whether or not tech giants prevent old photos from the Danish 1970s left wing from spreading on the web. And it is almost comical to follow how, for example, Facebook's struggle against nudity has migrated into the world of art and cultural history removing, among other things, classical works of art such as Delacroix's emblematic "La Liberté guidant le Peuple" (1830), where goddess of freedom Marianne leads revolutionary France in battle, equipped with the French tricolore, a bayonetted musket and bare breasts. Another removal was Courbet's famous painting from 1866, "L'Origine du Monde", featuring a close-up of a straddling woman, as well as iconic press photos from modern times such as "Terror of War", Nick Ut's Pulitzer Award-winning photo of naked Vietnamese children fleeing from an American napalm attack in 1972. Even Hans Holbein's drawing of Erasmus by Rotterdam's naked hand from around 1532 did not make it through.[4] Over the past ten years, an extensive and still ongoing confrontation has emerged between Facebook's removal policy and activist groups of breastfeeding mothers who, not entirely without reason, consider Facebook's removal of their happy selfie photos of babies sucking their breasts as just another element in a major suppression of breastfeeding mothers in the public sphere. The fact that Facebook categorizes such photos of mother-child idyll with relatively limited nudity as "obscene" or "adult" has probably offended these mothers just as much—if not more—as those images offended the sensible users who felt they needed to complain about them

---

[3] Kjær, B. "Facebook strammer censur-skruen over for Peter Øvig" *Politiken*. 10-03-16.

[4] Jones, J. "Facebook banned Holbein's hand – but it isn't even art's sauciest" *The Guardian*. 08-31-16.

to begin with.[5] In terms of nudity in advertisements, Facebook's policy is even more restrictive, which has made Belgian museums desperate—they can no longer advertise classic masterpieces such as "Adam and Eve" by Rubens. Therefore, they submitted an official complaint to Mark Zuckerberg in July 2018.[6]

However, the somewhat comical fear of nudity illustrates a much bigger and more fundamental problem: the tech giants' increasing removal of user content. To a large extent, the tech giants long managed to keep their machinery of removal hidden from the public, but as communications researcher Tarleton Gillespie points out, content moderation is one of the essential services provided by the platforms—it might even be part of what defines them.[7] Although the companies do not produce content, their reason for being—and what separates them from the remaining unfiltered web around them—lies in their services of moderation, prioritization and content curation. In the eyes of the tech giants, the fact that most users do not discover this machinery and perceive the platform as open and uncurated is a sign of the very success of the removal: when many users perceive the platforms as open to all ideas, it is because they have never run into problems themselves. This is not the case for the many users who have actually had their content removed and their accounts blocked. With a number of users in the billions, the number of removals can of course not be a marginal task; on the contrary, it is so extensive that the machinery of removal must take place on an industrial level. Due to a lack of transparency, it is difficult to get quality numbers on these removals, but in a 2014 TED Talk, Twitter Vice President Del Harvey said that "Given the scale that Twitter is at, a one-in-a-million chance happens five hundred times a day. (...) Say

---

[5] In Chapter 6, Gillespie (2018) maps the course of events in the breastfeeding controversy.

[6] "It's Rubens vs. Facebook in Fight over Artistic Nudity" (AP) *New York Times*. 07-28-18.

[7] Gillespie's *Custodians of the Internet* (2018) is the first comprehensive and thorough study of "content moderation" on social media.

99.999 percent of tweets pose no risk to anyone whatsoever. There are no threats involved ... After you take out that 99.999 per cent, the tiny percentage of tweets remaining, works out roughly 150,000 per month."[8] Obviously, this number has increased since. In March 2017, Mark Zuckerberg mentioned that Facebook gets "millions" of complaints each week (for more exact 2018 numbers, see ch. 12).[9] Although the percentage of controversial posts may be small, in absolute numbers they are enormous and many users are exposed to removals and sanctions which it takes a lot of resources to decide on and deploy.

As noted by Gillespie, most removal activity by the tech giants takes place on a number of levels, as part of an intricate collaboration scheme.[10] At the highest level is the company top management. Right below is the department responsible for ongoing updates of the removal policy, which consists of only a few highly placed persons. Below them is the management and recruitment of the crowdworkers who do the actual implementation of the rules by removing and making sanctions against users who have posted non-standard content. They are usually low-paid and loosely employed people, who can be hired and fired according to the given workload, far away from the lush main offices in Palo Alto, in places like Dublin in Ireland, Hyderabad in India or Manila in the Philippines. In addition, there is an increasing amount of automated artificial intelligence that—unlike the human censors working with already posted material—flags uploaded material *before* it is posted online so that it can be removed immediately, in some cases even without human involvement. In this context, the efficiency of AI is exaggerated, however. In 2016, it was reported that Facebook's AI now finds more offensive photos than the hired staff does.[11] However, the

---

[8] Quoted from Gillespie (2018) p. 74.

[9] Ibid. p. 75.

[10] Ibid. p. 116ff.

[11] Constine, J. "Facebook Spares Humans by Fighting Offensive Photos with AI" *TechCrunch*. 05-31-16.

computers merely flag the photos which then still need subsequent human check by a removal worker.

Although the development of such AI is highly prioritized in the companies' R&D departments, Gillespie points to its inherently conservative character. AI still suffers from the problem that the machine-learning process that the software is trained by can only teach the artificial intelligence to recognize images and text that are closely analogous to the applied set of training examples. Which essentially are selected by people. Moreover, the AI software is not semantically savvy—it recognizes proxies only for the problematic content, not the content itself. For example, large areas of skin surface tones are a proxy for nudity and sex. The exact wording of certain sexual slang, pejoratives, swearwords or threats are proxies for the presence of porn, "hate speech" or threatening behavior. This means that the AI detectors have large amounts of "false positives" (e.g. sunsets with color nuances of pale skin) as well as "false negatives:" (e.g. porn images mostly featuring dressed models). It also implies that they are easy for creative users to fool by writing "fokking" instead of "fucking"; "bo@bs" instead of "boobs", etc., or by coloring the pornographic models in colors far from that of pale skin. Something similar applies to political and religious terms, where it is possible to just write "mussels" instead of "Muslims", "migr@nts" instead of "migrants", etc. Of course, the programs can be revised so as to crack down on such creative spelling as well, but this requires ongoing human input and revision which cannot in itself be automatized. Another way is to identify controversial content individually, piece by piece—images can, for instance, be identified by a pixel sequence so that they can also be recognized as parts of edited or manipulated versions. This technology was developed to curb child pornography, but it requires that an extensive "library" of such banned images is kept, against which elements found online can then be automatically checked. Such technology was used in 2016 to fight terrorism, as part of a collaboration between Facebook, Microsoft, Twitter, and YouTube. They set up a shared database of already identified terrorist content, so that online reuse of this content could be removed automatically.[12] However, said technology is of course only able to recognize already identified content and it takes continuous human effort to update the database with new content found online. It is another variant of the overall fact that the software can not recognize e.g. pornographic, terrorist, threatening content, otherwise instantly recognizable to humans, unless the material has been anticipated in the software's training syllabus. Despite the techno-optimism inherent to the industry, it does not seem as if AI will be able—any time soon at least—to respond to new types of controversial content without human monitoring. For example, AI will not perceive new terrorist threats with a different political agenda than already known ones.

In addition to these human and mechanical removal procedures, most tech giants also rely on the contribution from users who have the option to complain about content they have witnessed on the platform by flagging it.[13] The use of this option makes up, in a sense, user co-creation of the site as a way to patrol its borders, fitting nicely into many of the tech giants' idyllic self-description as self-organized "communities". This is not free from problems, however. The users are no neutral, impartial police force. It is better to compare it to a self-organized militia or "posse" of a particular group or urban neighborhood, who might be capable of carrying out certain protective tasks, but who may also have its own agendas and who is not obliged by the rule of law, let alone knowing about the law. Of course, the trend is for the most annoyed or quarreling users to be the ones filing the most com-

---

[12] Perez, S. "Facebook, Microsoft, Twitter and YouTube collaborate to remove 'terrorist content' from their services" *TechCrunch*. 12-06-16.

[13] In addition to "flaggers", Gillespie points to yet another group of moderators—community managers, who are leaders of, for example, Facebook groups and the so-called "redditors" on Reddit. They may help enforce the companies' policies and add their own, as long as they do not contravene those of the company.

plaints—rather than just leaving the content in question. No one is forced to stick around and watch. There is no guarantee whatsoever that complainants primarily complain to defend the platform policy. In fact, there is no guarantee that complainants even know about the policy. Other motivations for complaints range from diffusely sensing something to be inappropriate, to perceived offense (whether or not the offense is a violation of any given rule), to offense on behalf of others (one is not personally offended but believes that the content may offend someone else, who complainants feel more or less in their right to defend), to moralist pushiness, to taking action against views that one is in disagreement with, to private revenge against people belonging an opposing group. Sometimes groups of users even join forces to carry out coordinated flagging of specific persons, groups, or views, simply to have them removed from the platform. What is more, there is not even any guarantee that the complaint in fact relates to the content in question. These circumstances are supported by the fact that the complainant remains anonymous both to the removal staff and the accused party, the latter of which is not informed about who reported and over what exact content aspect—users are completely free to complain in the sense that they cannot be criticized or accused of fake complaints. In most cases, communication to the proscribed user seems rudimentary. Often it is not made clear exactly what content is deemed problematic or what rule was allegedly violated, appeals mechanisms are not mentioned, and with most tech giants it is notoriously difficult to get in contact with staff members to object to an unfair decision.

Some additional details seem to affect this flagging procedure and the subsequent brief checks by the tech giant staff members (often outsourced to other companies such as TaskUs, which have specialized in content removal): the use of "super users" whose complaint pattern enjoys particular confidence and whose complaints are almost automatically favored. For example, YouTube has a "Trusted Flagger" category, in 2016 expanded and renamed as nothing less than

"YouTube Heroes". The program turns flagging into a kind of computer game with points and prizes. Conversely, tech giants appear to be working with lists of particularly suspect users who could somehow be expected to post questionable content—possibly based on posts previously complained about and removed, or simply based on their suspicious behavior on the site or anywhere else on the Internet. Subsequently, such problematic users may be subject to special monitoring aimed at quick and consistent crackdowns.

Finally, this entire complex internal structure is continuously affected from outside by leaked cases discussed and criticized on the site, elsewhere on the web or in traditional media—which, in some cases, may put pressure on or jeopardize the reputation of the tech giant in question, who may then modify the set of rules or practices, in public or concealed fashion. Given the large amount of complaints and the many odd levels of the complaint mechanism, nobody can expect consistency in the decisions, and there are many reports of people who have had their accounts deleted for posts that are nevertheless still up on other user profiles.

User flagging has several advantages to tech giants. In a certain sense, it outsources an enormous and unforeseeable task to the users who work for free. It may also seem to support the belief of tech leaders that the removal of content is made by a self-regulating "community"—as if the complainants were in mutual agreement and as if they were not complaining about widely differing things and with widely differing motives. Sometimes, the tech elite comes off as if by definition there are no other problems on their platform than the ones flagged by users—such as when Zuckerberg spoke at the congressional hearings. These romantic ideas are of course contradicted by the simple fact that it is the companies who make and enforce the rules and not the users who act as reviewers only, some would say snitches.

Different deviations and varieties of this general scenario are found. Filtering can be a supplement or an alternative to removals so that certain content categories are reserved for certain users. For example, some platforms use filtering for certain categories—such as Tumblr with porn—in a setup[14] where users rate their posts themselves based on how pornographic or not they are. That way only users who have previously accepted it have access to that content category. Certain services have "safe search", an option in which users beforehand deselect different categories of content from their search. However, as noted by Gillespie, not enabling "safe search" does not mean that the user gets access to all content when doing neutral searches (porn movies do not appear when searching "movies", only "porn movies"), so even with "safe search" disabled, moderation takes place. Filtering is of course a milder kind of control than the far more widespread policy of removal, but if it is not done according to very explicit principles, making the user aware of what is going on, it naturally increases the risk of filter bubbles.

Even Tumblr's relatively liberal stance towards porn has come under attack. In December 2018, the platform announced full prohibition of all pornographic material. The new rule prohibits "Adult Content. Don't upload images, videos, or GIFs that show real-life human genitals or female-presenting nipples — this includes content that is so photorealistic that it could be mistaken for featuring real-life humans (nice try, though). Certain types of artistic, educational, newsworthy, or political content featuring nudity are fine. Don't upload any content, including images, videos, GIFs, or illustrations, that depicts sex acts."[15] The argument behind seems to be that in order to accommodate the App Store policy against child pornography, it was deemed safest to remove the much larger category of pornography in general, in order to avoid the issue of borderline cases between child porn and normal porn. This antiliberal step gave rise to outcry from the LGBT community, which had seen Tumblr as a forum of self-expression and experiments. Simultaneously,

---

[14]The categories have changed over time. At one point there were two markings beside the neutral standard: *NSFW* ("Not Safe For Work") for "occasional" nudity and *Adult* for "substantial" nudity.

[15]Tumblr "Community Guidelines" modified 12-17-18. Last visited 12-20-18: https://www.tumblr.com/policy/en/community

this step seems to corroborate the suspicion that Apple is increasingly setting the limits for online expression – and applying it to other tech companies – because of the central role of the App Store as a gateway to Apple devices for the other tech giants.

All in all, content removal is a complex process involving many levels. Coordination and communication between layers is a problem in and of itself, aggravated by the existence of different versions of the same set of rules. One may ask why content removal — not only on Facebook but with most tech giants — must be kept so secret. Media researcher Sarah Roberts highlights several reasons behind this: the fact that removal is concealed so users do not know the detailed removal criteria may prevent users from trying to bypass or game the rules, and it also hides the elementary fact that the entire platform is a result of ongoing active selection based on monetary motives.[16] One might add that the whole ideology of a free self-organizing community is probably best maintained if the extent of the removal industry does not see the light of day. At the same time, secrecy gives users intolerable conditions when the rules approach the status of laws—since the Renaissance, a core aspect of the idea of rule of law has been that laws must be public.

For a long time now, websites have been around documenting this censorship, as it is often directly dubbed—e.g. https://onlinecensorship.org. When looking at how hyper-detailed and sensitive the services are when it comes to targeting content and ads at individual users, it is curious to see how insensitive their community standards have generally been. By default, they apply to the whole world, to "our entire community", as the Danish Facebook spokesperson said in sugar-coated terms. The standards are not in any way adapted

---

[16] Roberts, S.T. "Commercial Content Moderation: Digital Laborers' Dirty Work" *Scholarship@Western Media Studies Publications* 2016. Roberts quotes an anonymous content moderator working for one of the tech giants: "We have very, very specific itemized internal policies ... the internal policies are not made public because then it becomes very easy to skirt them to essentially the point of breaking them" p. 5.

to cultural, geographical let alone jurisdictional differences. They largely reflect the worldview of a small elite of wealthy men and software engineers at the top of Silicon Valley. In most Western countries, these community standards are more stringent than local laws on expressions, whereas in other cases, especially in the Middle East and Asia, they may be more lenient. But the principle that the standards should be the same throughout the world gives them a natural tendency to be organized by the lowest common denominator. If something is tabooed or feels offensive in one part in the world, then via the community standards that something is expanded to all users across the world. Øvig's harmless images of naked hippie breasts did not raise many eyebrows in Denmark where his book was initially published. But they became a problem because in other, more straitlaced places of the world, there are people who claim to be shocked at the sight of people's natural bodies. Something similar goes for the critique of religion, which is widely used in some places and even regarded as an intellectual endeavor of a certain standard, while elsewhere in the world it is regarded as blasphemy and may even invoke the death penalty. In that arena, the tendency is also for the lowest common denominator to prevail. When it comes to "hate speech", there are very different standards—as mentioned, it is not a crime in the US, but in many European and other countries it is, and it usually also appears among expressions regulated by tech giant standards.

Although by default the same standards apply to the whole world, in recent years pressure from dictator states and authoritarian regimes has made several tech giants tighten the criteria to align them with local laws. For instance, Facebook gave in to Turkish pressure by forbidding specific critique of Islam on their Turkish Facebook—including a ban on caricature images of prophet Muhammad. That happened in January 2015, only two weeks after Zuckerberg proudly, prompted by the *Charlie Hebdo* massacre in Paris, had stated the following: "We never let one country or group of people dictate what people can share across the world."[17] In 2010, American illustrator Molly Norris announced "Everybody Draw Mohammed Day". It was based on the idea that if the Internet drowned in drawings of Muhammad, censorship of them would be practically impossible. Pakistan filed protests to Facebook and threatened to close down the service. Morris' initiative was not covered by Facebook's rulebook, so Facebook's improvised reaction was to remove Norris's big Facebook group with hundreds of thousands of users in Pakistan, India and Bangladesh. Even Google agrees to such local concessions: on the Russian version of Google Maps, Crimea is now a part of the Russian Federation. Thus the tendency is that in cases where the principle of one and the same standard for the whole world is departed from, the departure is towards further local narrowing of what can be said, not liberalization.[18] There is no general openness or transparency about the range and nature of these local compromises made with non-democratic regimes. Gillespie points out that such modifications—just like personal filter bubbles—are invisible because not only is content removed, but there is no mentioning of said removal: the problem is "... the obscured obscuring of contentious material from the public realm for some, not for others." It creates filter bubbles on the national or religious level, so to speak. The "global community" may now look completely different in differ-

[17] Dewey, C. "Mark Zuckerberg's Facebook censors images of the Prophet Mohamed in Turkey – two weeks after he declared 'Je Suis Charlie'" *Independent*. 01-28-15.

[18] Facebook is allegedly entering into restrictive agreements with Pakistan on completely removing blasphemy (which is subject to the death penalty in the country), with Vietnam on removing comments critical of the government, and with Thailand on removing criticism of the royal family, cf. Gillespie (2018) p. 38. In this respect, Facebook seems more adaptable than Google, who pulled out of China due to that country's demand for censorship.

ent countries and may not be as global as once proclaimed.

Looking at the standards of the different tech giants, we find something striking. From the Pinterest "Terms of Service": "You grant Pinterest and our users a non-exclusive, royalty-free, transferable, sublicensable, worldwide license to use, store, display, reproduce, save, modify, create derivative works, perform, and distribute your User Content on Pinterest solely for the purposes of operating, developing, providing, and using Pinterest. Nothing in these Terms restricts other legal rights Pinterest may have to User Content, for example under other licenses. We reserve the right to remove or modify User Content, or change the way it's used in Pinterest, for any reason."[19] As with other tech giants, users give the company the right, to a surprising extent, to use their personal uploaded content in a number of ways, including commercial ones. But the crucial part here are the last three words: "for any reason." The right to remove or modify user content is reserved *for any reason*. Similar unspecified formulations are found in many tech giant policies, which may talk about removing content "at any time" or launching lists of critical content with the phrase "... including (but not limited to)."[20] This is analogous to censorship laws which fail to specificy exactly which types of statements are in fact criminalized. In the absence of such specification, the laws may be applied to an unlimited amount of undefined infringements; potentially to all kinds of statements. The legal protection of the user is non-existent if the extent to what can be removed remains unknown. In a Danish context, we are somehow back

[19] Pinterest "Terms of service" Most recent visit 06-25-18: https://policy.pinterest.com/en/terms-of-service.

[20] For instance, the conditions of Facebook-owned Instagram: "Also, Instagram reserves the right to remove any Content from the Service for any reason, without prior notice." Last visited 12-19-18: https://help.instagram.com/478745558852511, or "Spotify reserves the right to remove or disable access to any User Content for any or no reason." Last visited 12-19-18: https://www.spotify.com/legal/end-user-agreement/

at the Danish police-issued censorship of 1773, in which a police commissioner had the sovereign right to confiscate which books he deemed illegal, without any prior court decision. It is also characteristic that content removed by the tech giants *for any reason* is removed offhand, without the criteria being clear, without knowing whether it was done manually or automatically, without the user being informed why, without anything that looks like a court decision in which arguments pro and contra can be put forward based on a sound legal basis and finally without any formal or clear appeal path. When it comes to Pinterest's "Terms of Service", the policy on prohibited content fits on one single line: "Do not post pornography or spam or act like a jerk in front of others on Pinterest." This may sound funky, idiomatic and straightforward, but it exposes a lack of more precise description of what types of actions makes one considered "to be a jerk". This gives that particular company a legal license to do as it pleases.

The standard procedure for content removal on Facebook starts with users view content that they find problematic or offensive. They then decide to flag, to submit a complaint, which then constitutes the basis for removal. Then it is up to Facebook's safety and security staff—a team as per early 2018 consisting of 7,500 people, but which after Facebook's crisis in the spring of 2018 was set out to a quick expansion to around 30.000, many of which are allegedly based in the Philippines— to check the given content and determine which complaints should be favored. This essentially means that the needs of "offended" users are met—but it also means that only problems visible to the users can be addressed.[21] At the congressional hearings in April 2018, when commenting

[21] However, far from all potentially problematic cases are visible from the point of view of the individual user. For example, if an ad is only targeted to white buyers, non-white buyers will never know anything about, simply this because they do not see the ad. Many issues regarding targeted and personalized content may escape notice because users have no transparency when it comes to personalization.

on various problematic issues raised by US politicians, Zuckerberg repeatedly said that Facebook would obviously take care of these issues if, it should be noted, any users filed relevant complaints. This is to say that if no users were complaining, then there could be no real problem and the politicians need not worry. According to this logic, it is the complainants (and the advertisers) who set the agenda and that they in fact comprise the sole specification or correction of the company guidelines. Many have discovered this and are able to abuse it to organize social media shitstorms against views and people they dislike—who may then be removed from the platform by its speedy representatives, see below. According to the same logic, structural, general, and statistical aspects of the algorithms – invisible from the viewpoint of single users – could never appear as real problems the company ought to address.

As mentioned earlier, manual removal of content, as a response to complaints, is increasingly supported by the automated removal of content based on algorithms constantly developed and modified. There has been no public access to, neither the algorithms themselves nor the exact criteria on which removals are carried out. The criteria are revised and modified on a regular basis, and rarely communicated to the public. At the hearings in April 2018, Zuckerberg placed the main responsibility for the recent removal of "terrorist" content from Facebook on the algorithms, claiming that 99% of ISIS-related material was now removed automatically. He repeatedly cited further development and sophistication of AI-based algorithms as the solution to many of the issues highlighted by members of congress—including the removal of many different types of content, both those already covered by the standards and content found problematic by different politicians. But the public has no insight into or guarantee that all the aforementioned deleted ISIS posts actually contain serious acts such as threats, incitement to violence, organization of terrorist cells, etc. Needless to mention, nothing could be farther from the writers of this book to have the remotest sympathy with ISIS, but that is exactly the reason these cases are suitable to illustrate the problem. Interpretations of for instance the ISIS theology, its understanding of government, politics, strategy, propaganda etc. should *not* be removed, in our opinion, and certainly not automatically and without control. The classic line of argument to defend the position that such content should also be tolerated goes as follows: if not all views—also abominable ones—are allowed, the result is a public sphere characterized by dishonesty, pretense and hypocrisy, because people are forced to hide what they really mean. If certain views are banned, they will not just disappear, but instead get organized in the underground—for instance on The Dark Web—where they may gain a sheen of martyrdom, become radicalized and even more difficult to control. The result is fragmentation of the public sphere. It makes it harder both for the public, for researchers and for secret services to understand, for example, what kind of phenomenon ISIS is, if no one has access to their distorted views. And if radical views are rejected, supporters of such views are more likely to conclude that democracy does not include them; therefore, they must take anti-democratic action. One could also add that the presence of grotesque and extreme views in the public sphere has a diversity of functions. This does not only make for the recruitment of more supporters. It also gives the public the opportunity to be aware of, disgusted at and renounce such positions—like a vaccine that makes society ready to battle against such positions, a readiness which may lose force if these ideologies develop in more clandestine fashions.

The censorship procedure not only includes the removal of content, be it algorithmically by censorship before the fact or manually by censorship after the fact. It also happens by categorizing certain types of users as suspicious and then subjecting them to special monitoring of their online behavior. Categorization of someone as suspicious can of course be the simple fact that on repeated occasions the person has had content removed, manually or algorithmically. But it can also just be a significant change in one's metadata—data mapping one's network connectivity and online behavior. If that behavior suddenly involves new groups, not to mention groups in contradiction to one another, or if it comes off as striking in any other way, then the "standing" with the tech giant can be changed from light green to red, which means that the user's behavior is subject to special monitoring in order to immediately crack down, if the user posts something that violates the community standards. Monitoring users happens, of course, primarily for advertising and commercial purposes—but it also has a political dimension, so to speak, in the way that it categorizes users before the fact, if they are thought to possibly violate the community standards.[22] In August 2018, the public was given a small taste sample of this when Facebook announced its use of a Trust Index to rate users on a scale between 0 and 1. The purpose is to identify malicious users to crack down upon. The index most likely includes repeated violators of the community rules. According to Facebook, this credibility assessment also seems to include whether users have reported something as false which in fact was only a matter of disagreement—apparently the first attempt at possible sanctioning against abuse of the flagging feature. Similarly, the index also includes which publishers are considered credible by users. As always, there is no transparency about how these comprehensive credibility assessments are arrived at, whether all users are assigned a credibility score—and there is also no indication of whether it is even possible for users to gain insight into their own index and potentially file an appeal in case of error.[23]

The overall picture is that by using their de facto monopoly, the tech giants are actually in the process of turning their community standards into the new limits of the public sphere.

---

[22] We have this description of the categorization of users from an expert source who has visited and interviewed the tech giants on several occasions and who has had profiles closed; we are aware of the identity of the person who, however, has preferred to remain anonymous.

[23] E. Dwoskin. "Facebook is the Trustworthiness of its Users on a Scale from Zero to 1" *Washington Post.* 08-21-18.

From their origin as editorial principles these guidelines slowly transform and become de facto censorship legislation. And these new limits are far narrower than the broad limits for freedom of speech generally set out in modern liberal democracies.

Chapter 11
Facebook's Handbook of Content Removal

Due to the recent crises, Facebook is restructuring to restore the company's reputation, which is, according to Zuckerberg, a three-year process. On April 24, 2018, Facebook published its updated internal guidelines for enforcement of the company's community standards.[1] It was the first time the public gained direct, "official" insight into this comprehensive hidden policing inside the company. The only glimpses behind the curtain provided before then came from confidential documents leaked to *Gawker* magazine in 2012, to *S/Z* in 2016—and in 2017, when *The Guardian* published "The Facebook Files". They included comprehensive removal guidelines featuring a mixture of parameters, decision trees and rules of thumb—illustrated by many concrete examples of content to be removed, most likely taken from real ousted material of the time.[2] As a contrast to this, the 2018 document is much more sparse, orderly and void of examples, and it is tempting to think that this is a combed-down version aimed for publication. Still, the document gives unique insight into the detailed principles for the company's content removal—albeit not the enforcement procedure itself. One can only

[1] Facebook "Community Standards". Last visit 08-04-18: https://www.facebook.com/communitystandards/; the quotes in this chapter are taken from here. See also Lee, N. "Facebook publishes its community standards playbook" *Engadget*. 04-24-18.

[2] Cf. Gillespie (2018) p. 111f.

F. Stjernfelt, A. M. Lauritzen, *Your Post has been Removed*,
https://doi.org/10.1007/978-3-030-25968-6_11

guess as to whether this surprising move away from secrecy can be attributed to the increasing media storm throughout 2017, culminating in the Cambridge Analytica revelation of March 2018 and the congressional hearings in April of the same year. The document contains six chapters: (1) "Violence and Criminal Behavior", (2) "Safety", (3) "Objectionable Content", (4) "Integrity and Authenticity", (5) "Respecting Intellectual Property" and (6) "Content Related Requests."

The first chapter features reasonable restrictions regarding criminal acts such as threats and incitement to violence. The second, "Safety", is more problematic. Here, for instance, child pornography and images of naked children are treated as if they were but varieties of the same thing, i.e., no posting of photos featuring "nude, sexualized, or sexual activity with minors." This means that images of diaper-changing and pedophilia fall into the same category. The stance towards "self-injury" is also problematic, because Facebook believes itself capable of preventing suicide by banning content which "promotes, encourages, coordinates, or provides instructions for suicide, self-injury or eating disorders." For one, this excludes serious discussion of the ongoing political issue of voluntary euthanasia—and in the same vein, one can ask whether it would not also exclude many fashionable diets. The sections "Bullying" and "Harassment" and the right to privacy are less problematic. There is, however, an issue with the following wording: "Our bullying policies do not apply to public figures because we want to allow discourse, which often includes critical discussion of people who are featured in the news or who have a large public audience. Discussion of public figures nonetheless must comply with our Community Standards, and we will remove content about public figures that violates other policies, including "hate speech" or credible threats." This can easily be used as a cop-out to shield public figures from criticism many would find completely legitimate.

The fourth item is "Spam", "Misrepresentation", "False News" and "Memorialization." It is funny how a basic guideline within the "Spam" category says: "Do not artificially increase distribution for financial gain." It is hard not to read this as an exact characterization of Facebook's very own business model, but obviously the company cannot have users invading the company's own commercial turf. Indeed, spam is by far the largest category of content removed.

"Misrepresentation" refers to Facebook's policy stating that all users must use their own real name. In democratic countries, the reasoning behind this policy is understandable; the very name "Facebook" is based on the requirement of presenting a somewhat authentic picture of the user's face. But it may be acutely dangerous for users in non-democratic countries. However, even in democratic countries, certain people such as anonymous media sources, whistle blowers or others might have very legitimate reasons not to appear with their own name and photo. In 2017, a major case put Facebook and the LGBT community at loggerheads. Many Drag Queens who appeared on the platform under their adopted transgender names had their accounts blocked (it would later turn out that they had all been flagged by one and the same energetic complainant) with reference to the requirement to appear under their own real name. The problem is not peripheral. In the first months of 2018, Facebook had to close as many as 583 million fake accounts, while still estimating that 3–4% of the remaining billions of users are fake.[3] Creating and selling fake user accounts has become a large independent industry which can be used to influence everything from consumer reviews of restaurants, books, travel, etc., to more serious and malicious things such as political propaganda disguised as personal views originating from real users. When you read a good review of a restaurant online, it is potentially written by the owner, with a fake user as intermediary. As tech writer Jaron Lanier pointed out, there are numerous celebrities, businesses, politicians and others whose presence on the Internet is boosted by large numbers of fake users who

[3] That is, around 100 million fake users; "Facebook shut 583 million fake accounts" *Phys Org.* 05-15-18. Last visited 06-25-18: https://phys.org/news/2018-05-facebook-million-fake-accounts.html.

"follow" or "like" their activities.[4] He believes that the large amount of fake users represents a fundamental problem for tech giants because so much other false communication—fake ads, "fake news", political propaganda—is disseminated though these non-existent people. These are dead souls that can also be traded. As of early 2018, the price of 25,000 fake followers on Twitter was around 225 USD.[5] In this light, it is understandable that Facebook wants to tackle fake users, but it is unsettling if this can only be done by an encroaching ban on anonymity, especially earnest and necessary use of anonymity. Serious media regularly need to guarantee anonymity of sources or writers to even get them to participate, which then happens on the condition that the editorial staff know the identity of the person.

Regarding the strongly disputed concept of "fake news", the following phrase from the document might seem reassuring: "There is also a fine line between false news and satire or opinion." This could lead one to believe that Facebook does not feel called upon to act as judge of true and false. But the very next sentence goes: "For these reasons, we don't remove false news from Facebook but instead significantly reduce its distribution by showing it lower in the News Feed." So false news is not removed, but still the people in the background consider themselves capable of *identifying* false news, inasmuch as such news stories are downgraded in the news feed and thus marginalized. This reveals a shocking level of conceit: Facebook believes that its some 30.000 moderation inspectors —probably untrained— should be able to perform a truth check on news within 24 hours. It is self-evident that news is new, and society's established institutions—with their highly educated specialists in serious journalism, courts and academia—often spend a very long time determining and documenting what is true and false in the news flow. How would a platform with no experience in the production and research of news whatsoever be a credible clearinghouse for

---

[4] Lanier (2018) p. 34.

[5] According to *New York Times*, cit. from Lanier, op.cit.

truth? Perhaps the company is realizing this as of late. In December 2016, when the "fake news" debate raged in the wake of the US presidential election,[6] Facebook announced a collaboration with various fact-checking organizations. They were tasked with tagging certain news (primarily about American politics) as "disputed". The idea was, however, abandoned in December 2017, when it was found that this tagging attracted *more* attention and traffic to those news stories rather than scaring users off.[7]

Despite the public promotion of Facebook's new fact-checking cooperation, it is still a very closed procedure with few details given. The collaborating organizations are fact checker companies PolitiFact, FactCheck.org, Snopes and the two news outlets ABC News and Associated Press—cf. Mike Ananny's comprehensive 2018 report *The partnership press: Lessons for platform-publisher collaborations as Facebook and news outlets team to fight misinformation*.[8] Some collaborators work for free, while others receive a symbolic amount from Facebook. The report is based mainly on anonymous interviews with fact checkers and according to it, the collaborations between Facebook and the five organizations works as follows: "Through a proprietary process that mixes algorithmic and human intervention, Facebook identifies candidate stories; these stories are then served to the five news and fact-checking partners through a partners-only dashboard that ranks stories according to popularity. Partners

[6] It has since become clear that Facebook was the biggest source of "fake news" during the 2016 presidential election, cf. Guess, A., Nyhan, B. & Reifler, J. "Selective Exposure to Misinformation: Evidence from the consumption of fake news during the 2016 U.S. presidential campaign" Dartmouth. 09-01-18. Last visited 07-30-18: https://www.dartmouth.edu/~nyhan/fake-news-2016.pdf.

[7] BBC "Facebook ditches fake news warning flag" *BBC News*. 12-21-17.

[8] Ananny, M. "The partnership press: Lessons for platform-publisher collaborations as Facebook and news outlets team to fight misinformation" *Tow Center for Digital Journalism*. 04-04-18. Last visited 07-30-18: https://www.cjr.org/tow_center_reports/partnership-press-facebook-news-outlets-team-fight-misinformation.php#citations—the following quotes are taken from this.

independently choose stories from the dashboard, do their usual fact-checking work, and append their fact-checks to the stories' entries in the dashboards. Facebook uses these fact-checks to adjust whether and how it shows potentially false stories to its users." Thousands of stories are cued up on the website, and each organization has the capacity to control a handful or two per day.

The procedure for selecting critical news stories seems to consist of Facebook users flagging them as fake, in combination with automated warnings, which are based on previous suspicious links. Once again, a lot of responsibility is put on users flagging other users—but the details of the selection remain protected, as mentioned above. Ananny's report could access neither the central "dashboard" website nor the principles behind it, and many of the fact checkers interviewed in the report are dissatisfied with various aspects of the opaque procedure dictated by Facebook. Among other things, they complain of not being able to flag pictures and videos as fake.[9] Among the interviewees, for example, there is suspicion that Facebook avoids sending them false stories if they have high advertising potential. In general, there is skepticism among fact checkers regarding Facebook's motives and behavior around the design of the dashboard website and the classification and selection of its content: "We don't see mainstream media appearing [in the dashboard]—is it being filtered out?" And: "We aren't seeing major conspiracy theories or conservative media—no *InfoWars* on the list, that's a surprise." (*InfoWars* is a site dedicated to conspiracy theories, which had more than 1.4 million Facebook followers before Facebook finally shut down the site in August 2018—see Chapter 12).[10]

In the absence of a transparent process, several fact-checkers suspect that Facebook avoids sending certain types

---

[9] On iconic material in truth-based assertions, see Stjernfelt (2014).

[10] *InfoWars* host Alex Jones had his account on Facebook and other sites shut down on 6. August 2018, cf. Vincent, J. "Facebook removes Alex Jones pages, citing repeated hate speech violations" *The Verge*. 08-06-18. Apple, Spotify and YouTube also closed InfoWars on the same day.

of news through the fact-check system in order to avoid their labelling. If that is the case, then some false news stories are removed or de-ranked while others are not even sent to check. The suspicion seems justified, as in July 2018, an undercover reporter from *Channel4 Dispatches* revealed how popular activists from the extreme right get special protection from Facebook. The documentary showed how moderators, for example, let right-wing movement Britain First's pages slip through, simply because they "generate a lot of revenue". The process is called "shielded review". Typically, a page is removed if it has more than five entries violating Facebook rules. But with shielded review, particularly popular pages are elevated to another moderation level, where the final removal decision is made by Facebook's internal staff.[11]

In Ananny's report, fact checkers are also quoted as complaining that they have no knowledge of the actual purpose of Facebook's checks or what impact they have. Facebook has publicly stated that a negative fact check results in 80% less traffic to the news in question. But as a fact checker says, this claim itself is not open to fact-checking. Others complain that the process has the character of a private agreement between private companies and that there is no openness about its ideals or accountability to the public. With so little transparency about Facebook's fact-check initiatives, it is difficult to conclude anything unambiguously, but the whole process seems problematic from a free speech standpoint, given the lack of clear criteria regarding which stories are sent to check and which are not. The efforts do not seem to be working well, either. The number of users visiting Facebook pages with "fake news" was higher in 2017 than in 2016.[12] As part of its hectic public relations activity in Spring 2018, Facebook announced that it would begin to check photos and videos, this time in collaboration with the French media agency

---

[11] Hern, A. "Facebook protects far-right activists even after rule breaches" *The Guardian*. 07-17-18.

[12] According to a *Buzzfeed* survey: Silverman, C., Lytvynenko, J. & Pham, S. "These are 50 of Fake News Hits on Facebook in 2017" *BuzzFeed*. 12-28-17.

AFP.[13] Details about the procedure and results of this initiative remain to be seen. In December 2018, after Facebook had used the Definers spin company to smear opponents became known, former managing editor of Snopes, a fact-checking company, Brooke Binkowski expressed her disappointment with the company's two-year collaboration with Facebook: "They've essentially used us for crisis PR." She added: "They're not taking anything seriously. They are more interested in making themselves look good and passing the buck […] They clearly don't care."[14] By February 2019, Snopes quit the Facebook factchecking partnership.[15]

The next clause of the Facebook removal manual concerning intellectual property rights does nothing more than make explicit the company's responsibility disclaimer—much like Google and other tech giants. It puts all responsibility on users, who are assumed to have made the copyright situation clear for all posts they upload (cf. Ch. 14).

The last section of the clause, "Content-Related Requests", covers users' right to delete accounts—as expected, there is no mention of the right to ask Facebook to delete their detailed data profiles including their general online behavior, data purchased, etc. Also, the section does not address the issue of how the tech giant will respond if asked by intelligence agencies and police for access to user data—a touchy subject concerning anything from relatively unproblematic help with criminal investigations to much more debatable help with politically motivated surveillance.

Crucial to freedom of expression, however, is the third item: "Objectionable Content". It features the subcategories "Hate Speech", "Graphic Violence", "Adult Nudity and Sexual

---

[13] Ingram, D. "Facebook begins 'fact-checking' photos and videos" *Reuters*. 03-29-18.

[14] Levin, S. "'They don't care': Facebook factchecking in disarray as journalists push to cut ties" *The Guardian*. 12-13-18.

[15] Coldewey, D. "UPDATE: Snopes quits and AP in talks over Facebook's factchecking partnership" *TechCrunch*. 02-01-19.

Activity" and "Cruel and Insensitive".[16] Each category is described in detail. "We define hate speech as a direct attack on people based on what we call protected characteristics—race, ethnicity, national origin, religious affiliation, sexual orientation, sex, gender, gender identity, and serious disability or disease. We also provide some protections for immigration status. We define attack as violent or dehumanizing speech, statements of inferiority, or calls for exclusion or segregation. We separate attacks into three tiers of severity, as described below."[17] Facebook's list of "hate speech" examples is characteristic in its attempt at a definition based on a random list of groups of people who for some reason should enjoy particular protection beyond other groups in society. Such a break with equality before the law is one of the classic problems of "hate speech" regulation, both because different legislators choose and select different groups for special protection, but also in practice: usually, it is humor or other remarks about certain, selected skin colors, ethnicities and religions, that are considered as bad taste. But then there are others of whom it is considered acceptable to make fun. This changes with the spirit of the times and is often a matter of which groups yell the loudest—groups that do not have the zeitgeist in their favor notoriously do not even expect to find protection in "hate speech" paragraphs. Although "race" is a crucial concept on the list, for instance, the Caucasian race is rarely

---

[16] Facebook's "Community Standards 12. Hate Speech" p. 18. Last visited 07-30-18: https://www.facebook.com/communitystandards/objectionable_content/hate_speech.

[17] Many tech giants have similar formulas that directly cite the range of groups that enjoy special protection in US anti-discrimination legislation. Although the United States has no criminalization of hate speech (and may not have it because of the First Amendment), companies thus, in a certain sense, generalize and extend the existing law to include hate speech. It is worth noting that the characteristics (ethnicity, gender, religion, etc.) used in this legislation do not distinguish between minority and majority groups—unlike what is often assumed, the protection here is *not* aimed at protecting minorities specifically, and as a matter of principle majority groups supposedly have right to equal protection according to such laws and regulations.

mentioned as worthy of protection from attacks related to skin color, and attacks on Islam is often taken very seriously which is seldom the case with Christianity. Also, Facebook's "hate speech" definition does not include a reference to the concept of truth, as we find in libel—thus, a true statement can be classified as "hate speech" if someone claims to feel offended by it.

It is a well-known fact that Facebook and other tech giants have had a hard time deciding how to deal with statements which merely *cite* or *parody* the hateful statements of others. This problem is now openly addressed in the following segment: "Sometimes people share content containing someone else's hate speech for the purpose of raising awareness or educating others. Similarly, in some cases, words or terms that might otherwise violate our standards are used self-referentially or in an empowering way." Irony and satire are not mentioned explicitly but are referenced in the part about "fake news", and one must assume that they are addressed in the "self-referential" use of "hate speech". Such statements are, of course, difficult to process quickly or automatically because their character cannot be determined based on the simple presence or absence of particular terms but require a more thorough understanding of the whole context. Facebook's solution goes: "When this is the case, we allow the content, but we expect people to clearly indicate their intent, which helps us better understand why they shared it. Where the intention is unclear, we may remove the content."[18]

Quotes or irony are allowed, then, but only if this is made completely clear, with quotation marks and explicit or implicit underlining. An ironic post about Christians and white Danes was exactly what sprung the Facebook trap on Danish journalist Abdel Aziz Mahmoud in January 2018.[19] As

---

[18] Facebook's "Community Standards 12. Hate Speech" p. 18. Last visited 07-30-18: https://www.facebook.com/communitystandards/objectionable_content/hate_speech.

[19] See Abdel Mahmoud's Facebook post in Pedersen, J. "Kendt DR-vært censureret af Facebook: Se opslaget, der fik ham blokeret" *BT.* 01-28-18.

a public figure with many followers, he had posted a comment aimed at highlighting the double standard among many players in public Danish debate. However, after several users reported the post as offensive, Facebook chose to delete it and throw the journalist off the site. Facebook does not seem to understand that irony works best in a delicate balance, causing its addressee to wonder what exactly the idea may be—and not by overexplaining and spelling out. The reason for this removal was, of course, that no one can expect sophisticated text interpretation from underpaid staff working under pressure on the other side of the globe, just as it has not yet been possible to teach artificial intelligence to understand irony. But apparently Facebook has concluded that some of the most elegant and artistically and politically effective instruments—irony, parody and satire—cannot come to full fruition. In a Danish context, we need to dig deep in the history books and go all the way back to the Danish Freedom of the Press Act of 1799. Its Article 13 established that irony and allegory were penalized the same way as explicit statements. At the time, the idea was to protect the Monarchy. In the case of Facebook, the reasons are financial, as the company cannot afford to deploy the procedures necessary to really differentiate such challenging statements.

Since 1790, crimes of press freedom in Denmark have, at least as a general rule, been decided publicly in the courts, allowing for thorough arguments pro et contra to be presented, and for the intention and meaning of a contested statement to be clarified. One of the key challenges of the new online censorship is that this is not the case. It is performed automatically, without transparency, and thus far removed from any real appeal option, unless the affected person—as in the case of Abdel Mahmoud Aziz—is fortunate enough to be a publicly known figure with the related opportunities of contacting the traditional press to raise public awareness about a problem, pressuring tech giants to respond and apologize for the removal.

Another example from Denmark of a public figure clashing with Facebook's foggy policies was Jens Philip Yazdani, former chairman of the Union of Danish Upper Secondary School Students. During the 2018 Soccer World Cup, Yazdani, whose background is part Iranian, weighed in on the debate on national identity and what it means to be Danish. In a post he wrote that he found it easier to support the Iranian national team than the Danish one, because of the harsh tone of the immigration debate in Danish society. The post was shared vividly on Facebook, garnering many likes and a glowing debate in the comments. Against all reason, Facebook decided to remove the post—including its many shares and comments—after several complaints, because the post had allegedly violated Facebook's guidelines on "hate speech". One may agree or disagree with Yazdani, but it is indeed hard to find anything per se offensive in the post whatsoever. With the press of a button, Facebook managed to kill a relevant contribution to the Danish debate in society. Only journalist Mikkel Andersson's public criticism of Facebook's decision led to a concession from Facebook, who put Yazdani's post back online.[20]

The "hate speech" clause details three levels and therefore requires a larger quotation here:

> Do not post:
>
> **Tier 1** attacks, which target a person or group of people who share one of the above-listed characteristics or immigration status (including all subsets except those described as having carried out violent crimes or sexual offenses), where attack is defined as
>
> Any violent speech or support in written or visual form
>
> Dehumanizing speech such as reference or comparison to:
>
> Insects
>
> Animals that are culturally perceived as intellectually or physically inferior
>
> Filth, bacteria, disease and feces
>
> Sexual predator
>
> Subhumanity
>
> Violent and sexual criminals

[20] Andersson, M. "Når Facebook dræber samfundsdebatten" *Berlingske*. 07-25-18.

Other criminals (including but not limited to "thieves," "bank robbers" or saying "all [protected characteristic or quasi-protected characteristic] are 'criminals'")

Mocking the concept, events or victims of hate crimes even if no real person is depicted in an image

Designated dehumanizing comparisons in both written and visual form

Tier 2 attacks, which target a person or group of people who share any of the above-listed characteristics, where attack is defined as

Statements of inferiority or an image implying a person's or a group's physical, mental, or moral deficiency

Physical (including but not limited to "deformed," "undeveloped," "hideous," "ugly")

Mental (including but not limited to "retarded," "cretin," "low IQ," "stupid," "idiot")

Moral (including but not limited to "slutty," "fraud," "cheap," "free riders")

Expressions of contempt or their visual equivalent, including (but not limited to)

"I hate"

"I don't like"

"X are the worst"

Expressions of disgust or their visual equivalent, including (but not limited to)

"Gross"

"Vile"

"Disgusting"

Cursing at a person or group of people who share protected characteristics

Tier 3 attacks, which are calls to exclude or segregate a person or group of people based on the above-listed characteristics. We do allow criticism of immigration policies and arguments for restricting those policies.

Content that describes or negatively targets people with slurs, where slurs are defined as words commonly used as insulting labels for the above-listed characteristics.

We find these straitlaced∗, American∗ moderators on Facebook despicable∗. We hate∗ their retarded∗ attempts to subdue free speech. We think that such idiots∗ ought to be kicked out∗ from Facebook and from other tech giants∗.

In this short statement, we have violated Facebook's "hate speech" criteria in Tiers 1, 2 and 3 (marked by ∗). Despite the amplified rhetoric, the sentiment is sincere, and we consider the statement to express legitimate political criticism. It is instructive to compare Facebook's weak and broad "hate speech" criteria with Twitter's radically different narrow and precise definitions, beginning with: "You may not promote violence against or directly attack or threaten other people on the basis of race…" (and then a version of the usual well-known group list is added).[21] The only strange thing here is that it implies that users are indeed *allowed* to promote violence against people who happen not to belong to any of those explicitly protected groups. At Twitter, the focus remains on "harm", "harassment", "threats" and—unlike Facebook's list—it does not operate with a diffuse list of fairly harmless linguistic terms, statements and metaphors.

Regarding "Violence and Graphic Content", Facebook's policy goes as follows:

> Do not post:
>
> Imagery of violence committed against real people or animals with comments or captions by the poster that contain
>
> Enjoyment of suffering
> Enjoyment of humiliation
> Erotic response to suffering
> Remarks that speak positively of the violence; or
> Remarks indicating the poster is sharing footage for sensational viewing pleasure
> Videos of dying, wounded, or dead people if they contain
>
> Dismemberment unless in a medical setting
> Visible internal organs
> Charred or burning people
> Victims of cannibalism

It is no wonder that the company wants to ban snuff videos where people are actually killed in front of rolling cameras,

[21] Quot. from Gillespie (2018) p. 58.

essentially for profit. But the paragraph seems to completely overlook the value of war journalism and other serious reports on torture, crime or disasters—such as Nick Ut's already mentioned press photo "Napalm Girl", featuring a naked child running from a US napalm attack, a photo that at the time contributed to a radical turn in the public opinion on the Vietnam War.[22] Or what about Robert Capa's famous photos from the Spanish Civil War? Facebook seems to assume that all images featuring, for example, "charred or burning people" necessarily have a malignant purpose as opposed to an enlightening, medical, journalistic, documentary or critical purpose. In any event, this section of the policy has no counterpart in the legislations of most countries.

The section on nudity and sex contains the following interesting concessions:

"Our nudity policies have become more nuanced over time. We understand that nudity can be shared for a variety of reasons, including as a form of protest, to raise awareness about a cause, or for educational or medical reasons. Where such intent is clear, we make allowances for the content. For example, while we restrict some images of female breasts that include the nipple, we allow other images, including those depicting acts of protest, women actively engaged in breast-feeding, and photos of post-mastectomy scarring. We also allow photographs of paintings, sculptures, and other art that depicts nude figures." Facebook seems to be realizing that fighting against the Delacroix painting, breast-feeding selfies, and so on is going way too far. Still, as recently as 2018, the company had to apologize for repeatedly deleting photos of one of humanity's oldest sculptures, the tiny 30,000-year-old stone figurine known as "Venus from Willendorf", an ample-

[22] Ingram, M. "Here's Why Facebook Removing That Vietnam War Photo Is So Important" *Fortune*. 09-09-2016. Norwegian newspaper *Aftenposten* went to great lengths to attack Facebook's removal of the photo when its Editor-in-Chief published an open letter to Zuckerberg, which gained international impact. Critics added that the effect of Facebook's removal of the photo reiterated the Nixon administration's attempts many years ago to label the photo as a fake.

bodied fertility symbol with highlighted labia.[23] And August 2018 saw the story of the removal from the Anne Frank Center page of a Holocaust photo featuring naked concentration camp prisoners.[24] The very long list of things that this section disallows is very detailed and would probably still include Peter Øvig's hippie photos from 1970. In a subclause such as the following, there are two interesting things to make a note of among the list of sexual content which users are not allowed to post:

Other sexual activities including (but not limited to)

> Erections
> Presence of by-products of sexual activity
> Stimulating genitals or anus, even if above or under clothing
> Use of sex toys, even if above or under clothing
> Stimulation of naked human nipples
> Squeezing naked female breast except in breastfeeding context

The recurring phrase "but not limited to" (cf. "for any reason") gives the platform a license to expand the list of prohibited subjects as it sees fit. Thus users, despite the quite explicit and detailed descriptions of examples worthy of a porn site, are not given any real clarity about where the boundary actually lies. Another interesting ban is that against "the presence of by-products of sexual activity"... the most widely known and visible byproduct of sexual activity being—children. However, photos of children (unless nude) do not seem to be removed from people's Facebook pages—the sloppy choice of words shows that the platform's detailed community standards are still a far cry from the clarity one normally expects of real legal texts. This is no minor issue, inasmuch as these standards are in the process of supplementing or even replacing actual legislation.

---

[23] Breitenbach, D. "Facebook apologizes for censoring prehistoric figurine 'Venus of Willendorf'" *dw.com*. 01-03-18.

[24] The photo was put back up after a complaint filed by the museum. Brandom, R. "Facebook took down a post by the Anne Frank Center for showing nude Holocaust victims" *The Verge*. 08-29-18.

The last form of forbidden content has been given the enigmatic title "Cruel and Insensitive" (which seems to be missing a noun, by the way). It is only briefly elaborated: "Content that depicts real people and mocks their implied or actual serious physical injuries, disease, or disability, non-consensual sexual touching, or premature death." Is this to say that making fun of someone's death is okay, as long they died on time? Perhaps this rule against mockery of disabilities was also what allowed Facebook to remove a caricature drawing of Donald Trump with a very small penis, believing that it was an offense against the poor man. Again, a more context-sensitive reader or algorithm would know that this was an ironic political reference to the debates during the presidential primaries of 2016, where an opponent accused Trump of having small hands (obviously referring to the popular wisdom that a correlation exists between the size of men's hands and their genitals).

In the spring and summer of 2018, Facebook seems to have been hit by almost a panic of activity in the wake of the Cambridge Analytica scandal—hardly a week went by without new, ostentatious initiatives from the company, probably in an attempt to appear serious and well-behaved enough to avoid imminent political regulation. However, many of the initiatives come off as improvised and uncoordinated—the principles of the removal manual from April were thus already being revised in August. During the Alex Jones case (see Chapter 12), the application of the "hate speech" policy was further tightened, and a few days after the Jones ban, on August 9th, Facebook came out with another sermon, this time with the title "Hard Questions: Where Do We Draw The Line on Free Expression?", signed by the company's Vice President of Policy Richard Allen. The document takes its departure in a defintion of freedom of speech as guaranteed by the government. The spread is noted between American freedom, acknowledged by the First Amendment, and at the other end, dictatorial regimes. However, in the message Facebook takes care to remind us that it is not a government, but that still the company wants to draw this line in a way "...

that gives freedom of expression the maximum extension possible."[25] It seems that leaders at Facebook have finally begun to look to the political and legal tradition of freedom of expression. Now there are references to Article 19 of "The International Covenant on Civil and Political Rights" (ICCPR) as a source of inspiration. The United Nations joined this covenant in 1966, but even back then, the agreement was already surrounded by a lot of discussion and criticism, partly due to its Article 20 calling for legislation on "hate speech". It was heavily criticized by many Western countries for its curtailment of free speech. There is some irony to the fact that this convention, which Facebook now invokes, was promoted by none other than the former Eastern Bloc, led by the Soviet Union.[26] One may wonder why Facebook does not prefer to seek inspiration in the US tradition of free speech legislation and case law, a country which has gained important experience practicing freedom of speech over a long period of time. In the short term, however, what is worth noting is another bit: "we do not, for example, allow content that could physically or financially endanger people, that intimidates people through hateful language, or that aims to profit by tricking people using Facebook." In mere casual remark, Facebook here introduces a new removal criterion that was not included in the removal handbook: "financial danger", i.e. content that tries to gain a profit by fooling Facebook users.[27] Again, the sloppy steps of the approach are spectacular: A whole new removal criterion is introduced in passing, with no clear definition or examples of what would comprise a violation of the new rule. If we did not know any better, the many ads through which Facebook generates its huge profits could easily be characterized as tools to gain profit by fooling people into buying something they do

---

[25] Facebook: "Hard Questions: Where Do We Draw The Line on Free Expression?" *Facebook Newsroom.* 08-09-18.

[26] See also Mchangama & Stjernfelt (2016) p. 781ff.

[27] Constine, J. "Facebook now deletes posts that financially endanger/trick people" *TechChrunch.* 08-09-18.

not need. This is yet another piece of improvisation when formulating policy—one must hope that American and European politicians realize that such measures cause more problems than they solve, and that such measures call out for regulation rather than make it superfluous.

The bottom line is that Facebook's belated publication of more detailed content removal guidelines is a small step forward—probably triggered by the congressional hearings of Zuckerberg a few weeks before their publication. It is commendable that a little more public light is shed on the mix of reasonable and strange, common-sense and unconsidered pondering that lie beneath this key political document. We still do not know much, however, about the safety and security staff, at present counting some 30.000 people, and their training, qualifications and working conditions, or what equips them to perform this task so crucial for the public. Many of the content moderation departments of the tech giants work mostly for a low pay (3–500 dollars a month) in third-world countries like the Philippines and under non-disclosure agreements.[28] There is indeed some distance between the luxurious hipster life of table soccer and free organic food and drinks at the Facebook headquarters in California and the work lives of stressed subcontractors stuffed closely side-by-side in shabby surroundings. One might reasonably ask how they should be able to understand the motivation behind a user posting a picture, especially when that user is in a different country, posting in a different language and a different context. Is the staff being trained, and if so then how? Image, video and text are often intertwined, commenting on each other: Does the company have personnel with the appropriate language skills to cover a global circle of users posting in hundreds of different languages? Does Facebook give moderators productivity bonuses—how many cases does an employee need to solve

[28] Chen, A. "The Laborers Who Keep Dickpics and Beheadings out of Your Facebook Feed" *Wired*. 10-23-13.

per hour? And, respectively, how many accounts need to be blocked? And how much content is removed per hour?

An average time of five to ten seconds spent on each image is often mentioned; in such a short span, aspects like context, culture, quotation or irony of course cannot be taken into account. But the actual time frame may be even shorter. Dave Willner, who worked for Facebook as a moderator from 2008 to 2013, processed 15,000 images per day; on an eight-hour workday, that makes around two seconds per image.[29] Since doubtful cases presumably take a little longer, the average time for most decisions is even shorter. Is there any effective, overall assurance that the many employees actually follow the guidelines, or are they to some extent left to their own rushed decisions and assessments based on taste? In an interview with ProPublica, Willner's description of how the removal work began in 2008 points to a great deal of judgment involved: "... [Facebook's] censorship rulebook was still just a single page with a list of material to be removed, such as images of nudity and Hitler. At the bottom of the page it said, 'Take down anything else that makes you feel uncomfortable.'" This is an extremely broad censorship policy, leaving a considerable amount of judgment on the shoulders of the individual employee—and very little legal protection for the user. Willner continues with a thoughtful remark: "'There is no path that makes people happy. All the rules are mildly upsetting.' The millions of decisions every day means that the method, according to Willner, is 'more utilitarian than we are used to in our justice system. It's fundamentally not rights-oriented.'"[30] The utilitarian attitude weighs damage against utility. So if a number of users' rights are violated and their content is removed, the act can be legitimized by the fact that a larger number of *other* users, in turn, experience a benefit—for example, if they feel that a violation has been avenged.

[29] Angwin, J. & Grassegger, H. "Facebook's secret censorship rules protect white men from hate speech but not black children" *Salon* (originally appeared on ProPublica). 06-28-17.

[30] Ibid.

Questions of guilt and rights drift to the background, as what matters is the net number of satisfied users. Obviously, such a balancing system tends to favor the complainant, since he or she is the one heard by the moderators, while the accused party is not heard and has no means of defense. Therefore, it is inherent to this system that the expressing party, the utterer of a statement, has no right—no real freedom of expression.

The community standards of the tech giants are becoming the policies guiding a new form of censorship. Removal of content by an algorithm before it even becomes visible to users takes us all the way back to the pre-censorship which was abolished in Denmark in 1770 by J.F. Struensee. On large parts of the Internet, this "formal" freedom of speech is not respected. The manual removal of content upon complaints can be likened to post-censorship and is comparable to the police control practiced in Denmark from 1814 until the Constitution of Denmark came into effect in 1849—with it came a number of laws against material freedom of expression, such as the sections on blasphemy, pornography and "hate speech." Unlike Danish law going as far back as 1790, however, in the legal environment of the tech giants there is no judicial review, no public court case, and appeal options are poor, unsystematic, or non-existent.

Of course, Facebook's rule-book is not a proper legal document, but still it is bizarre to note that this pseudo-legal text, with its vagueness and many hyper-detailed bans, now comprises the principles governing the limits of expression of millions—if not billions—of people for whom Facebook's de facto monopoly is the only way they may reach the public sphere and access their news.

In the April 2018 document, Facebook had also promised a new appeal option for users whose content has been blocked and their accounts suspended. In a November 2018 missive to Facebook users, Zuckerberg elaborated on the idea. Here, he promised the long-term establishment of an independent appeal institution in order to "[...] uphold the principle of giving people a voice while also recognizing the reality of keeping people safe."[31] We are still waiting for the details on how that attempt of squaring the circle will work—particularly how the board will be selected and how independence of Facebook's commercial interests will be granted. Given the amount of flaggings, one can only imagine how many staffers would have to be employed in this private "supreme court". Even if this idea may be a virtual step in the right direction, such an appeal organ, of course, will still have to function on the basis of the much-disputed detail of the Facebook community standards.

In the same pastoral letter, Zuckerberg articulated a new theory on the regulation of free speech. No matter where one draws the line between legal and illegal, he claimed, special user interest will be drawn to legal content which comes *close* to that borderline. No matter whether you are prudish or permissive in drawing the line, special fascination will radiate from borderline posts. To mitigate this fact, Zuckerberg now proposes a new policy: such borderline content, legal but in the vicinity of the border, will be suppressed and have its Facebook circulation reduced—with more reduction the closer to the line it comes: "[...] by reducing sensationalism of all forms, we will create a healthier, less polarized discourse where more people feel safe participating."[32] The idea echoes de-ranking "fake news", only now spreading to other types of content. Introduced in the same letter as the appeal institution, this idea begs some new unsolved questions: will people posting borderline content be informed about the reduced distribution of their posts? If not, a new zone of suppression without possibility of appeal will be created. Furthermore, as soon as this reduction is realized in the community, more interest is sure to be generated by posts on the borderline of the borderline—a slippery slope if there ever was one.

One might ask why there should even be detailed rules for content removal at all. It was not an issue with the communi-

---

[31] Zuckerberg, M. "A Blueprint for Content Governance and Enforcement" *Facebook Notes*. 11-15-18.

[32] ibid.

cation technologies Facebook is helping to replace: the telephone and mail former generations relied on to "connect" with their "friends". The postal services of the free world do not refuse to deliver certain letters after examining their content, and the telephone companies do not interrupt calls based on people talking about things the phone companies do not like. These providers of communications infrastructure were even obliged *not* to censor users; they were seen as companies that help communicate content, not moderate it.[33] It is primarily for commercial reasons that companies like Facebook introduce restrictions on what their users have to say. But a harmful consequence of this is that it has turned out to be conducive to the desires for censorship of certain political forces.

---

[33] Cf. the distinction in American law between "conduit" and "content", responsibility for transfer and responsibility for content modification, respectively.

Chapter 12
Facebook and Google as Offices of Censorship

On May 15, 2018, Facebook continued its springtime campaign to restore its reputation in the aftermath of the Cambridge Analytica scandal. A "Transparency" report was published, which included statistics on the extent of content removal, organized by category. Let's look at for instance the category "Graphic Violence": "In Q1 2018, we took action on a total of 3.4 million pieces of content, an increase from 1.2 million pieces of content in Q4 2017. This increase is mostly due to improvements in our detection technology, including using photo-matching to cover with warnings photos that matched ones we previously marked as disturbing. These actions were responsible for around 70% of the increase in Q1".[1] The numbers may seem high, but they only tell half the story. Another graph in the report shows that 71.56% of the 1.2 million users were tracked by Facebook itself, until user complaints started flooding in; in the first quarter of 2018, this figure rose to 85.6%. The fact that the number of removals tripled means that content removed because of user complaints rose from 341,000 to almost 500,000, in absolute figures, despite the decrease in percentage. So, the increase can be attributed not only to better tracking equipment, but also to more complaints favored. These numbers are a testimony to content removal on a disproportionately large scale, also known as censorship.

[1] Facebook "Community Standards Enforcement Preliminary Report."

F. Stjernfelt, A. M. Lauritzen, *Your Post has been Removed*,
https://doi.org/10.1007/978-3-030-25968-6_12

In other categories, the numbers are even higher. The category "Pornographic nudity and sexual activity" remains constant over the two quarters: 21 million posts censored in each quarter. "Terrorist propaganda" increased from 1.1 to 1.9 million cases, out of which 99.5% were removed before even appearing, that is, as acts of pre-censorship. "Hate speech" went up from 1.6 to 2.5 million cases over the course of the two quarters. Out of these cases, only 23.6% and 38%, respectively, were found by Facebook itself. The majority of these were identified by flagging users, so the company goes to great lengths to accommodate users' sense of violation. In those Q4 and Q1, respectively, 727 and 936 million cases of spam were deleted, while 694 and 583 million false accounts were shut down. The total number of posts removed increased over the two quarters, rounding a billion, which amounts to more than 10 million per day—the vast majority of them spam.

Given the speed of the procedure, some questions should be asked: How accurate or indicative can these numbers be? Is there a reason to believe that all the removals can be attributed to someone actually noticing the alleged norm-breaking content? And if not, do some—or maybe even many—removals happen as a result of accusation alone, that is, without going through the actual content? Of the content-based complaint categories, nudity-and-sex is the most frequent one. This could explain why in some cases the category seems most liable to be used politically by users to have their opponents silenced. There seems to be systematic use of the complaints option. If a group of people agree to complain against someone voicing something, it seems fairly easy to have that person thrown off of Facebook. It also seems that the plausibility of the complaint filed is not always given the highest attention.

In 2016, the Council of Ex-Muslims of Britain claimed that 19 different Facebook groups or sites organized by Arabic ex-Muslims or freethinkers had either already been shut down or underwent attacks via organized abuse of the flagging system.[2] Thus, it seems that Islamist groups (or even governments in the Middle East?) use the flagging system, in an organized manner, in order to remove democratic Muslim or anti-Islamist sites from Facebook. In the conservative online magazine *American Thinker*, it has been claimed that such shutdowns often happen in the following way: Massive complaints of pornography are filed by many complainants at the same time against a given page, which is then shut down.[3] From the look of it, the reason is that sheer number of complaints is taken as an indication of the complaint's justification, and/or that the pressure on the staff is so high that not all cases can be properly handled. Among the deleted accounts in 2013 were "Ban Islam", "Islam Against Women", "Islam Free Planet". The interesting thing is that the majority of pages hit in this way do not contain pornography at all, since they are in fact politico-religious pages. Experience seems to suggest that sex complaints are easily accepted, so that large amounts of complaints almost automatically will trigger the blocking of the targeted Facebook page, with no review of whether there is even sex on the page. Such abuse may comprise anything from spontaneous actions to systematic flagging of political opponents, and such cases are obviously invisible to the Facebook stats, where systematic weeding out of democratic voices in the Middle East is then represented in the stats simply as removed pornography.

No one knows the extent of coordinated abuse of the flagging feature. Gillespie mentions cases like "Operation Smackdown", organized by a group of YouTube users to attack pro-Muslim content on the platform by complaining against it for featuring acts of terrorism. The attack was orchestrated with a long list of videos to target, detailed instructions on how to file complaints and a Twitter account

[2] "Facebook: Stop Censoring Arab Ex-Muslims and Freethinkers NOW" *Council of Ex-Muslims of Britain*. 02-20-16.

[3] Murphy, P. "Blasphemy Law Comes to Facebook" *American Thinker*. 06-27-13.

featuring the dates on which the videos were to be attacked. This operation was active from 2007 to 2011.[4] Obviously, surrendering an important part of the removal process to the users' own reporting activity is dangerous, since user groups can abuse the feature to foment their own agendas. We have not been able to find clear estimates of how widespread this low-intensity online culture war is. Notes Tarleton Gillespie: "There is evidence that strategic 'flagging' has occurred and suspicions that it has occurred widely.""[5]

Thanks to the flagging system, Facebook's own removal reports may thus hide censorship and let the company off the hook. Evidence suggests that Facebook's current set of rules and statistics does not contain the whole truth. In many cases, the enforcement of the policy is not consistent with equality before the law—sometimes criticism of Islam is removed with greater enthusiasm than, for example, anti-Semitism or criticism of the state of Israel. In 2016, New York-based Jewish website *the algemeiner* quoted Amos Yadlin, former chief of Israel Defense Forces, an Israeli intelligence service, for saying that "The most dangerous nation in the Middle East acting against Israel is the state of Facebook." Yadlin, who now heads the Institute for National Security Studies in Tel Aviv, continued: "It has a lot more power than anybody who's operating an armed force. Unlike before, there's no longer an existential military threat facing Israel. Rather, it's a strategic threat."[6] Since then, Facebook and Israel seem to have reached an agreement to remove "incitement" from the platform, but the details of the agreement are not known to the public.[7] However, as mentioned, there is no reason to expect that the many removals taking place will remain consistent,

---

[4] Gillespie (2018) p. 92.

[5] Ibid.

[6] Sherman, E. "Ex-IDF Intel Chief: 'State of Facebook' Greatest Mideast Threat to Israel" *the algemeiner*. 01-31-16; translated into English from the Hebrew website *nrg*.

[7] Kaye, D. "Report of the Special Rapporteur on the promotion and protection of the right to freedom of opinion and expression" *UN Human Rights Council*. 04-06-18. Chapter 20.

and certainly not over time, as Facebook may be easily influenced by lobbyists, campaigns and pressure from both Israeli and Arab sides.

Similarly, Catholic associations in the US have complained about their Facebook accounts being shut down. Facebook probably did not take a classic and uncomfortable fact from the history of religion into account: that many of the large religions practice, as a natural and central custom, insults, mockery and ridicule of other religions, or worse: they may have a strong tradition for calls to violence against the followers of other religions or against infidels—sometimes such practices even take place in the sacred texts of certain religions.

There is an increasing number of cases where Facebook in fact removes seemingly legitimate political views, such as support for Russia or support for Trump's more unusual bills. In January 2018, Uffe Gardel, a Danish Eastern Europe journalist, reported on a peculiar experience. He describes it: "I participated in a passionate debate on my own Facebook page: the topic was the Russia-backed war in Eastern Ukraine. We participated around five users, all of us Danes: two pro-Russian views and three pro-Ukrainian views. We debated in a lively and matter-of-fact way. Suddenly, not a word came from one of the pro-Russian participants. He did not respond when addressed. Not a word from him, and moreover his previous posts were suddenly gone."[8] Gardel was surprised that his debate opponent Jesper Larsen suddenly withdrew from the debate. When he returned, Larsen wrote that Facebook had informed him that his posts had been deleted as spam. A new test post from him was deleted in a matter of seconds only. However, it was not spam, but a short comment featuring a link to Ukrainian television. Could it be thinkable that Facebook had begun removing pro-Russian posts? Maybe after the ongoing Russian bot campaigns interfering in American politics had become known?

---

[8] Gardel, U. "Når Facebook censurerer" *Journalisten*. 01-11-18.

Gardel contacted the Danish branch of Facebook, whose representative Peter Andreas Münster explained: "The point here is that 'real' people can easily risk triggering our anti-spam systems if they post stuff very frequently and very quickly." No information was provided on whether the removal was influenced by user complaints. What also remains unclear is whether Jesper Larsen had posted hyperactively, and whether Facebook's explanation is trustworthy, given the fact that Facebook is the only source of this information. As Gardel adds, this is not the only recent case of political content leading to deletion. He quotes Danish writer and debater Suzanne Bjerrehuus, who was sanctioned with a three-day quarantine from Facebook that same winter. She had posted the following comment on a series of gang rapes in the Swedish city of Malmö: "Brutal and abhorrent violence and then they get away with it. The police are powerless. [...] The Swedes ought to break with those politicians who have ruined Sweden." Facebook's "hate speech" clause was only made public a couple of months later—but at the time, Bjerrehus received the explanation that her post was in breach of the company's ban on "posts attacking people based on race, ethnic background, national origin, religious affiliation, sexual orientation, gender or disability." The many separate problems of this clause aside, it is in fact peculiar that her opinion should fall within the scope of that clause. Gardel rightly states that one needs not agree with Larsen's or Bjerrehuus' views in order to find the removal of their statements extraordinarily problematic. He concludes that tech giants such as "[...] Facebook have gained such a strong position that regulation is needed. A still increasing proportion of the Danish debate on public matters is now taking place on Facebook. Facebook pages become actual media, which are then enrolled in the Danish Media Ethical Commission. In some cases, established web media use Facebook's debate forums to control user comments; currently, this is what's happening with the newspapers of media outlet Syddanske Medier. These media organizations end up in fact leaving parts of their editing rights in the hands of

Facebook, and this alone should alarm everyone in the publishing industry." Concludes Gardel admonishingly: "In any case, it must now be clear that we cannot have both a safe Internet and a free network. And it's an old truth that he who gives up freedom for security is at risk of losing both." We support this outcry—playing on Benjamin Franklin's classic words—to the fullest.

There is much to suggest that content with different political motivations is removed. Stories and documentation abound online of strange omissions, excessive removal and inconsistencies in Facebook's censorship.[9] However, it should come as no surprise that the removal does not have the same consistency as a court bound by precedence, given that the control is so speedy, comprehensive, reckless and carried out by legally untrained employees. At the congressional hearing in April 2018, Senator Ted Cruz (R) was critical, as he himself had experienced the tendency of Facebook to remove conservative more eagerly than liberal content, more republican than democratic. However, just because content critical of Islam is sometimes removed and content critical of Christianity is not, it does not follow that such a bias is systematic and a sign of double standards. Given the vast amount of content deletions, one does not exclude the other. Only whistleblowing or deep statistical surveys would be able to uncover explicit or implicit double standards. In December 2015, Israeli NGO Shurat HaDin[10] did a little experiment: They created two parallel Facebook pages entitled *Stop Israel!* and *Stop the Palestinians!* with identical setups, designs and rhetoric. Facebook shut down the anti-Palestinian page, but not the anti-Israeli one. The organization has since sued Facebook.

---

[9] See e.g. Tobin, A. &Varner, M. & Angwin, J. "Facebook's Uneven Enforcement of Hate Speech Rules Allows Vile Posts to Stay Up", *ProPublica*. 12-28-17.

[10] Melnick, O. "Facebook's Hate Speech Double Standard" *WND*. 01-11-16.

In 2016, technology site *Gizmodo* featured an article[11] based on statements from former Facebook employees who claimed that employees who edited incoming news content for the Facebook "Trending" column routinely removed conservative news, e.g. news on Republicans Ron Paul and Mitt Romney. The column claims that it algorithmically reflects "topics that have recently become popular on Facebook." But several of Facebook's former news curators, as they were called in the organization, also told *Gizmodo* that they were instructed to artificially "inject" stories into the trending news feed, even though they were not popular enough to even be there—in some cases the stories had no following whatsoever. These former curators, who all worked on contract, also said that they were told not to include news about Facebook, not even in the trending feature. An anonymous former employee kept a protocol of news stories that were buried in this way. *Gizmodo* therefore concluded that Trending on Facebook works like a plain opinion-based newspaper, except it maintains a surface of neutrality. Top management at Facebook rejected all these allegations as false.

Nevertheless, the allegations about what was happening on Trending Topics seem to have affected Facebook. As early as January 2015, the company had announced a campaign against the volume of "fake news" that abounded in the column. In August 2016, shortly after the revelation in *Gizmodo*, Facebook dismissed the 26 editors who had fed the news column and replaced them with an automatic algorithm. The algorithm would ensure that the news stories featured also reflected their actual popularity on the platform. However, this step did nothing short of opening the floodgates for viral spread of false news. Apparently, the company had overestimated ability or willingness of users to identify and reject false news. Just two days after the new algorithm was put to use, a false story about a Fox News journalist made it high up on the list: "Breaking: Fox News Exposes Traitor Megyn

[11] Nunez, M. "Former Facebook Workers: We Routinely Suppressed Conservative News" *Gizmodo*. 05-09-16.

Kelly, Kicks Her Out for Backing Hillary."[12] According to a *Washington Post* survey covering a three-week period in September 2016, five fake and three highly misleading news stories ranked high on the Trending Topics section of four different Facebook accounts (of course, there may have been even more on other accounts because of the personalization of each account). In January 2018, in the aftermath of the chronic problems that had turned Facebook into a main supplier of "fake news" during the presidential campaign, the company attempted to shift the news feed balance from journalistic news to local news from "friends". In June, a further step was taken when Facebook announced the complete elimination of Trending Topics.[13]

At the same time, the company met new problems due to a policy introduced on May 24, 2018. The policy gives political ads a special label and collects such ads in a separate archive containing information on their ad budget, number of users who have seen them, etc.[14] This goes for ads related to candidates and elections, but also political issues such as "abortion, arms, immigration and foreign policy". The intention was, of course, to increase transparency around political ads. However, newspapers and media associations, led by *New York Times*, protested fiercely over the fact that their articles *about* politics were given the same categorization and labeling on Facebook, the "political ad" warning. Media representatives argued that since the media pays to have such articles promoted as a way of selling their own product, Facebook must respect the boundary between political ads on the one hand and ads for quality journalism *about* politics on the other, instead of trying to erase it. After this, *New York Times* and other leading media stopped paying to place their content on the platform. At the same time, reports came out

---

[12] Solon, O. "In firing human editors, Facebook has lost the fight against fake news" *The Guardian*. 08-29-16.

[13] Kastrenakes, J. "Facebook will remove the Trending topics section next week" *The Verge*. 06-01-18.

[14] Constine, J. "Facebook and Instagram launch US political ad labeling and archive" *TechChrunch*. 05-24-18.

showing that people had less confidence in news coming from social media than from all other media, and that news consumption via Facebook was declining (hardly surprising in light of the suppression of "real" news earlier that year).[15] CEO of *New York Times* Mark Thompson called Facebook's categorization a "threat to democracy". In an angry debate, he accused Campbell Brown, Head of Global News Partnerships at Facebook, of supporting the enemies of quality journalism.[16] It is rather ironic that *real* news was turned into political ads as the result of an attempt to make political ads explicit and the extent of them public – thus hoping to eradicating "dark ads" in the form of targeted political ads visible only to their receiver. The case also shows Facebook's ongoing conflict with the media. Despite its many attempts at forming alliances, by categorizing journalism as ads Facebook unilaterally launched a new and secretly developed policy, without having consulted their supposed media allies beforehand. In July 2018, researchers from New York University demonstrated that from May to July, the first two months of the new ads archive, Facebook's largest political advertising client was ... Donald Trump.[17]

Only a few days later, another scandal broke: Zuckerberg "accepted" Holocaust denial and claimed that it "deserved" its place on the platform. This made him the target of a veritable shitstorm in both the offline and online media. However, he had not used these words. He was interviewed for an hour and a half by Kara Swisher of *recode* on the topic of Facebook's "annus horribilis",[18] an interview unsurprisingly circling around news, "fake news", disinformation, etc. The irony is that in the interview, Zuckerberg goes to great lengths to defend free speech on his platform: "There are

---

[15] "Digital News Report 2018". Last visited 07-30-18: http://www.digitalnewsreport.org.

[16] Moses, L. "How The New York Times' Mark Thompson became the latest thorn in Facebook's side" *DigiDay.* 07-11-18.

[17] Frenkel, S. "The Biggest Spender of Political Ads on Facebook? President Trump" *New York Times.* 07-17-18.

[18] Swisher, K. "Zuckerberg: The Recode interview" *Recode.* 07-18-18.

really two core principles at play here. There's giving people a voice, so that people can express their opinions. Then, there's keeping the community safe, which I think is really important. We're not gonna let people plan violence or attack each other or do bad things. Within this, those principles have real trade-offs and real tug on each other." If what is meant by "attack" is real, violent attack, there is hardly a single free speech supporter out there who will disagree with this—parallel to the limits to freedom of expression drawn at "incitement to imminent lawless action".[19] In the following sentence, however, Zuckerberg changes course: "In this case, we feel like our responsibility is to prevent hoaxes from going viral and being widely distributed." He then goes on to present the news that verifiably "fake news" must be downgraded in the news feed, but not removed from it. The journalist does not comment on Zuckerberg's mix-up of misinformation and planning violence but instead asks him why "fake news" should be downgraded and not simply eliminated entirely. To this, Zuckerberg again defends freedom of expression: "... [A]s abhorrent as some of this content can be, I do think that it gets down to this principle of giving people a voice." This prompted the journalist to give an example of a post she felt should just plainly be removed: the claim that "Sandy Hook never happened" (a tragic school shooting in 2012, which later became the subject of an *InfoWars* conspiracy theory claiming that the event never took place but was staged by

[19]The classic American phrase from 1919 famously states that the limit is "clear and present danger" (from iconic Supreme Court Justice Oliver Wendell Holmes' turn of phrase in *Schenk v the US*). The current phrase goes like this: "[...] the constitutional guarantees of free speech and free press do not permit a State to forbid or proscribe advocacy of the use of force or of law violation except where such advocacy is directed to inciting or producing imminent lawless action and is likely to incite or produce such action" – a quote from the *Brandenburg v Ohio* case of 1969. In the case *Hess v Indiana,* the Supreme Court made clear that unless statements made "... were intended to produce, and likely to produce, imminent disorder, those words could not be punished by the State on the ground that they had a 'tendency to lead to violence.'" Cf. Freedom Forum Institute: "Incitement to Imminent Lawless Action". 05-12-08.

anti-gun activists). Zuckerberg defended why this conspiracy theory was not removed from Facebook — and then went on to compare it to the Holocaust: "I'm Jewish, and there's a set of people who deny that the Holocaust happened. I find that deeply offensive. But at the end of the day, I don't believe that our platform should take that down because I think there are things that different people get wrong. I don't think that they're *intentionally* getting it wrong, but I think .." Then he is interrupted by the journalist. He continues: "It's hard to impugn intent and to understand the intent." He is certainly right about that — but he is just as certainly wrong in claiming that Holocaust deniers innocently make a mistake the same way he himself could make a mistake publicly. Deflating Holocaust deniers' motives in this way caused a scandal, and the day after he had to pull back: "I personally find Holocaust denial deeply offensive, and I absolutely didn't intend to defend the intent of people who deny that."[20]

In the midst of this media shitstorm, many people thought it obvious that conspiracy theories such as the one about Sandy Hook should be deleted as a matter of routine. But these people were never able to come up with a clear principle as to where to draw the line between conspiracy theories, lies, false statements, satire, irony, quotations, and random mistakes, and how such a line should then be monitored. Although Zuckerberg went quite far to defend freedom of expression, he expressed himself in covert and unclear fashion, confusing violent attacks with false statements and presenting a half-baked theory that people's sincerity—which is not easy to measure—should act as thermometer to assess whether statements should be allowed, downgraded, or altogether removed. It is not comforting that a man in his position is unable to express himself more clearly, and it calls for a reminder of a classic warning: hazy words cover up hazy thoughts.

---

[20] Swisher, K. "Mark Zuckerberg clarifies: 'I personally find Holocaust denial deeply offensive, and I absolutely didn't intend to defend the intent of people who deny that.'" *recode.* 07-18-18.

The defense of free speech did not last long, however. On August 6, 2018, after weeks of heated public discussion, Facebook blocked four accounts belonging to Alt-right talk show host Alex Jones and his *InfoWars* podcast shows. Apple was the first tech giant to block *InfoWars* and was quickly followed by Facebook, YouTube, Pinterest and even YouPorn, all on the same day in what may resemble a coordinated action. This is probably the biggest act of online censorship to date—Jones had 1.4 million followers on Facebook and 2.5 million on YouTube. In a public statement, Facebook argued that Jones' pages were removed for "glorifying violence, which violates our graphic violence policy, and using dehumanizing language to describe people who are transgender, Muslims, and immigrants, which violates our hate speech policies."[21] The banning process is ugly and devoid of principles: as usual, no one is given information on exactly which statements are deemed unacceptable. Only a few weeks earlier, Zuckerberg had even defended Jones' presence. Jones was punished for accumulating "too many strikes", but there is nothing about how many that is, and which strike was the final blow. If Jones really fell under the scope of Facebook's "hate speech" policy, why had it not happened before? For years he had presented his huge audience with grotesque opinions on the platform.[22] The other tech giants made similar references to "hate speech" rules. Rumor spread fast that Apple's action made the other tech giants follow suit because Apple threatened to throw them out of its App Store, which has strict regulations. Commentator Brian Feldman wrote: "What the *InfoWars* decisions represent is a capitulation—not to censors, not to the public, not to the deep state, but to the only entity left that has any real power over Facebook

---

[21] Shaban, H., Timberg, C. and Stanley-Becker, I.: "YouTube, Apple, Facebook and Spotify escalate enforcement against Alex Jones" *Washington Post.* 08-06-18.

[22] Facebook's statement on the Alex Jones case: "Enforcing our community standards". 08-06-18.

and YouTube: Apple."[23] The exception was Twitter. For eight days they hesitated, until finally blocking *InfoWars*. But it was only a week long suspension and it was not for "hate speech", but more explicitly for encouraging violence, as Jones had urged his followers to have their "battle rifles" ready to fight mainstream media.[24]

Commentators point out that Jones and his supporters will see the ban as evidence of their claim of a coordinated political attack against them—and that it will only strengthen Jones' position as a right-wing martyr.[25] Jones and his followers will most likely regroup in underground networks, separated from the general public. Predictably, Jones was infuriated by the removal: "We've seen a giant yellow journalism campaign with thousands and thousands of articles for weeks, for months misrepresenting what I've said and done to set the precedent to de-platform me before Big Tech and the Democratic Party as well as some Republican establishment types move against the First Amendment in this country as we know it."[26] Jones is especially known for spreading provable untruths. Most famous were "Pizzagate", the claim that Hillary Clinton ran a pedophile ring out of a Washington pizzeria, or Jones' assertion that the Sandy Hook school shooting in 2012 never took place. Jones went on to harass parents of children killed at the massacre—not to mention spreading fake conspiracy theories about teenagers who survived the Parkland school shooting in Florida of February 2018. Recently, he has tried to convince the public that the Democrats wanted to start a civil war on the 4th of July.

---

[23] Feldman, B. "The Only Pressure Facebook Understands Comes from its Megaplatform Rivals" *New York Magazine*. 08-06-18.

[24] Kang, C. and Conger, K. "Twitter Suspends Alex Jones and Infowars for Seven Days" *New York Times.* 08-14-18.

[25] See e.g. Lapowsky, I.: "Why Big Tech's Fight Against InfoWars is Unwinnable" *Wired.* 08-06-18.

[26] Shaban, H., Timberg, C. and Stanley-Becker, I.: "YouTube, Apple, Facebook and Spotify escalate enforcement against Alex Jones" *Washington Post.* 08-06-18.

There is no doubt that Jones has repeatedly peddled abominable lies, false accusations and bizarre conspiracy theories. Still, Facebook's argument for banning Jones is not based on his "fake news" but on the murkier concept of "hate speech"—presumably in an attempt to avoid taking the seat of judge between true and false. As stated by several observers, nevertheless, "hate speech" is not only a vague, politicized and subjective category. It is also full of double standards, because it does not equally protect all groups defined by race, gender, religion and so on.[27] It is an all-purpose category with no clear limits, so it can be stretched to accuse points of view that are simply not liked. As pointed out by Robby Soave, no one will miss *InfoWars*—the serious issue raised by this event is that completely unclear rules and procedures now govern the removal of content on the giants' platforms.[28] The Jones case seems to be triggered by public pressure, and one thing remains particularly unclear: are there also plans to crack down on other right-wing extremists with similar views but fewer supporters operating on the same platforms out of the public eye? There is no shortage of those. Perhaps a less problematic cure against characters like Jones would be to bring the removal criteria closer to existing US legislation. That would make it possible to intervene, assisted by proper authorities, against clearly illegal acts such as slander, libel, threats and harassment. In Jones' rhetoric alone, there is more than enough of these.[29]

---

[27] Shapiro, B. "What Tech Giants' Alex Jones Ban Got Wrong" *National Review.* 08-07-18.

The fact that Facebook now express a wish to be inspired by the International Covenant on Civil and Political Rights (ICCPR) from the 1960s is puzzling, inasmuch as that law helped many countries introduce hate speech laws (see Chapter 11) and the United States was among the countries that chose *not* to comply with ICCPR.

[28] Soave, R. "Banning Alex Jones" *Reason.* 08-07-18.

[29] Cf. French, D. "A Better Way to Ban Alex Jones. *New York Times.* 08-07-18.

All in all, the presentation of news through Facebook has been characterized by recurring problems with "fake news", mixing up news with ads, political bias and content deletion, not to mention improvised reactions to public and political pressure. Various remedy initiatives have not produced any successful cure, neither of a human nor algorithmic form (see Ch. 11 for a discussion of fact checkers).

The secretive, opaque and shifting removal procedures obviously make tech giants subject to political pressure from international top players who wish to influence the removal policy—not to mention journalistic Kremlinology trying to interpret what is really going on behind the scenes, based on small signs, rumors and stand-alone issues. When Zuckerberg met with Angela Merkel in Berlin during the European migrant crisis of 2015, she apparently encouraged him to crack down harder on "hate speech", to which he is said to have made the following response: "Yeah." This was interpreted by some media as Facebook committing itself to suppressing critical news coverage of migrants in Europe.[30]

The spring of 2019 was characterized by an increasing effort to censor different types of Facebook content, particularly "fake news" and "hate speech". In March, after repeated criticsm from journalists and lawmakers, Facebook announced that it was diminishing the reach of anti-vaccine posts.[31] Later the same month, Facebook announced it would ban white nationalist content.[32] These developments clearly indicate the ad hoc character of the company's removal policy, without clear principles.

A radical change in the overall Facebook vision was announced by Mark Zuckerberg March 6th: "As I think about the future of the internet, I believe a privacy-focused communications platform will become even more important than

---

[30] David, J. E. "Angela Merkel caught on hot mic griping to Facebook CEO over anti-immigrant posts" *CNBC*. 09-27-15.

[31] Matsakis, L. "Facebook will crack down on anti-vaccine content" *Wired*. 03-07-19.

[32] Stack, L. "Facebook announces new polity to ban white nationalist content" *New York Times*. 03-27-19.

today's open platforms. Privacy gives people the freedom to be themselves and connect more naturally, which is why we build social networks."[33] Zuckerberg defined privacy in terms of six headlines: privacy of interactions in selected communication types; end-to-end encryption extending from WhatsApp over the whole platform; extended possibility for posting information for shorter periods of time only; increased safety; interoperability in the sense of communication ability across Facebook's different platforms; increased protection of data in countries violating human rights. This general declaration of intent, of course, is an attempt to preempt oncoming government regulation. Simultaneously, it is striking that the core business model seems all but untouched by the new principles—nothing is said about data sharing and ad targeting.[34] Late March, however, Zuckerberg gave in to looming regulation in a surprising op-ed in *Washington Post* where he called for some sort of external regulation. In the face of increased political pressure, Zuckerberg now chose the tactics of delimiting regulation to four specific areas: harmful content, election integrity, privacy and data portability. "I've come to believe that we shouldn't make so many important decisions about speech on our own. So we're creating an independent body so people can appeal our decisions," he said.[35] The degree of independence of a voluntary Facebook-invented body will of course be a matter of contention. Zuckerberg, however, also envisions some kind of cross-platform authority to standardize removal practices over the internet at large. Again, Facebook's sudden willingness to abandon responsibility can be seen as a preemptive move as against threatening anti-trust initiatives.

Only a couple of weeks later, Facebook announced a series of new measures to ensure "integrity" in its much-debated

[33] Zuckerberg, M. "A Privacy-Focused Vision for Social Networking" *Facebook.* 03-06-19.

[34] Lapowsky, I & Thompson, N. "Facebook's pivot to privacy is missing something crucial" *Wired.* 03-06-19.

[35] Zuckerberg, M. "Mark Zuckerberg: The Internet needs new rules. Let's start in these four areas" *Washington Post.* 03-30-19.

news feed—of which the most important device was the so-called Click-Gap.[36] It will influence the determination of the ranking of a given post in the feed. The idea is to limit the dissemination of websites which are deemed disproportionally viral on Facebook in comparison with the net as a whole. A given news content of that sort will be limited in reach on Facebook. The controversial and contested news feed is sought domesticated by a conformity measure making it a mirror of the average traffic on the internet. This means that it provides no security against viral matters which are popular also outside of Facebook. During little than one month, Facebook announced a handful of new initiatives, most of all giving evidence of increasing panic in the head office of 1 Hacker Way.

Facebook has always had a very comprehensive removal policy. By contrast, Google has held the free speech banner quite high. For example, in 2010 Google pulled out of China after several years of hacking attempts and pressure to enact censorship. But Google has also been accused of outright censorship. In 2016, Robert Epstein, a professor of psychology and Google critic, came up with an overview of at least nine different blacklists at work in Google's content filtering.[37] Especially Epstein's first blacklist is relevant—it

---

[36] Dreyfuss, E. & Lapowsky, I. "Facebook is changing news feed (again) to stop fake news" *Wired.* 04-10-19.

[37] Epstein's nine blacklists read as follows:

1. The autocomplete blacklist, which automatically blocks the guesses that follow when certain keywords are entered.
2. The Google Maps blacklist—maps with disputed geographic areas, which without explanation are not shown—military zones, wealthy people who paid to have their land exempt.
3. The YouTube blacklist—for instance in Pakistan featuring what the government demands to be removed from the platform.
4. The Google Account blacklist—blocking users who have not complied with the "Terms of Service", which can typically be terminated "at any time" and with no real appeal option.
5. The Google News blacklist, which has been accused of leaving out news critical of Islam (see below).
6. The Google AdWords blacklist—certain words cannot appear in ads, or entire industries whose ads Google does want on the platform.

concerns the autocomplete feature, which was introduced in 2008 and which works by completing entered keywords with a variety of suggestions generated by an algorithm. This feature blocks, for example, obscene words. But Epstein also found political effects in the auto-complete feature. For example, when writing the word "Lying" during the American election campaign in 2016, what followed was "Ted" (Trump's nickname for Ted Cruz, "Lyin' Ted"), but when writing "Crooked", what was then suggested was *not* "Hillary" (Trump's nickname for Hillary Clinton, "Crooked Hillary") – and thus Google served as a protection of Clinton but not of Cruz. Others, however, have pointed out politically conflicting biases—if someone wrote "Feminism is" or "Abortion is", then the suggestions that came up were "cancer" and "sin", respectively.[38] After Google was incriminated for caving in to censorship in hardliner Islamic countries, the company has been accused of favoring a rosy description of Islam, also in other countries. It does indeed cause concern that in Denmark, in June 2018, when googling "Islam is", the first four suggestions are "Islam isimleri",[39] "Islam is Peace", "Islam is ..." and "Islam is a peaceful religion". By comparison, the first four auto-suggestions for "democracy is" are "bad", "dead", "failing" and "not good", respectively.

---

7. The Google AdSense blacklist—concerning websites paid by Google for their skill at attracting users to ads—in these cases Google is accused of withdrawing from the agreements right before payments are due.
8. The search engine blacklist—it sends search results to the bottom ranks, potentially ruining companies affected.
9. The quarantine list—blocking anything from individual users to entire sections of the Internet, sometimes taking a very long time to be restored.

Se Epstein, R. "The New Censorship" *US News*. 06-22-16.

[38] Solon, O. & Levin, S. "How Google's search algorithm spreads false information with a rightwing bias" *The Guardian*. 12-16-16.

[39] "Islam isimleri" is Turkish for "Islamic names". The auto-completion suggestions are of course personalized and relative to the searcher and time.

A central battlefield within Google is its crucial ranking system. It determines which search results end up at the top of the results list. As described above, it has been personalized since 2009. But there is also a long and growing list of other conditions, pressures and forces that influence rankings. It is believed that more than 200 different principles now govern rankings, including how old a website is, the length of its URL, a special preference for YouTube links, emphasis on local websites in a geographical area, and many more; some innocent, others causing suspicion.[40] It has become a large independent industry to try to "trick" Google's ranking criteria, enabling companies and others to pay to rank high on search lists—called Search Engine Optimization, SEO. The method makes use of various tricks, such as creating lots of artificial links between websites that one would like to see promoted, repeating keywords throughout a text, automatically copypasting from—and then adding a few changes to—already successful sites, which are then given other titles, and much more ("spamdexing"). In 2016, SEO was already a $70 billion industry in and of itself. Google is said to be constantly struggling to make its ranking principles more sophisticated and coordinated in efforts to eliminate the possibility of capitalizing on the system in this way—in which is, of course, an infinite arms race with increasingly sophisticated responses from SEO companies. But if companies can game Google's ranking algorithms and place interested customers on the top of the list, this can be used by political interests in the same way as commercial ones. *The Guardian* has thus mapped out how extreme right-wing sites in particular seem to have figured out how to take advantage of the complicated ranking procedures to come up high on the search rankings.[41]

---

[40] Dean, B. "Google's 200 Ranking Factors: The Complete List (2018)" *Backlinko*. 05-16-18.

[41] Cadwalladr, C. "Google, democracy and the truth about internet search" *The Guardian*. 12-04-16.

But these principles can also be politically influenced by the company itself.[42] Already in 2002, critics of Scientology were being removed from search results.[43] In 2009, searches on then-First Lady Michelle Obama resulted in high ranking of a photo where she had been morphed with a monkey. At first, Google refused to do anything, referring to the company's neutrality policy, but after much criticism in the media, the image was removed and replaced with an explanation as to why.[44] Political battles in recent years seem to have intensified political censorship. In August 2017, neo-Nazi site *Daily Stormer* was deleted from the web-hosting platform GoDaddy because it had mocked one of the victims of the Charlottesville riots. The site shifted to Google, which blocked it after only three hours. *Daily Stormer* is undoubtedly a detestable site, but once again the removal conflicted with Google's tradition of claiming full neutrality regarding content, including political content.

In November 2017, company CEO Eric Schmidt announced that Google would downgrade Russian propaganda in its ranking system: "'We're working on detecting this kind of scenario ... and de-ranking those kinds of sites', Schmidt said, in response to a question at an event in Halifax, Canada. 'It's basically RT and Sputnik. We're well aware and we're trying to engineer the systems to prevent it.'"[45] The Cato Institute, a libertarian think tank, immediately took note of this initiative and asked whether Google itself was really concerned about

---

[42]The Black feminist Safiya Noble highlights cases of algorithmically driven data failures that are specific to people of color and women and argues that marginalized groups are problematically represented in erroneous, stereotypical, or even pornographic ways in search engines. See Noble (2018).

[43]Hansen, E. "Google pulls anti-Scientology links" *Cnet*. 04-22-02.

[44]Google's explanation was: "Sometimes Google search results from the Internet can include disturbing content, even from innocuous queries. We assure you that the views expressed by such sites are not in any way endorsed by Google"., cf. Ahmed, S. "Google apologizes for results of 'Michelle Obama' image search" *CNN*. 11-25-09.

[45]Hern, A. "Google plans to 'de-rank' Russia Today and Sputnik to combat misinformation" *The Guardian*. 11-21-17.

Russian influence, or if the company was rather acting on overt or maybe hidden political pressure from the US Government.[46] The Cato Institute referred to a recent congressional hearing where Senator Dianne Feinstein (D), a senior member of the Senate Select Committee on Intelligence, had blamed Google Vice President Kent Walker for not responding to Russian propaganda long ago: "... I think we're in a different day now, we're at the beginning of what could be cyberwar, and you all, as a policy matter, have to really take a look at that and what role you play." As noted by The Cato Institute, such a political imposition would not only violate the First Amendment guarantee of free speech; it would also violate Google's judicially protected freedom to be in charge of managing its service, that is, prioritizing search results.[47]

There are two conflicting problems at play here: government intervention in the tech giant's freedom of expression, but also potentially Google's own opaque, politicized prioritization of search results—depending on which of the two explanations is the correct one (one of them, of course, needs not exclude the other). In the first case, the perspective is that we need to settle for getting only search results approved by the US government. In the second case, we must settle for search results in alignment with Google's political stance or the company's voluntary or involuntary permissiveness in the face of pressure groups. The Cato Institute, focusing on a narrow definition of freedom of expression as closely linked to the actions of governments, seems to have no issue with the latter of the two scenarios just described. However, it seems to us that the prioritization of search results should in all cases adhere to openly available criteria, so that users are informed and aware of any political biases—if not the very searches themselves ought to be governed by principles of fairness and neutrality.

---

[46] Samples, J. "Censorship Comes to Google" *Cato Liberty*. 11-21-17.

[47] Sterling, G. "Another Court Affirms Google's First Amendment Control Of Search Results" *Search Engine Land*. 11-17-14.

Curiously enough, Google has been accused of favoring both critique of Islam and defense of Islam in its rankings. This might seem contradictory, but only on the surface. Both charges can actually be correct at different times, because if the platform has been pressured to modify the algorithm to de-rank one of the two, then other will be consequently favored. A similar accusation is based on a survey from *The Guardian*,[48] which showed that a search for "Jews" would direct the searcher towards radical anti-Semitic websites, the same way as entering "did the Hol" would lead to websites denying the Holocaust. The latter is probably because most serious studies of the Holocaust do not even question the fact that the event took place and so do not contain the letter sequence "did the Hol", making it a non-factor in the search ranking. However, in suggested videos on Google-owned YouTube, there is a tendency to prefer extreme results based on search words (see below), probably because extreme videos generate more clicks and are therefore better for advertising. If ranking algorithms are indeed set up to prioritize extreme views over moderate ones, it is ironic that they reflect the conscious targeting strategy of the Russian troll factories: not to support particular positions favored in the West, but to spread disagreement, controversy and disintegration in Western societies by supporting extremism across the political spectrum.

In March 2018, Google announced a new policy in the fight against "fake news": the creation of a "Disinfo Lab" meant to downgrade or remove misinformation among search results and rank serious journalism high. The intention behind this initiative is commendable, but the effects of it are yet to be assessed. We remain skeptical as to whether Google, even with its huge economic muscle, could be able to create a

---

[48] Cadwalladr, C. "Google is not 'just' a platform. It frames, shapes and distorts how we see the world" *The Guardian*. 12-11-16. Google seems to have reacted to this accusation by simply removing the "suggestions" when for instance entering "Jews are", "Americans are"—but not when entering "Danes are", which still prompts suggestions such as "reserved", "cold", "unfriendly" but also the happiest people in the world.

clearinghouse for truth that would surpass the existing networks of media, courts and universities. It is also hard to imagine such a lab as operating without political bias, if not favoring a particular party, then because its values will be based on a "Californian" outlook and the implicit platitudes of the Zeitgeist.

The idea of fact checking as something that can take place quickly and effectively is counteracted by the simple fact that there will always be important cases that remain undecided and moot—and even more so by the fact that some truths we take for granted today will be overthrown by new evidence tomorrow. That is, if indeed this new evidence is given the opportunity to come forward and is not fact-checked away in a flash. Take the process of Danish transitional justice after World War II.[49] Back then, a number of Nazi authors were punished for expressions made during wartime. This took place by recently adopted, retroactive legislation: they were sentenced for actions that were not criminal at the time of the deed. What is worse, when Harald Tandrup—writer and journalist at Danish Nazi daily newspaper *Fædrelandet (The Fatherland)*—was sentenced to three years in prison, a piece of "fake news" acted as crucial evidence. In the beginning of World War II, more than 8,000 Polish officers were rounded up and executed near Katyn, outside the city of Smolensk, Russia. After the massacre was discovered in 1943, Tandrup advanced in the Nazi press the scandalous assertion that the Soviet Army perpetrated the massacre. Everyone knew that Nazis were responsible for the Katyn massacre, so Tandrup's assertion was deemed Nazi propaganda. In 1952, however, an American commission of inquiry found that the Soviet Union was in fact behind it, and only in 1990 did the country, through Mikhail Gorbachev, admit that Soviet troops had indeed been responsible for the massacre. It turned out Tandrup had been right all along. One is of course free to believe that the freedom of expression and rule of law for Nazi suspects presents no major problem, despite the fact that abominable

---

[49] Cf. See Mchangama and Stjernfelt (2016) p. 665ff.

persons and their views are exactly what principles should be tested against. In the context of this book, the example goes to show that claims—even when put forward by a coherent and serious group of people who are entirely sure of its veracity—may later be debunked if new evidence comes to light. But there is only room for such knowledge gains if there is no commission or algorithm performing "fact checks", removing such evidence from the public sphere long before any thorough investigation can take place.

Compared to Facebook, Google seems more seriously concerned with freedom of expression, for example, in its year-long infight with Chinese censorship, but that has not prevented the company from making deals with a number of countries on local modifications of the algorithms aimed at removal of specific content. Currently, Google is resuming relations with China after the break in 2010, and possible censorship consequences of this new development remain unclear. Increasing rumors hint at the development of a specially censored search engine called Dragonfly which will automatically remove content based on dictates from the Chinese government; these rumors are taken seriously to the point that Senators from both US parties have asked Google's top leaders to explain.[50] This has also led to more than a thousand Google employees protesting against the management's plans.[51] Critics fear that if Google and China agree on such an arrangement, it might form a model for censored Google searches in a number of other countries, such as Pakistan, Iran, Saudi Arabia, etc. Whether Google, like Facebook, has already caved in to Pakistani requirements remains disputed. In the spring of 2018, Swedish newspaper *Expressen* began a campaign against the tech giant, claiming that as a publishing entity, Google was responsible for spreading hatred and that it should be subjected to censorship. This prompted the

---

[50] Yuan, L. & Wakabayashi, D. "Google, seeking a return to China, is said to Be Building a Censored Search Engine" *New York Times.* 08-01-18.

[51] Associated Press: "More than 1,000 Google Workers Protest Censored China Search" *Washington Post*. 08-17-18.

Swedish government to call Google up for a meeting. The government was represented by Justice Minister Morgan Johansson (Social Democratic Party) and Minister of Digitization Peter Eriksson (The Green Party). They expressed concerns that on the platform, Google allowed "illegal" and "harmful" content which could affect the Swedish elections. Note that the two legislators did not restrict their concerns to illegal content. Google promised to modify the algorithm and hire more staff to ensure that threats and hate were removed from search results and YouTube videos.[52] Other Swedish newspapers such as *Göteborgs-Posten* and *Ystads Allehanda* warned against the *Expressen* campaign and the government initiative, stating that "spring-cleaning" Google could be extremely damaging to freedom of expression.[53]

The bottom line is, however, that we know that Google has knowingly used the ranking algorithm in several cases to prioritize or deprioritize political and other content—but we do not know anything about how often it happens or of the principles behind it. The ranking algorithm and its constant development and sophistication remains part of Google's innermost secret DNA. But one wonders if a de facto monopoly on a piece of public infrastructure such as Google should be based on principles entirely opaque to the public, or if algorithms should instead be publicly accessible and subject to discussion.

In August 2018, the possible lopsidedness of Google's searches was questioned again, now as part of the Alex Jones case. President Trump posted one of his infamous tweets, based on an article by Paula Bolyard in *PJ Media*. She had searched for "Trump news" on Google, looked at the first 100 results and claimed that the 96 of them linked to left-wing media — based on a definition that ranked virtually all main-

[52] "Censorship by Google" *Wikipedia*.

[53] Boström, H. "Hatet mot Google" *GP*. 19-03-18; "Rensa nätet försiktigt" *Ystads Allehanda*. 03-12-18. Last visited 08-03-18: http://www.ystadsallehanda.se/ledare/rensa-natet-forsiktigt/

stream media as "left-wing".[54] Three days later, Trump posted a stream of tweets: "Google search results for "Trump News" shows only the viewing/reporting of Fake News Media. In other words, they have it RIGGED, for me & others, so that almost all stories & news is BAD. Fake CNN is prominent. Republican/Conservative & Fair Media is shut out. Illegal? 96% of results on "Trump News" are from National Left-Wing Media, very dangerous. Google & others are suppressing voices of Conservatives and hiding information and news that is good. They are controlling what we can & cannot see. This is a very serious situation-will be addressed!"[55] The statement was backed by the White House, which announced government checks against Google and the other tech giants. This naturally caused a heated debate, indicating that such control would squarely violate the freedom of expression protection of the First Amendment. Also, a very reasonable objection was made: if one labels all media who have criticized Trump as left-wing, it is no surprise that one reaches conclusions like that of Bolyard. At the same time, an equal number of search results for and against a given subject cannot count as a criterion of fairness: Should a search on "Flat Earth" then return an equal number of websites claiming the Earth is flat versus round?

Google's own response to Trump's criticism showed, nevertheless, how difficult it was for the company to come up with a clear defense: "When users type queries into the Google Search bar, our goal is to make sure they receive the most relevant answers in a matter of seconds. Search is not used to set a political agenda and we don't bias our results toward any political ideology. Every year, we issue hundreds of improvements to our algorithms to ensure they surface high-quality content in response to users' queries. We con-

---

[54] Bolyard, P. "96 Percent of Google Search Results for 'Trump' News Are from Liberal Media Outlets" *PJ Media*. 08-25-18.

[55] Cit. fra Wemple, E. "Google gives Trump a look at reality. Trump doesn't like it" *Washington Post*. 08-28-18. The President is not himself a computer user, so it is believed that his numbers come from Bolyard's article.

tinually work to improve Google Search and we never rank search results to manipulate political sentiment."[56] What is meant by the fluffy words "relevant" and "high quality", on which this argument relies? Google's weak response shows that, in a sense, the company had it coming, exposing itself to attacks like Trump's: when the company operates with an opaque, increasingly complicated algorithm, it is no wonder that it calls out for conspiracy theories, and with Google's history of actual political manipulation with searches, it is hard to muster much trust in the company's defense. Trump's idea of state censorship is terrifying and unconstitutional, but his confused tweet contains the correct observations that Google defines what we see, and its workings are not transparent.

Interestingly, the accusations of liberal bias among the tech giants caused a group of internal critics on Facebook to surface, who pointed to a left-wing trend among the company staff. Brian Amerige, top Facebook engineer, wrote in an internal memo: "We are a political monoculture that's intolerant of different views. We claim to welcome all perspectives, but are quick to attack—often in mobs—anyone who presents a view that appears to be in opposition to left-leaning ideology."[57] There is little doubt that Amerige's observations apply also to staff at the other tech giants in famously liberal Silicon Valley. Whether this imbalance is reflected in the product is of course another question. But the combination of the staff's bias and the lack of transparency in the companies' procedures makes them a natural target for conspiracy theories such as Trump's, theories which—for that very same reason—the companies have more than a hard time repudiating.

In July 2018, three representatives from Google, Facebook and Twitter were summoned to testify before the House Judiciary Committee about the content moderation proce-

---

[56] Cit. fra Ohlheiser, A. og Horton, A. "A short investigation into Trump's claims of 'RIGGED' Google results against him" *Washington Post*. 08-28-18.

[57] Cit. fra Conger, K. & Fraenkel, S. "Dozens at Facebook Unite to Challenge Its 'Intolerant' Liberal Culture" *New York Times*. 08-28-18.

dures of the companies. During the hearing, the tech giants were repeatedly accused of censoring conservative voices. An interesting thing about this hearing was that it became increasingly apparent that several legislators present did not understand how beneficial certain legislations on technology has been to these companies, and whose benefits are only recently being seriously questioned. Tech giants have always been able to enjoy full freedom from responsibility when it comes to the communication of their users. They remain under the political and legal radar because of the Safe Harbor Act—also known as Section 230—of 1996. The law is extremely convenient for tech giants. Firstly, it ensures that platforms that provide access to content are not accountable for the the expressions and actions of users on the platforms. This means that the platform providers do not have to control what their users are doing. Secondly, the second part of the law includes the decisive detail that if the platforms actually do decide to control what their users are expressing or doing, they do not lose their protection under Safe Harbor. This means that if a platform removes or moderates content, it will not suddenly be categorized as a publisher with associated responsibilities.[58] At the time, the second part of the law was considered an encouragement for tech companies to take on the difficult task of limiting online pornography or other unwanted content without being held responsible if the task seemed impossible to solve. But with Section 230, the principle that control implies liability was dissolved. The law—captured by the phrase "you have the right, but not responsibility"—leaves legislators without political leverage because it immunizes the tech companies, regardless of whether they restrict and censor user communication or not.

The law gives rise to some confusion because its second part is less known. During the hearing, Congressman Matt Gaetz (R) questioned whether tech companies can claim to be exempt from liability under Section 230 while at the same time asserting their freedom of expression with reference to

[58] Gillespie (2018) p. 30.

the First Amendment, which guarantees publishers the right to freely restrict content on their platforms. Gaetz's reasoning was that calling upon the Section 230 protection necessarily means giving up the right to be a publisher.[59] But this reasoning is a sign that the law was misunderstood, and Gaetz is not the only one. Due to the aforementioned detail in the second part of the law, it does not prescribe neutrality, which is the underlying premise of Gaetz's criticism.

Supporters of Section 230 have raised serious concerns due to increasing criticism of the law among Members of Congress combined with its widespread misinterpretation. One of the alarmists is Eric Goldman, a leading researcher on Section 230. He points out that the First Amendment prohibits the government from intervening in freedom of expression, and that this protection applies to both private companies and publishers as well as tech companies. Goldman says: "Private entities can engage in censorship. We call that editorial discretion." He then added: "When the government tells publishers what they can and can't publish, that's called censorship."[60] It is Goldman's point that by threatening to compromise the moderation practices of tech companies, congress is likely guilty of committing the very censorship they accuse the tech companies of doing. This is, however, a drastic warning, as tech companies would very much prefer not to be categorized as publishers. In order to highlight this dilemma, we point to the comprehensive responsibilities that the European Union is beginning to impose on tech companies — measures which do not leave the freedom of expression of users any better off. An example of this was a decision by the European Court of Human Rights in the case *Delfi v Estonia* in 2015. It was concluded that an Estonian website could actually be held responsible for reader comments in a debate posted on the forum without that being a violation of Article 10 of the European Human Rights Declaration on

[59] Lapowsky, I. "Lawmakers Don't Grasp the Sacred Tech Law They Want to Gut" *Wired*. 07-17-18.

[60] Op. cit.

Freedom of Expression – a somewhat excessive publisher responsibility.

This mess suggests that it is difficult to modify and adjust Section 230 without any clear definition of "tech giants". Are they publishers, distributors, a public sphere, or something entirely different? This is one of the major problems with tech companies—they do not fit into existing categories. Practically all tech giants make their own content policies and police their platforms themselves. With 230 in hand, the giants have the freedom to arbitrarily decide when, to what extent, and why they should take responsibility for their users' content. As previous chapters of this book have shown, this freedom to restrict often goes far beyond what is legally required. Often, it is just the result of economic strategy. One thing is certain: Section 230 is outdated.

Section 230 was adopted as part of the Communications Decency Act of 1996. Not only does it pre-date Facebook, Twitter and Google, but also platforms such as MySpace, Friendster and Napster. The point is that the law is in no way designed for social media, which did not exist in 1996.[61] It does not take into account Google's ranking algorithm that prioritizes or downgrades specific content, YouTube's filtering technology which, despite claims to the contrary, could identify copyrighted material, or Facebook's personalized news feed algorithm and removal handbook. And, most particularly, it does not take into account the emerging monopoly status of tech giants that has developed in the course of the 2010s. Tech giants are a hybrid of many existing business categories, which makes it extremely difficult to carry out a political and legal review of the nature of platforms' responsibilities. There is quite simply no clear point from which to consider them in existing legal terms. In April 2018, a study by the Pew Research Center showed that over half of Americans support tech companies that take the initiative to limit false information in the fight against misinformation,

[61] Gillespie (2018) p. 33-34.

"even if it limits public freedom to access and transmit information."[62] This is not the right way forward.

In the fall of 2018, a new wave of censorship swept through the main tech giants. In September, Twitter adopted new guidelines under the nauseating motto "Be Sweet When You Tweet"[63]. It prohibits "[...] content that dehumanizes others based on their membership in an identifiable group, even when the material does not include a direct target" and adds a version of the standard list of selected groups to be granted special protection: "Dehumanization: Language that treats others as less than human. Dehumanization can occur when others are denied of human qualities (animalistic dehumanization) or when others are denied of their human nature (mechanistic dehumanization). Examples can include comparing groups to animals and viruses (animalistic), or reducing groups to a tool for some other purpose (mechanistic). Identifiable group: Any group of people that can be distinguished by their shared characteristics such as their race, ethnicity, national origin, sexual orientation, gender, gender identity, religious affiliation, age, disability, serious disease, occupation, political beliefs, location, or social practices."[64] The description of "dehumanization" is extremely vague and wide-ranging and it is obviously it can be used to stifle much standard political debate—such as claims that such and such political group has been instrumentalized by lobbyists.

In October, a long-held internal Google memo with the title "The Good Censor" was leaked.[65] The memo is a blend

---

[62] Mitchell, A., Grieco, E. & Sumida, N. "Americans Favour Protecting Information Freedoms Over Government Steps to Restrict False News Online" *Pew Research Center*. 04-19-18.

[63] Matsakis, L. "Twitter Releases New Policy on 'Dehumanizing Speech'" *Wired.* 09-25-18.

[64] Twitter: "Creating New Policies Together"09-25-18. Last visited 12-18-2018: https://blog.twitter.com/official/en_us/topics/company/2018/Creating-new-policies-together.html.

[65] Bokhari, A. (upload) "The Good Censor – GOOGLE LEAK." Last visited 12-18-2018: https://www.scribd.com/document/390521673/The-Good-Censor-GOOGLE-LEAK#from_embed. More details:

of interviews and contributions from academics, journalists, and cultural critics, arguing for narrowing the scope of Google's traditional free speech stance. Here, the introduction of censorship is portrayed as a balance between free speech and the protection of users from "harmful conduct". The memo discusses whether users can be protected the users against negative phenomena like bots, trolling, and extremism while still being a platform for all voices. The memo does not yet conclude in terms of a new rulebook, but clearly the tendency goes in the direction of less rather than more freedom of expression. The general, hard-to-solve tension between liberty and security is the same conundrum as encountered by all the tech giants in the wake of the Alex Jones case in August 2018.

Moderation, content deletion, censorship by the tech giants—call it what you will—is undoubtedly here to stay. The Internet must be policed for criminal activities such as threats, harassment, extortion, incitement to violence, organization of violence, or forming terrorist cells. However, it does not follow that control should spread from such illegal activities to a wide variety of other types of content. It is also not obvious that the control, as is the case today, should remain hidden. Finally, there is no reason such control and its principles should be the privilege of tech companies themselves. The tech giants, often relying on a simplified and romantic idea of representing a "community" of common values, must realize that their vast populations of users are highly complex and represent strong, often opposing currents and values that also exist and act offline. The companies should instead realize that such contradictions are real, and not only the result of poor communication which will magically disappear through mantras such as "connecting people". Their task is rather to make available the many widely different, incompatible positions and values and provide a forum for serious clashes to take place and develop in a clear and unfeigned manner, one

---

Statt, N. "Leaked Google Research Shows Company Grappling with Censorship and Free Speech" *The Verge* 10-10-18.

that is free of violence and free of crime. This means forming public spaces rather than "communities"—and bringing the policies closer to ordinary, transparent standards of free expression.

However, strong trends are unfortunately heading in a completely different direction. With the law in hand, this tendency seeks to expand the deletion practice and responsibilities of the tech giants and thus—somewhat unwittingly—hand them even *more* power over the public.

Chapter 13
Entrusting Government Control to Private Tech Giants

Seen from the offices of the CEO's, the current public turmoil faced by the tech giants must be rather confusing. On the one hand, agitated politicians and intellectuals demand that the companies engage still more in the *removal* of content—of "hate speech," "fake news," extremism, defamation, Russian bots, nipples, pejoratives and a wide range of other things. On the other hand, a number of politicians and intellectuals—among them the authors of this very book—are accusing the giants of already removing *way too much* content, applying their narrow but at the same time vaguely worded community standards and the murky and uncontrollable enforcement of them. Unfortunately, the former of the two tendencies seems to have the upper hand at the moment.

Many of the critical questions made to Zuckerberg during the congressional hearings he faced in 2018 revolved around *more* removal of content, and it seems politicians are able to use the problems with the tech giants as a pretext to demand de facto censorship, otherwise impossible to carry out against the constitutions of most countries. Oftentimes the point is put forward that tech giants must acknowledge their status as actual media outlets—that they have to assume publisher responsibility, make targeted edits to their content and assume the same legal status as print media. We think that is going down the wrong road. Tech giants are not media and they produce news or other content only marginally (Google,

F. Stjernfelt, A. M. Lauritzen, *Your Post has been Removed*,
https://doi.org/10.1007/978-3-030-25968-6_13

Amazon) or not at all (Facebook, Twitter). We will return to how they should indeed be categorized.

Still, the idea of tech giants as media outlets naturally leads decision makers to imagine how, as subjects of political monitoring, the giants should take over responsibility for the content that is uploaded on their platforms. In this matter, Europe leads the way. In May of 2016, the European Union convinced Facebook, Microsoft, Twitter and YouTube to accept a "code of conduct" on "hate speech", which required that the companies subject themselves to more detailed control and agree to respond to complaints within 24 h.[1] The most ominous example of this tendency is the German legislation carrying the nebulous name "Netzwerkdurchsetzungsgesetz"—Networks Implementation Law – nicknamed "The Facebook Law" or "The Heiko Maas Law", after the German Minister of Justice. It was adopted during 2017 and entered into full force on January 1st, 2018. Its purpose is to comb social networks for smear campaigns and "fake news" (it does not, however, include email services and edited news sites). The law obliges social network providers of a certain size—such as Twitter and Facebook—to remove all statements from their servers that are "clearly illegal" within 24 hours by establishing and staffing a permanent reporting service. In more complex cases, a 7-day deadline may be allowed so as to hear the user's side of the matter. In not so clear cases, the service can initiate "regulated self-regulation", to be monitored by the Justice Department in the form of reports twice a year, but also this regulation is run, staffed and paid for by the service provider

---

[1] "European Commission and IT Companies announce Code of Conduct on illegal online hate speech" *European Commission, Justice and Consumers*. 05-31-16. Certain organizations may here assume status of "trusted flaggers" whose complaints over content receive special treatment in a certain channel unaccessible for normal users. The deal not only concerns removal of terrorist content, but also the promoting of "counter-narratives", which may be difficult to distinguish from state propaganda Cf. Kaye, D. "Report of the Special Rapporteur on the promotion and protection of the right to freedom of opinion and expression" *UN Human Rights Council*, section 21. 04-06-18.

itself. Objectionable statements not caught by the still more advanced algorithms will have to, for instance on Facebook, be reported by vigilant users. A person reports a posting he does not like, indicates what violation he thinks the given content is guilty of and adds a description of the context in which it appears. Subsequently, Facebook—or some subcontractor entrusted with the task of control—decides within 24 hours on the removal of the utterance in question. If the company fails to take measures to remove controversial content, fines of up to 50 million euros can be issued, along with €5 million fines levied on individual employees of the social media in question who are deemed guilty. Even during the preparation of this law, heavy criticism was voiced: it would breach the German constitution's article on freedom of speech, and the short deadline and high fines would put pressure on the networks to remove all content under even the tiniest suspicion of containing reprehensible material. Another big problem is that this law actually privatizes parts of the judicial as well as the executive powers, by leaving tech giants to decide what falls within the scope of German law and whether or not to penalize users by removing content and enforcing short termed, long termed or indefinite exclusion from the networks. Finally, it is extremely problematic that all of this takes place in a semi-automated fashion, without any public scrutiny or control, except for generic half-yearly reports.

One would think these issues might be serious enough. However, it gets worse. The German newspaper *Frankfurter Allgemeine* decided to investigate how this new informer service works. If and when a user wishes to complain about another's posting, he is taken to a website containing 14 different categories of violations and has to classify the offending post. According to *Frankfurter Allgemeine,* the informer can choose between the following categories of violations: (1) spreading propaganda material from unconstitutional organizations; (2) using features of unconstitutional organizations; (3) preparing a serious act of violence against the state; (4) instigating the public to commit criminal acts; (5) disrupting the public space by threatening to carry out criminal acts; (6) forming terrorist associations; (7) inciting hate and violence ("Volksverhetzung"); (8) reproducing violent acts; (9) insulting faiths, religious organizations or ideological associations ("Weltanschauungsvereinigungen") ; (10) disseminating, acquiring or possessing child pornography (if disseminated via the Internet); (12) rewarding and accepting criminal acts, (13) unspecified "violation"—but, as the newspaper states, also otherwise not criminalized acts such as (14) "treasonous falsifications".[2] However, it is not correct that treasonous lies are not punishable. They come under the rarely used Article 100a of the German Criminal Code.[3]

In general terms, these infractions concern anything from planning and threatening to commit very serious crimes—to things normally associated with ordinary debate, such as criticism of religions and ideologies, representations of violence, and unspecified violation ("Beleidigung"). These examples are indeed included because they appear in the German Criminal Code. But in the absence of court cases with experienced and skilled judges, prosecutors and defense attorneys, how are we to trust that the newly hired staff at the German branch of Facebook are capable of making a distinction

---

[2] "Verbreiten von Propagandamitteln verfassungswidriger Organisationen, Verwenden von Kennzeichen verfassungswidriger Organisationen, Vorbereitung einer schweren staatsgefährdenden Gewalttat, Anleitung zur Begehung einer schweren staatsgefährdenden Gewalttat, öffentliche Aufforderung zu Straftaten, Störung des öffentlichen Friedens durch Androhung von Straftaten, Bildung terroristischer Vereinigungen, Volksverhetzung, Gewaltdarstellungen, Beschimpfung von Bekenntnissen, Religionsgesellschaften und Weltanschauungsvereinigungen, Verbreitung, Erwerb und Besitz von Kinderpornographie (sofern über Telemedien verbreitet), Belohnung und Billigung von Straftaten, Beleidigungen – aber auch selbst für Juristen eher unbekannte Tatbestände wie die „Landesverräterische Fälschung"". Quote from Wieduwilt, H. "Löschgesetz verlangt Facebook-Nutzern viel ab" *Frankfurter Allgemeine*. 12-30-17.

[3] One of this book's authors (Stjernfelt) was once misled by *Frankfurter Allgemeine*'s mistake about this matter when he claimed that these 14 items included content not punishable under German law. That is not the case.

between "dead letter" articles of the law and still applicable ones? How are we to trust that relevant precedence is considered when applying particular articles and weighing contradictions between them? And how are we to trust that the people involved understand that the article of the German Constitution on freedom of speech historically has kept the articles on, for instance, criticism of religion and insults within strict limits? Would one not think it more likely that Facebook will interpret these articles in the light of their own community standards and the associated combination of tighter procedures and more vague wordings?

The entry into force of the law was not impaired by the fact that *Reporters sans Frontières* and a growing freedom-of-speech movement in Germany have pointed to the resulting serious encroachments on basic human rights. At the time of writing, the German branches of Facebook, Twitter etc. are busy cleaning out content of the aforementioned kind, a job carried out by a large influx of new employees. Critics have dubbed this law an autocratic mechanism of censorship, referring to totalitarian states and their control of the public. They point to the fact that the Belarusian dictator Lukashenko is inspired by this legislation. And as early as July 2018, Russia drafted legislation which basically copy-pasted the German law made public months before. German chair of *Reporteurs sans Frontières* Christian Mihr said: "Our worst fears have become reality. The German law on Internet" hate speech "now serves as a model for non-democratic states wishing to restrict debates online."[4] Eight out of ten experts summoned to the German Bundestag claimed that enforcement of this law must be the responsibility of the government and not of private contractors. They point to a breach of the principle of proportionality regarding punishment, given the imbalance between the enormous fines and the nature of the actual offense. Observers estimate that the implementation of the required control systems will cost social media in

---

[4] "Russian bill is copy-and-paste of Germany's hate speech law" *Reporters-Without-Borders.* 07-19-17.

Germany around 500 million euros per year. At the time of writing, the EU Commission has blocked access to documents examining whether this law is even compatible with EU legislation, the European Human Rights Convention, and European laws on information society service.

However, the most unsettling aspect of this rushed legislation is that responsibility for this new form of censorship is left to private actors and their opaque employee and subcontractor setups. Content is now removed from the public space without any warning, without any open case process, without the right of defense of the person responsible—and with limited recourse to appeal, a recourse to be decided by the networks. No court, trial or sentence is involved—something which, mirrored in a Danish context, would bomb us back to before 1790 when court sentences became standard in matters of press freedom crimes. We have no reason to believe that tech giants solely focused on profit possess the journalistic, scientific or legal expertise to judge whether a reported statement is criminal or merely controversial. Or *true*, for that matter: How would a provider of computer services, with such skills, be able to decide whether a piece of news is "treasonous falsification"? As pointed out by critics of the German law, which threatens to allow for fines of up to 50 million euros, the most likely scenario is that the tech giants will remove content in cases with even the slightest doubt about their nature. For obvious reasons, both the German right and left have opposed this legislation—surely both sides envision how their political statements can end up among those deleted by faceless hordes of content moderators.

An example from December 2017 illustrates the problem: a videoclip of a pedestrian breaking into foul and racist language while passing a Jewish restaurant in Berlin. It was shared vividly on Facebook, only to be quickly removed. After a while, the video returned to the platform. Facebook gave no information about the motivations behind the removal nor the reappearance of the video. But as stated in *Frankfurter Allgemeine*, one may assume it was removed because the passer-by was thought to be carrying out an act of "incitement to hate and violence". Yet later it was uploaded again, once it became clear that people shared it in order to shame the individual in the video rather than support his views, turning sharing it into a kind of shunning by quotation. Merely from the primitive tools "share" and "like", one cannot tell whether such clicking actually means that the clicker agrees with what is being liked or shared. Without any public insight into procedures and decisions, is there any way of knowing for sure that such subtle contextual reasoning will be applied in each individual case? We have no reason to believe that such flash justice performed by the German branch of Facebook is capable of distinguishing quotation or irony from direct statements.

The law on these networks appears to rely on the entirely untenable idea that to identify "clearly" criminal or controversial points of view is an easy and straightforward matter, even possible to turn into an object of automatized control. The law completely overlooks the fact that in modern societies, such elementary distinctions are only put into use thanks to the ongoing and demanding work done by the judicial systems, serious media and scientific research—and that there can be no shortcut to handle this justice via automated algorithms[5] or anonymous, privately employed moderators stressed for time and with dubious qualified training.

It is important to emphasize that the new German censorship practiced by social media has come about despite the wishes expressed by the tech giants, and that it puts considerable economic and administrative burdens on them. It is the German government and Bundestag which have resorted to this peculiar, panic-like measure. It forces the outsourcing of a crucial and important part of the legal enforcement of freedom of speech online to private, formally incompetent and reluctant players. The legal rights for large parts of the German public sphere remains entirely undefined and insufficient. These days, much of this public sphere is practiced online via social media—including the many "traditional" media engaging with their audiences via pages on Facebook

[5] Cf. Garapon and Lassègue (2018).

or Twitter. One might fear that the legislations currently being drafted in France, and the tech regulations possibly underway in the United States, could be inspired by the German government and hand over *more* power to the tech giants rather than less.

At present, we know only the outline of the suggested French legislation, which is set to include a newly established Internet tribunal with fast-track case processing as well as tightened legislation and control of political ads, especially around election time. Unlike the German law, case processing is here maintained within the judicial system. On the other hand, this new tribunal may be given very vast competences. Among other things, the scary possibility of simply closing down media found guilty of "fake news" is currently being discussed.

In March 2019, a white supremacist assassin from Australia attacked two mosques in Christchurch, New Zealand, simultaneously livestreaming his crime on Facebook. That incident provoked a new wave of strong demands for regulation of so-called "harmful content", an umbrella term for "fake news", "hate speech" and graphic violence. Inspired by the German legislation, Australia passed a new law in the beginning of April. The law threatens social media with heavy fines and jail sentences for their top executives if they do not manage to remove rapidly "abhorrent violent material" from their platforms. Such material comprises videos that show terrorist attacks, murder, rape or kidnapping; fines are up to 10% of annual profit, and employees can face up to three years in prison.[6] Similar legislation is underway in New Zealand. In the UK, an even more comprehensive law is drafted in a whitepaper, targeting harmful content including child exploitation, "fake news", terrorist activity and extreme violence. British officials claim that UK will be the "safest place in the world to be online".[7] The legislation will be policed by an inde-

---

[6] Cave, D. "Australia Passes Law to Punish Social Media Companies for Violent Posts" *New York Times.* 04-03-19.

[7] Romm, T. "U.K. unveils sweeping plans to penalize Facebook and Google for harmful online content" *Washington Post.* 04-07-19.

pendent regulating body with the power to impose fines against tech companies and hold individual executives personally liable. Increasingly, tech giants are categorized after the lines of traditional media with publishing responsibities. What began as internal regulation in individual companies is quickly developing in the direction of traditional centralized state censorship. The strange thing is that these tendencies are rarely discussed in the context of fundamental political liberties in existing constitutions. Why should special legislations be developed for the internet when well-functioning, clearly defined free speech legislation exists in most Western countries, e.g. the First Amendment in the US?

Chapter 14
The First Digital Losers

As we have seen, censorship is a real and serious problem when it comes to the tech giants. However, when they use the word "censorship" themselves, they often have something completely different in mind. That other something is copyright. Not surprisingly, the tech giants oppose copyright protections, since they wish to attract users by offering free access to a world of alluring content. Thus, by praising copyright infringements as though they were a matter of practicing free speech, they end up abusing the honorable name and reputation of free speech itself.

In the early years of the Internet, the push for the free exchange of information and software boasted the motto "Information wants to be free." But the word "free" may mean both "without restraint" and "without cost," and on tech platforms, free information tends to be interpreted as the right to access films, music and text *without cost*. Oftentimes, it is in the very name of free speech that popular content is uploaded and made available. The call for free access to a world of information may come off as a blessing for knowledge. It has never been as easy to get ahold of so much knowledge and treasured material as it is today—without even having to pay for it. But the dogma of no cost has enabled the tech giants to neutralize the economic value of knowledge and art. First, the traditional paid media have grown desperately dependent on the platforms of these giants. Second, the intellectual property of musicians, writers and other content makers has been

F. Stjernfelt, A. M. Lauritzen, *Your Post has been Removed*,
https://doi.org/10.1007/978-3-030-25968-6_14

robbed from them. The latter consequence has already claimed its first victims: the digital losers. The success of the motto "move fast and break things" has drained the income sources of many artists.[1] It is the consequence of the tech giants' powerful position to dictate the rules of how to access and share content. For many years, Silicon Valley has waged war on copyright legislations, propagandizing the issue by framing these laws as a kind of censorship machine which aims to put an end to freedom of expression. However, this is Orwellian *doublespeak*—as a form of rhetoric, it plays on fear sentiments in an attempt to stir up resistance against political intervention. This line of thought puts writers who want an income for their work up there with totalitarian regimes curbing free speech. The truth of the matter is that these laws serve to protect the incomes of content makers and their opportunity to create new and valuable material.

Large chunks of the traffic toward traditional media sites run through Google. Pieces of writing are easily and quickly accessed via social media, especially Facebook's news feed. As mentioned earlier, a *Reuters* mapping of news consumption in 2017 showed that a little over half the Danish population go to social media weekly for their news. The Internet has changed our behavioral patterns as news consumers. Newspapers and magazines have tried to rethink their business strategies to adapt to the changes brought on by the advent of the Internet. The Internet was, after all, this information superhighway that would open the door to a huge readership hitherto out of reach, back when traditional marketing strategies were applied. Wanting to fit in and adjust, many articles were published online for free, while the media were waiting for new and better online business model to emerge. Charging for these articles would mean letting a revolutionary opportunity slip by. Their hope was to reach a larger readership and then generate more traffic on their own websites—and thus more advertising income. That was just

---

[1]The first major elaboration of this problem is found in Taplin's *Move Fast and Break Things* (2017).

not what happened. As an unforeseen consequence of this strategy, many newspapers and magazines burst into pieces. They had to abandon large parts of the editorial line and accept the role of simple piles of decomposed and decontextualized articles. In the traditional print versions of newspapers, the editorial layout of articles represented a strong strategy: readers interested in the cultural section only of, for instance, *Washington Post,* would also have to pay for international politics, sports, local news, cartoons, op-eds and the rest of the obligatory package that came with the newspaper. This was the classic "omnibus" newspaper, catering to all kinds of readers, which practically sold itself with its optimal "mix" of many kinds of news and features. But online, many articles were now accessible individually, à la carte and, let us not forget, for free. Users no longer needed to pay subscription fees or even buy an entire copy. Thus, readers became used to jumping from page to page and from one link to the next. The result was that online news outlets and magazines ceased to exist in the form of coherent anthologies of articles offered by the classic general-interest daily newspaper. Now each individual article was to be self-sustaining, measurable by its numbers of clicks.[2] Articles may no longer be sheltered by the more or less coherent editorial line of an entire newspaper. In came new and powerful gatekeepers such as Facebook, Amazon and Google, who opened the gates to a full supply of news articles, books and videos, gathered in bundles. Out of the many fragmented parts, they made a useful and somewhat coherent product. Obviously, this is a hugely successful business model for the tech giants: Google and Facebook never pay for the articles they offer to their users, and they can offer a much larger selection than traditional media outlets, and even customized to the individual user.

Most of the media organizations that were not seduced by the Internet mantra of free information were punished by the

[2] Foer (2017) pp. 86–87.

algorithms run by Facebook and Google.[3] Newspapers and magazines charging a subscription for access to their product tend to drown in the enormous supply of information controlled by the algorithms. The articles do not generate the decisive likes, comments and shares that are rewarded with promotion and exposure. In other words, articles hidden behind paywalls tend to lose the online popularity contest. In 2006, Jonathan Rosenberg, then Senior Vice President of Products at Google, said that his company should "pressure premium content providers to change their model to free."[4] This is a clever business strategy, since the value of the giants depend upon offering a free shortcut to an enormous supply of valuable information and entertainment.

The problem today is that journalism and newspapers have become unhealthily if not pathologically dependent on Google and Facebook, which have made them financially vulnerable. The news media have entered into anti-competitive agreements, which initially seemed essential to their survival. Unfortunately, however, these agreements have made the giants even more powerful. The media outlets have accepted that Facebook sells accompanying ads, traditionally the media's own main source of revenue, and Google has been allowed to publish the articles quickly and directly on their own platform rather than allowing traffic to go through the media's web sites. The agreements are particularly sensitive because of the well-known capriciousness of the giants: they quickly change direction if it benefits their bottom lines or reputations. The problem is that such changes may have major consequences for the media, who now depend upon the traffic flowing from the platforms.[5] For example, in January 2018, Zuckerberg changed the news feed algorithm radically, so that content from "friends" and family took priority over news content, and more local news was

---

[3] Foer (2017) p. 90.

[4] Cleland, S. "Grand Theft Auto-mated! Online Ad-Economics Fuel Piracy &amp: SOPA Opposition" *Forbes*. 11-30-11.

[5] Foer (2017) p. 132.

given higher priority.[6] The purpose of this radical change was to create more "meaningful interactions" and avoid inappropriate content such as misinformation and hateful comments. As a result, the disempowered media naturally saw a sharp drop in traffic and in revenues derived from it.

In 2014, Mathias Döpfner, CEO of the large German media group Axel Springer, wrote an open letter to Google CEO Eric Smidt expressing his concern that Google's dominant position as a search engine has lead to companies small and large living in constant "fear of Google". Frequent changes to the search algorithm unpredictably affect all businesses that have become dependent on the heavy traffic flowing through the platform. Döpfner wrote: "Our business relationship is that of the Goliath of Google to the David of Axel Springer. When Google changed an algorithm, one of our subsidiaries lost 70 percent of its traffic within a few days." With bitter irony that is possibly lost on Google, Döpfner added: "The fact that this subsidiary is a competitor of Google's is certainly a coincidence."[7] Reaching $14 billion, Google's annual profits are about twenty times bigger than Axel Springer's. Financially, they do not compare; even as a giant in Germany, Springer is a dwarf as compared to Google. One could say that Google does not need Springer, while Springer—and with them all other larger and smaller media companies—most definitely need Google.

Besides causing financial vulnerability, the giants even dictate the actual work patterns of journalism. Journalism is increasingly subject to Google's and Facebook's algorithms. If a story is important, it must be shared at exactly the right time, have exactly the right headline and the right status update to go with it. And still it is not certain that the article will get attention. The point is that stories important in themselves do not gain popularity unless they are also curated to fit into the model of each tech giant. Pandering to the

---

[6] "Facebooks News Feed Algorithm History" *Wallaroo Media.* 06-04-18.

[7] Döpfner, M. "Why we fear Google" *Frankfurter Allgemeine.* 04-17-14.

algorithms may affect the quality of the news. In his book *World Without a Mind* (2017), Franklin Foer writes about his time at American political magazine *New Republic*. The magazine's growing dependence on tech giants gradually undermined the integrity of its journalism. In the pursuit of clicks—of survival—even major news providers began to embrace sensationalism, publish more or less dubious stories and give attention to propagandists and conspiracy theorists, including Donald Trump.[8]

Journalists are continuously and instantly measured by how many clicks their stories generate, sometimes openly, via a single screen in the editorial office. An infinite cycle of feedback is established: priority is given to stories that spread online, all other material is downgraded even if it is supposed to be important according to classical journalistic news criteria. Easily digestible content has become a whole new genre that appeals to people who are bored at work or on the train. It includes various top-ten lists, videos, and short, quick reads.[9] The subject may be serious, but it is published in a fast and entertaining way so that it may generate reactions on Facebook and thus be shared. Another side effect is that many media outlets get caught in the clickbait trap, preferring to high click rates over solid news. Headlines such as "you'll never guess …" have become commonplace online. These mischievous teaser headlines activate in the reader an almost primal hunger for the information suggested, which is quickly and easily accessed with a click or two. Contrary to traditional print media, the headline no longer contains the gist of the article but may be enigmatic and inspire curiosity, act as bait, and keep the user busy clicking, sometimes generating a whole series of clicks, which increases both the time spent by the user and the number of possible companion ads. The classic journalistic criterion that the headline should condense the most important information in the article is abandoned in favor of riddle-like headlines. The result is that the reader

[8] Foer (2017) pp. 6–7.

[9] Ibid. pp. 139–140.

loses the freedom to determine the relevance of the article based on the headline. In the United States, *Upworthy*, *Buzzfeed* and *Vox* gained incredible success by developing insights, through the analysis of data, into how audience-winning content is created. Since then, most of the media community has followed suit—even highly respected media outlets like *Time* and *Washington Post.*

In general, tech giants have created a novel news system that aims to offer products pandering to the tastes of users. This may ultimately lead to a homogenization of the news industry through a leveling of opinion and taste. The founder of *Vox Media* and *The Verge*, Joshua Topolsky, bemoans this tendency: "Everything looks the same, reads the same, and seems to be competing for the same eyeballs."[10] Most media outlets write about the same scandals and cling to the hot topics of the day. Foer gives a spot-on example in his book. Many people may remember the rather inconsequential story of Cecil the lion. The story became very influential online, with its picture of a smiling hunter posing proudly in front of his prey, which he had shot with his bow and arrow in Africa. It had social media in a frenzy. The American dentist and hobby hunter became the object of hatred on Twitter under the hashtag #WalterPalmer, and the story generated more than 3.2 million other pieces of content from both private users and from major media outlets. Everyone tried to steer traffic in their direction. It was almost comical to witness the many clumsy attempts to find new angles on the weak and hackneyed story. Most media outlets made an honest attempt. The news outlet *Vox* wrote: "Eating Chicken is morally worse than killing Cecil the lion" and *BuzzFeed*: "A Psychic Says She Spoke With Cecil The Lion After His Death." Even a more traditional magazine like *The Atlantic* wrote "From Cecil the Lion to Climate Change: A Perfect Storm of Outrage".[11] The list goes on, and international media also followed suit. The unhealthy dependence of journalism on the

---

[10] Topolsky, J. "Hello again" *Joshua Topolsky blog*. 07-11-15.

[11] Foer (2017) p. 148.

tech giants causes them to be in constant danger of losing control. If the ethos of journalism is to be protected, no-cost content and data fetishism is not the right way to go.

Not only journalism suffers under the giant idea that the word "free" in "Information wants to be free" should be understood as "free of charge". It is even worse for other content creators such as authors and musicians. Back in 2004–05, Google discreetly launched its digitization project. The goal was to create the largest collection of knowledge ever seen on the Internet, by scanning millions of library books and indexing them in one massive digital archive; Google Books. It was part of their mission to "organize world information". A Google spokesperson said: "Google was founded on the principle of making information more accessible to more people. From the beginning, we've envisioned a future where students, researchers, and book lovers could all discover and access the world's books online. We believe that this agreement represents a giant step toward realizing that vision."[12] Many international universities participated in the project, which has indeed provided useful access to a vast amount of literature from before 1900. The digitalization project sounds so magnificently philanthropic that we almost miss the fact that this philanthropy turns into piracy when moving into the literature of twentieth century.[13]

In Google's opinion, copyright rules should not hold anyone back. Google's chief lawyer once described the company's attitude as follows: "Google's leadership does not care terribly much about precedence or law."[14] This statement alluded to the traditional protection of intellectual property. This reckless attitude has the power to destroy the publishing industry, and it will obviously be disastrous to writers

---

[12] Pilkington, E. "Google's book project faces growing opposition" *The Guardian*. 08-19-09.

[13] Most countries' copyright legislations operate with an expiration date, for example 70 years after the death of the author. Thus, the copyright restrictions of most texts from before 1900 have expired and they are now free to be used by anyone.

[14] Foer (2017) p. 54.

dependent on that industry. Put bluntly, with its digitization project Google was planning an intellectual coup of historical dimensions. By 2015, 25 million[15] of the estimated 130 million existing books (2010 numbers) were scanned,[16] but the ambitious goal to finish scanning all of them by 2020 disappears on the horizon due to copyright conflicts that have significantly reduced the scanning pace.

The interesting thing is that Google's path to success was created by copying material without asking or paying for permission to do so. The pattern consists of a "Don't ask permission" strategy and, subsequently, confidence that users will love the results as soon as they see them. Ergo, Google will do whatever it wants. Better to ask for forgiveness than permission. Just think of Gmail, with which Google offered free email and storage. Would users have accepted the terms as easily if Google at the same time had asked them permission to scan all emails in order to sell the content for custom-made ads? Or what about Google Street View, taking photos of everyone's front yards and matching them with people's addresses? If Google had asked permission to do this, the streets would most likely be dotted with pixelated houses due to the many rejections they would receive.

The "Don't ask permission" strategy is also why virtually any song in the world is available for free on the video-sharing website YouTube. The platform is the largest music streaming service in the world with a market share of 52%, even though YouTube only pays 13% of the total music streaming royalty costs paid by the music industry.[17] Co-founder of YouTube Chad Hurley wrote the following email regarding one of the company's early copyright disputes: "So, a way to avoid the copyright bastards might be to remove the 'No copyrighted or obscene material' line and let

---

[15] Heyman, S. "Google Books: A Complex and Controversial Experiment" *New York Times.* 10-28-15.

[16] Jackson, J. "Google: 129 Million Different Books Have Been Published" *PC World.* 08-06-10.

[17] Taplin (2017) p. 99.

the users moderate the videos themselves. Legally, this will probably be better for us, as we'll make the case we can review all videos and tell them if they're concerned they have the tools to do it themselves."[18] He seems well aware that he is building his business on illegal material. YouTube has a consistently lax attitude towards pirated material. It has been able to get away with this for years. Due to the United States' Safe Harbor provision and the EU's Electronic Commerce Directive (2000), the giants can move under the radar when it comes to copyright politics because legislation places the legal responsibility for the material with the users who share it and not with the companies that provide the platforms. This legislation was originally adopted with the reasonable aim of finding a balance between the rights of copyright-holders and the interests in transmitting content of the internet companies. The exemption of the companies from legal responsibility was counterbalanced by their duty to shut down accounts that contained unauthorized copyrighted material. However, the companies did not regard these two aspects of the law with equal seriousness. They do not police their platforms for illegal uploads, and they rarely remove accounts that violate copyright laws unless repeated complaints have been made. Therefore, without much difficulty, YouTube has been able to employ a strategy in which they simply close their eyes to illegal content uploaded by users, removing it only if reported by the copyright holders. Legislation in this area is outdated and as a consequence, the content owners are left alone with the responsibility of finding out if a website in some corner of the Internet is violating their copyright. Today, YouTube has made agreements with most copyright owners, but what it is paying is almost symbolic when looking at the profit the company gains from the use of the material, see figures above.

One is easily seduced by the arguments that information should be free and cultural products should be shared. Professor of Law and copyright expert Lawrence Lessig exposes the tech giant philosophy when he describes how the

[18]Taplin (2017) p. 100.

Internet is disrupting a long era in which greedy publishers, film studios, and record companies have "robbed the people of culture", reducing them to mere consumers, passive sofa-ridden recipients of movies, television and music. From this point of view, the Internet was supposed to be a showdown against the professionalization of creativity. And through this showdown, the creativity of millions of ordinary people would be released online, and all information and other content should become free, understood as "free of charge". This is a new interpretation of the old idea that "good artists copy, while great artists steal". Lessig thinks it is an established fact that every artist borrows, references and creates original works only on the basis on the work of others.[19] Lessig wants to dilute copyright rules, which, in his opinion, are based on a quaint, romantic, illusory idea of originality. He is seconded by Google and most of Silicon Valley because he strikes an important chord with tech giants: creativity is based on collaboration.[20]

It may sound alluring and beautiful, and it is tempting to be seduced by the idea when tech giant representatives talk about cooperation as opposed to the illusion of the romantic genius. But strangely enough, this point is put forward by the very same VIPs who honor Ayn Rand-like worship of the lonesome, heroic entrepreneur who creates a tech giant all by himself. When it comes to writers, thinkers and artists, collaboration is considered wonderful, as long as it does not demand remuneration. On the other hand, when it comes to programming, tech development, and funding, the solitary genius is worshipped, and the tech giants zealously defend the copyright on their own patents, algorithms and programs. All of a sudden, copyright legislation is a thing! In addition, it is important to keep in mind—even though it may seem counter-intuitive—that professionalism actually makes writing more democratic. It becomes more diverse because content producers are actually paid for their work by the very

[19] Lessig, L. "Laws that choke creativity" *TEDtalk* 2007.

[20] Foer (2017) p. 160.

companies Lessig attacks—unlike those he defends. Writing and artistic expression may become a way of life and a profession for a larger part of the population and thus not just a hobby reserved for the privileged class.[21]

Silicon Valley has long waged war against professional writers. It is a deliberate tactic to weaken the copyright laws that allow authors, musicians and artists to live off their profession. Consider Google—copyright protection is one of the company's biggest concerns because the company links to millions of copyrighted newspaper articles, books, magazines, etc. In 2012, the US House of Representatives discussed the Stop Online Piracy Act (SOPA). The intention behind the law was to curb copyright infringement by limiting access to pages that helped the exchange of pirated content. The law specifically targeted search engines like Google, which links to pirate pages. In response, Google put a picture on its homepage with the Google icon blocked by a black box that read "Tell Congress: Please don't censor the web!" with an accompanying link to a list of email addresses for all members of congress. In the 24 hours the icon and link were up on the search portal, this display of force was seen by 1.8 billion users. An overwhelming number of people responded to it and two days later, the proposal was withdrawn.[22] Misusing the "censorship" concept to attack legitimate rights holders proved effective.

Google deploys tremendous lobbying to moderate copyright legislation. In 2017, *Wall Street Journal* reported: "Over the past decade, Google has helped finance hundreds of research papers to defend against regulatory challenges of it market dominance, paying $5,000 to $400,000 for the work."[23] Academic experts can play a key role in supporting the policies promoted by specific stakeholders. During the Obama

---

[21] Foer (2017) p. 166.

[22] Taplin, J. "Why is Google spending record sums on lobbying Washington?" *The Guardian*. 07-30-17.

[23] Mullins, B. & Nicas, J. "Paying Professors: Inside Google's Academic Influence Campaign" *The Wall Street Journal*. 07-14-17.

administration, Google appears to have encouraged the firing of US Register of Copyrights Maria Pallente, who supported an update of the copyright legislation and thus opposed Google's efforts to weaken copyright protection for musicians, writers and artists. Google's lobbying was so massive that the Obama administration was sometimes referred to as "the Google administration".[24] The odd part is that when it comes to Google's own intellectual property, the double standard shines as clear as the sun: "Our patents, trademarks, trade secrets, copyrights and all of other intellectual property rights are important assets for us ... any significant impairment to our intellectual property rights could harm our business or our ability to compete."[25] World information is to be organized and made available to all for free, but of course there is one exception: Google itself. Google and Facebook's algorithms are among the best kept secrets in the world and have never been subject to successful hacker attacks.

It is untenable to claim that information should not only be free but also free of charge. Journalism and art are part of what challenges the powers that be every day, developing new experiences and knowledge, pushing boundaries. But today, content makers have seen a significant shrinkage in their opportunities to create new art and content and make a living on it. Their revenues have simply been channeled into the swelling money bins of the tech giants. Google tries to frame copyright legislation as a censorship machine that will suffocate freedom of speech, but that is simply wrong. On the contrary, the purpose of copyright legislation is to protect the rights of artists and other content creators on the Internet—and their continued opportunity to investigate the world and express themselves.

Since 2016, the EU Commission has been working on a new and disputed copyright legislation. At the core is an

---

[24] Pridham, D. "How Google Tries to Buy Government" *Forbes*. 07-19-17.

[25] Lanchester, J. "Googled: The End of the World as We Know It by Ken Auletta" *The Guardian*. 02-21-10.

attempt to modify the lucrative business model of the tech giants, which sneaks advertising sales into user-uploaded content like music, movies and books, not to mention allowing free access to original journalism content—in a certain sense providing it all without charge.

The proposal is controversial and its critics specifically focus on Article 11 and Article 13. The former grants news outlets copyright over the sharing of their content online and it is aimed at websites such as Google and Facebook, which use links to journalistic content as part of their business models. The proposal would require such websites to pay an amount for each link they post. Something critics claim is an effective "tax" on links. The latter article concerns websites such as YouTube and Instagram, which under the Safe Harbor provision have not been liable for the copyrighted material uploaded by their users. The users themselves are responsible. According to Article 13, the platforms would be responsible for the copyright infringement of the users unless they proactively prevent offending uploads. It is a call for content recognition systems or upload filters like Google's Content ID-system, which according Article 13 should be used to block copyrighted content such as images and videos that violate the rights of copyright holders.

However, the visions for copyright legislation has entered troubled waters. In July 2018, parliamentarians would cast their votes on the new and updated EU copyright directive—very similar to the one first proposed by the European Commission. But in the meantime, the directive was massively criticized. Particularly, Article 13 was dubbed nothing short of a censorship machine. Such rhetoric raised suspicions that the EU intended to undermine a free and open Internet. Seventy high-profile internet professionals, start-ups and tech companies got together to form a critical coalition and drafted an open letter asking European Parliament President Antonio Tajani to vote down the proposal. Among the activists opposing the proposal were Wikipedia founder Jimmy Wales, founder of the Internet Tim Berners-Lee, and net neutrality expert Tim Wu. In the letter, they said that "Article

13 takes an unprecedented step towards the transformation of the Internet from an open platform for sharing and innovation, into a tool for the automated surveillance and control of its users."[26] But this conclusion is too radical. The proposal from Parliament includes no *general* surveillance of uploads. Rather, it focuses on the right of authors and artists to have their works monitored.

There is real need for legislation that breaks with the unreasonable free rein given to the tech giants and the subsequent distortion of the market for art and journalism. There is no doubt that this is no easy task, and therefore it is important to listen to critical voices. In the open letter, the critical coalition sought more clarity and consistency in the proposal's attempt to define which tech platforms would have to comply with the provision and which could be exempted. First, they accused the law of hitting small- and medium-sized tech companies economically harder than the big ones, as the required automatic filtering technology would be both expensive and burdensome for the smaller players on the market. Second, the law would affect ordinary users who not only upload music and video, but also text, images and computer coding used in open collaboration on, for example, Wikipedia. Third, according to the coalition, the law would restrict freedom of expression and information because it would, in practice, have a much broader effect than what was intended, restricting how users share information.[27] These are all reasonable critical points and they must be taken into account in the ongoing work to modify the directive.

The mandate for the copyright directive in the European Parliament was voted down in July 2018—with 318 voters against and 278 in favour of the mandate. The European lawmakers did not vote *against* the proposal, but they wanted to have the opportunity to discuss more amendments and

---

[26] Cerf, V., Berners-Lee, T. m.fl. Open letter "Article 13 of the EU Copyright Directive Threatens the Internet". *Electronic Frontier Foundation.*

[27] Ibid.

details in plenary. When the proposal comes up for a final vote in early 2019, it is unlikely to lose.

The controversial proposal is not without its backers. In 2018, thirty thousand artists from all over Europe signed a statement of support for the EU proposal. French electronic music pioneer Jean-Michel Jarre, who was in charge of collecting signatures, said: "The biggest crime against freedom of expression would be to remove the artists' income—and thus their ability to create new art."[28]

[28] Lassen, A. "På med sølvpapirshatten - copyright-monstrene kommer!" *Jyllands-Posten.* 06-20-18.

Chapter 15
Distortion of the Public Sphere

In 2010, in an attempt to explore how technology promotes peace, Facebook launched a new feature 'Peace on Facebook': "Facebook is proud to play a part in promoting peace by building technology that helps people better understand each other. By enabling people from diverse backgrounds to easily connect and share their ideas, we can decrease world conflict in the short and long term."[1] Facebook keeps track of for instance how many "friendships" the company has helped create between people representing arch enemies such as Israel/Palestine, Pakistan/India and Ukraine/Russia under the headline "A World of Friends". All of them great stories. But Facebook speaks less loudly when it comes to the role of the company in the ethnic cleansing of the Rohingya minority in Myanmar. In 2014, Facebook moved into the country and within three years, the amount of users went from two to thirty million,[2] and since then Buddhist extremists have used the platform to spread misinformation, encouraging violent upheaval. In 2017, propaganda, threats and coordination via Facebook became a contributing factor in this extensive eth-

---

[1] Huffington Post "'Peace On Facebook' Tracks How Tech Promotes Peace" *Huffington Post*. 03-18-10.

[2] Ananny, op. cit.

F. Stjernfelt, A. M. Lauritzen, *Your Post has been Removed*,
https://doi.org/10.1007/978-3-030-25968-6_15

nic cleansing.[3] The fact that the conflict seems to have started with an Islamist massacre of Hindu villages in Rakhine state in August 2017,[4] does not exempt Facebook for parts of the blame for the following escalating violence. In August 2018, after the UN had pointed to Myanmar military leaders as responsible for genocide, Facebook finally chose to remove 20 accounts of individuals and organizations from Myanmar's top political management, among them General Min Aung Hlaing and the military television network *Myawady*—their Facebook pages were followed by as many as 12 million out of a total population of 53 million and had been used to encourage genocide. It was the first time Facebook banned political leaders from using the platform. The UN report criticized the role of Facebook as a useful instrument of the armed forces who incited the population to fight the Rohingya people. Facebook admitted that they had reacted too slowly.[5]

No one is claiming that Facebook is an evil company, planning to drive the world off a cliff. A more likely explanation of the tragic events can be found in the automated algorithm system and the business model of the giant. Despite the beautiful ideals, Facebook and the other giants are first and foremost ad brokers whose purpose it is to make money off of user attention. They have created a communication system where certain emotionally driven utterances are exposed while others are simply killed in the noise. It is a successful business strategy, but the side effect is disturbance of the public sphere. A contributing issue is that the spread of the business to new areas with new languages seems not to be associated with a corresponding linguistic training of the safety and security staff, skills which could more effectively

---

[3] Taub, A. & Fisher, M. "Where Countries Are Tinderboxes and Facebook Is a Match" *New York Times*. 04-21-18.

[4] Amnesty International "Myanmar: New evidence reveals Rohingya armed group massacred scores in Rakhine State" *Amnesty International.* 05-22-18.

[5] Bostrup, J. "Facebook blokerer Myanmars militære topledelse" *Politiken*. 08-28-18.

remove threats and coordinated campaigns of violence, rather than spending time on nipples and "hate speech" of a diffuse character.

Tech giants have created a public sphere with unlimited access to contributing to this sphere, at least in principle. Many people can communicate information and attitudes so that they become part of the common knowledge of societies. That was the ideal—verbalized in slogans like "a more open and connected world". But given the fact that the giants have almost reached monopoly power over user information flow, they have in their hands a very powerful tool to control and take advantage of precisely what becomes shared knowledge and what does not. It is a power that should be used with great care. The one who controls public space and the information in it can do good but also cause major harm. With information, or lack thereof, the character of the public sphere can even change. It makes it possible the amplification and dissemination of information phenomena such as information cascades and pluralistic ignorance.[6] The former arises from *too much* information. The user doubts the adequacy of his own information and turns to the other (presumably reasonable) users whom they trust and conclude that what the others do or feel must be the right thing to do or feel. The latter arises from *too little* information. It becomes legitimate for everyone to remain in the unknown as long as one observes that everyone else remains there as well. On these bases, it is possible to turn public opinion, create false agreement and make groups of consumers buy certain products—but also share political, social or religious views. Both individually and collectively, people can reproduce the mistakes of others and just jump on a train whose destination no one knows.

The public sphere of tech giants has become each individual user's very own customized public space. First and foremost, that space is characterized by conformism. The algorithms feed the users with content they like to read and

---

[6] Hendricks and Hansen (2011) p. 17.

share with others. But what is not to like about giving us what we like? The problem is that the algorithms serve the user text and video that confirm existing positions—or even existing attitudes in more extreme form, see below. At the same time, the algorithm calculation suppresses the opinions and positions that might challenge users. That is, content that could be instrumental in moving attitudes and providing insight into the views of other people and perhaps understanding them – in short, the classic role of the public domain as a meeting place in democracies, "the marketplace of ideas". But filter bubbles may develop, which tend to reinforce confirmation bias—believing in things that confirm already existing attitudes more so than things that go against them. After all, it is an easy thing to consume information which corresponds with one's own ideas and world view. However, it may be frustrating and difficult to consume information that challenges a person to think in new ways and question one's basic assumptions. In spite of Facebook's ideal to help connect people around the globe, the algorithms of the filter bubble are just not set to present the user to the diversity of ideas or people and new cultures.

Conformism has a tendency to flip over and turn into phenomena like polarization and radicalization. As professor of Law Cass Sunstein from Harvard University says: "When people find themselves in groups of like-minded types, they are especially likely to move to extremes."[7] Like-minded people can easily agree *too much*, because if not exposed to competing views and opinions, the views are more likely to becomes extreme—be they political, social, religious or cultural. On these terms, a discussion can streamline the attitudes of the entire group and that of the individual user into a more radical version than their initial point of view. In this polarization process, the algorithm does the user the dubious favor of making a thick preselection of the voices the individual users will likely listen to, the sources they will bother

[7] Sunstein (2009) p. 2.

reading and the people they feel like talking to. This form of information selection can become an actual echo chamber, where only persons already in agreement are let in. An echo chamber is a hospitable environment for various forms of bubble formation. Bubbles of opinion, politics or religion easily arise when a given matter is overheated and when substance or value are absent. Opinion bubbles can grow and trigger Twitter storms or hate campaigns on Facebook. The international media storm which hit the Copenhagen Zoo in 2014 is a good example. A lot of people had very strong opinions about Marius, a giraffe that had been put down, and "the Danish tormentors of animals". The media storm arose as a momentary storm of emotions, not considering the point that the zookeepers had to put Marius down in order to keep up the gene pool in the Copenhagen Zoo, since the genes of this particular giraffe were already well represented in European zoos. Of course, such effects do not violate freedom of expression in the sense of the right to express their point of view—but they are highly problematic when looking at the broader concept of freedom of information, especially since the bubbles are not noticed from the inside: you may not realize that alternative views are left out, and you also do not notice the filtering process itself.

With the algorithm behind YouTube's autoplay feature, the video service even has a tendency to speed up radicalization. By feeding users with gradually more extreme content, Google-owned YouTube increases the possibility that the user remains glued to the screen. Sociologist Zeynep Tufekci experimented with YouTube during the 2016 US presidential elections. She found out that no matter what content she was looking for, the recommended videos were always a bit more extreme and titillating than the previous ones. Jogging became ultra marathon, vegetarianism became veganism, and even more interestingly: Trump videos were followed by rants and svadas from supporters of white supremacy, Holocaust denial, and other content from the extreme right. On the other hand, videos of Hillary Clinton and Bernie Sanders would prompt extreme leftist conspiracy theories, such as accusations that 9/11 was orchestrated by the US Government. Tufekci illustrated this by an analogy of fat and sugar, making YouTube a happy junk food restaurant: "In effect, YouTube has created a restaurant that serves us increasingly sugary, fatty foods, loading up our plates as soon as we are finished with the last meal. Over time, our tastes adjust, and we seek even more sugary, fatty foods, which the restaurant dutifully provides. When confronted about this by health department and concerned citizens, the restaurant managers reply that they are merely serving us what we want."[8]

In addition to reshaping the framework of the public domain, tech giants also influence the way users interact. Users are rewarded for the expressions that engage the most. This happens because it gives them a dopamine hit every time they get likes, comments, shares, retweets, etc. You can say that tech giants *train* the user to cultivate a behavior that seeks confirmation. When, at the same time, the algorithms favor elementary activity-mobilizing emotions (anger, fear, awe and fascination), the consequence may be that the users get an intoxicating shot of energy from attacking the opponent, be it the other group, the other political party, or the other religion. The giants exploit the right of the users to express themselves by luring or downright manipulating the user to express negative feelings in anticipation of more social gain. A tempting hypothesis is that "conflicts and divisive material about everything from political views to religious beliefs to social inequalities have greater social transmission than consensus."[9] Conflict can be thought to—perhaps unintentionally—have become one of the main ingredients of the algorithmic laws of tech giants, cf. the Girard-Thiel hypothesis above.

The problem with the public sphere of the giants is that there is a dismal backside to their version of it. Conformism, radicalization and polarization are by no means new phe-

---

[8] Tufecki, Z. "YouTube, the Great Radicalizer". *New York Times*. 03-10-18.

[9] Hendricks, V. (2016) p. 153.

nomena, and divisive material has always gained attention. But this cocktail, plus the speed and global scope enabled by these technologies, inadvertently risk amplifying disruptive and in some cases downright dangerous tendencies in societies in different parts of the globe. Western countries are seeing increased political correctness, which has turned into a digital culture war between an aggressive identity political discourse on the one hand and extreme right-wing groups on the other; in developing countries there are disturbing examples of threats, incitement to violence and coordination between activists which turn into lynching in the streets; they are polarization processes with one thing in common – they all originate from Facebook.

In Western countries, the disturbance of public space is manifested in an online cultural war, where extreme right-wing movements battle against the front-line fighters of aggressive identity politics—and both parties are radicalized and made more simple-minded in the process. One of the first big clashes between the two sides was the controversy known as "Gamergate" in 2014, where attention was drawn to sexism and misogyny in the American gaming industry.[10] Feminist video game critic Anita Sarkeesian became the object of extensive hate campaign when she uploaded videos on YouTube where she introduced viewers to basic ideas within feminist media critique. She had a critical view on how video games depicted women. We are used to think that societies with free speech can discuss criticism of a classic work of art for being sexist without necessarily doubting its aesthetic or other value, and one can easily disagree with the quality of it without moving on threats of rape and death. But Sarkeesian would have to endure several years of not just harsh attacks, but also outright personal threats for this intolerable "crime". She was met with comments like "I'll rape you and put your head on a stick", vandalism of her Wikipedia page with pornographic images, threats, and a campaign to flag her social media accounts for spam, fraud and even for terrorism. These

[10] Nagle (2017) p. 19–24.

were serious attempts to ruin her career and reputation—including criminal acts such as harassment, slander and threats.

Meanwhile, fairly unknown video game developer Zoe Quinn released the game "Depression Quest", which was an ideological project to take video games in a more feminist direction. This would turn out to be the straw that broke the camel's back within the gamer community. Also Quinn was subjected to death and rape threats; she was hacked, her personal information was published and she was the victim of revenge porn. In the wake of this, attacks were directed at other feminist gamers and video game critics who dared entering the war zone. Journalists defended these feminists through articles on how the game culture had become a toxic community for misogynist men. The reaction from anonymous voices in the online world was even more vandalism and trolling. Everyone blamed each other for lying and having malicious intentions. #Gamergate was born and lines of battle were drawn. The controversy will be remembered as a turbulent culture war feeding on not only strong passions but also harassment and personal threats, which are criminalized in the legislations of most countries.

Writer and journalist Angela Nagle has examined this digital culture war, where two parties fight over anything from feminism to sexuality, gender identity, racism, freedom of speech and political correctness. According to her analysis, the conflict can be traced back to a discussion about the discourse on Facebook. The Alt-right, which in the United States is the umbrella term for the new extreme right of the 2010s, has developed by using old left-wing strategies like transgression, provocation, satire, and abysmal irony. Their behavior is a reaction to what they see as a politically correct finger constantly wagging on the social media. Former *Breitbart* editor and Alt-rights leader figure Milo Yiannopoulos has expressed it in this way: "The Alt-right for me is primarily a cultural reaction to the nannying and language policing and authoritarianism of the progressive left—the stranglehold that it has on culture. It is primarily—like Trump is and like I am—a reaction against the progressive left doing today what the religious right was doing in the 1990s—which is trying to police what can be thought and said, how opinions can be expressed."[11] In other words, some feel left out of the ranks. No one has to agree to the bizarre political ideas of the Alt-right in order to understand why they may be annoyed with the choking political correctness of their opponents. The limit of tolerance goes exactly where it glimpses intolerance.

The fraction of the left-wing concerned with identity politics is increasingly an anti-free speech, anti-free thinking and anti-intellectual online movement obsessed with policing speech. It is an emotional culture that aims to witness and expose the sufferings of oneself and others. Initially, the movement roamed on niche platform Tumblr, where floating genders and identities were broadly embraced. Over time, however, the movement has gained hold of the mainstream and now dominates parts of social media discourse. For example, in 2014, users could choose between 50 different genders on their Facebook profile.[12] It has even spread into "the real world" with Hillary Clinton assuming catchphrases from identity politics, for instance 'check your privileges' and 'intersectionality', as part of her presidential campaign. Particularly in American universities we have witnessed the emergence of a range of now well-established political demands and concepts going against free speech; *safe spaces* as in safe zones where women or African-Americans or other identities can meet screened off from groups and statements whom they prefer to avoid; *trigger warnings* which are clear expression of caution which the teacher is responsible for giving if a work of literature contains words or paragraphs with potentially offensive content, for instance violence, rape, dis-

[11] Nagle (2017) p. 65.

[12] Associated Press in Menlo Park, California "Facebook expands gender options: transgender activists hail 'big advance'" *The Guardian*. 02-14-14.

crimination, or particular offensive words; *no platform* which is a slogan used to prevent certain invited speakers from making their voices heard—by way of social media storms, harassment and pressure on university management; *cultural appropriation* which refers to majority persons who borrow or "steal" elements from another culture, and who are therefore accused of not respecting that other culture. A curious example of the latter was the public shaming that hit Caucasian pop star Justin Bieber when he got dreadlocks. These activities take place not only online but on campuses as well, in the classrooms and auditoriums—but the suppression of freedom of expression in these physical spaces is closely tied to social media storms organized online aimed at gathering loud masses who can interrupt and harass unwanted speakers or put pressure on weak university management to cave in to demands of censorship.

Rather than embracing diversity or hybrid identities, identity politics has developed an extreme worship of group affiliations. The battle is fought through words, and the goal is to achieve silence rather than agreement or disagreement. Nagle unfolds it this way: "They tried to move the culture in the opposite direction by restricting speech on the right but expanding the Overton window on the left when it came to issues of race and gender, making increasingly anti-male, anti-white, anti-straight, anti-cis rhetoric normal on the cultural left. The liberal online culture typified by Tumblr was equally successful in pushing fringe ideas into the mainstream. It was ultra-sensitive in contrast to the shooting irreverence of chan culture, but equally subcultural and radical."[13]

Policing the web from the perspective of identity politics has as a consequence that Facebook and Twitter hesitate to accommodate right-wing warriors from the Alt-right. Instead, the extreme right has absconded to anonymous niche platforms such as *4chan* and *8chan*, where they can freely practice their cynicism, nihilism, misogyny and fight for men's rights, white identity and the right to rebellion. The Alt-right has not

[13] Nagle (2017) p. 68.

lost its power in this process, quite the contrary. It has grown larger in isolation because its devotees know how easily digestible humor and content, when combined with explosive comments and debate threads can leverage broad and active communities. With Trump's election victory, they even felt represented in the White House by people like Steve Bannon. There are several examples reminiscent of Gamergate, where right-wing extremists hit back hard; where inhumane rhetoric turns into actual threats and violence. In 2015, a US student wrote on 4chan that the users of the site should stay home from school the following day, when that self-same student ended up committing a school shooting in Oregon.[14] The clash between the Alt-right and the cultural left has turned into a bitter and overheated cultural war with no peace dialog in sight. Each of these groups find themselves in each their own extreme bubble of opinion, where some matters overheat so much that they trigger media shitstorms, threats, shaming and slander campaigns.

Gamergate also helped make it clear that there is a big difference between the inaccurate concept of "hate speech" concerning pejoratives directed at certain groups—and actual persecution and harassment of individuals where groups single out an individual victim (cf. Girard's scapegoat), using techniques such as shifting accounts, coordinated networks on other platforms, systematic abuse of the flagging option, *doxxing* (revealing people's private addresses and other private data as a way of encouraging persecution and violence against them), sending private and compromising information to friends and colleagues, hacking and taking over the person's Internet accounts and *swatting* (calling the victim's address to the police based on invented reports)[15]—a list that includes criminal acts such as stalking, threats and harassment. Here, the tech giants ought to play a more active role in the criminal persecution of such acts, by helping identify the individuals responsible for the coordinated pursuits.

---

[14] Nagle (2017) p. 26.

[15] Cf. Gillespie (2018), p. 56f.

The consequence of Gamergate was that a number of tech giants made their removal procedures even stricter. During the online war, particularly Twitter had gained reputation as a place where hateful voices would gather and at an internal meeting in February 2015, CEO Dick Costolo came to a tough conclusion: "We suck at dealing with abuse and trolls on the platform and we've sucked at it for years. It's no secret and the rest of the world talks about it every day. ... We're going to start kicking these people off right and left and making sure that when they issue their ridiculous attacks, nobody hears them."[16] Hardly a cure without side effects for free speech on the platform.

In Gamergate, Facebook did not live up to its ideal of contributing to human understanding between people—quite the contrary. The digital culture war is a consequence of the polarization tendencies brought on by the automatic algorithm system of the technology giants. It reinforces a universal tendency towards tribalism. Groups dividing the world into "us" and "them" occur naturally, also outside of the Internet, but they are easily reinforced if Internet users are always floating in a stream of information which confirms already existing attitudes only. It is difficult to say why the public opinion on Twitter and Facebook has fluctuated so heavily towards identity politics. It is also difficult to tell whether Facebook has unintentionally picked sides in the conflict by prioritizing the "tone of debate" over freedom of expression in their community standards and in their responses to users flagging questionable content. But preferring peace and quiet over agreement and disagreement in the public sphere has its serious consequences. In her many years as president of the American Civil Liberties Union, Professor of Law Nadine Strossen has argued that free speech is the only cure against hateful utterances, and that prohibition and restrictions will only make thing worse. For years, when argu-

[16]This statement was leaked to *The Verge*, here quoted from Gillespie (2018) p. 24.

ing time and again with censorship-happy right wingers, she had to plead against censorship, but in more recent years she has had to argue also against her old comrades-in-arms on the left, who are leaning ever more towards censoring opinions they do not like, cf. Strossen's book *Hate: Why We Should Resist It with Free Speech, Not Censorship* (2018).

However, such Western problems with extremization pale in comparison with the growing amount of urgent cases seen in developing countries. Facebook's fast expansion in places like Indonesia, India, Mexico, Myanmar and Sri Lanka has resulted in some of the most frightening examples of serious, Internet-based social unrest. In those places, many people's access to the Internet goes through Facebook, oftentimes they may even consider Facebook as the very Internet itself. Emotional feelings run free on the platform because the institutions in some of those countries are weak and credible sources are few and far between. This means that content shared between friends, family and people of trust may easily become "common knowledge". When this is combined with people not relying on police and courts, panic originating from misinformation and calls for violence on Facebook may lead to violent riots and lynchings, because users take justice in their own hands. That recently happened in Sri Lanka. Facebook's inborn preference for negative feelings helped escalate the conflict between Buddhists and Muslims, because mutual hatred and threats frequently and freely dominated the flow of news on Facebook, which is now the Sri Lankans' primary source of news and information. The Muslims form a 10% minority on the island, speak predominantly Tamil, and many of them are immigrants.

In April 2018, *New York Times* ran the story. At the center of the storm was 28-year-old Muslim restaurant employee Farsith, who became the innocent victim of a seriously violent chain of event caused by a rumor gone viral on Facebook. According to rumors, the police had confiscated 23.000 sterilization pills from a Muslim pharmacist in the town of Ampara. For a while rumors had circulated of a

Muslim plot to sterilize and wipe out the Sinhalese majority in Sri Lanka. One day, when a Sinhalese restaurant guest yelled out that he had found a lump of something white in his food, everything went wrong. The customer furiously gathered a crowd around Farsith and accused him of having put sterilization medicine in the food. Farsith was unaware of the viral rumor and hesitantly commented, in his inadequate Sinhalese, something along the lines of: "Yes, we put?" Farsith thought they were yelling about the small lump of flour he could see in the dish. The crowd took his muttering as a confession of his crime, beat him up, terrorized the restaurant and burned down the local mosque. The story did not end there, because while the assault unfolded, Farsith's "confession" was recorded on a mobile phone, uploaded and quickly gained viral life. The 18 seconds video was uploaded to a popular Buddhist Facebook group as "proof" of the Muslim plot. With hasty shares, likes and comments, the video went viral and generated comments like "Kill all Muslims, don't even spare infants". Unintentionally, Facebook's algorithm system transformed Farsith into a nationwide villain. This tragic affair ruined his business, put his family in debt and nearly cost him his life.[17]

How could things turn out as badly as in the case of Farsith? Presumably because conflicts have higher social transmission than consensus—the algorithmic law. Because users move around inside an echo chamber which amplifies and radicalizes already existing positions—polarization. And because, as a group, we can easily end up following a norm (in this case extreme hate towards Muslims), which each of the members of the group might not individually dislike, but which they nevertheless end up persecuting because they mistakenly believe, that the everyone else in the group do the same—pluralistic ignorance. Because even if we personally believe otherwise, the mere fact that many others seem to believe the opposite (judging by the countless likes, shares

---

[17]Taub, A. & Fisher, M. "Where Countries Are Tinderboxes and Facebook Is a Match" *New York Times*. 04-21-18.

and comments a particular video has generated) makes us suppress what we actually used to believe—information cascades. There is a particular mean irony to the fact that these effects seem enhanced by the new policy introduced by Facebook during the winter of 2017–18, as a response to the whole debate on "fake news" online. A new calibration of the news feed was introduced: communication between "friends" was now prioritized, while news stories driven by the media were deranked—allegedly in order to emphasize the ideal of "connecting people" and build local communities rather than serve as the source of news of shifting quality. In Sri Lanka, however, the effect of this was that local rumors of evil Muslims circulated intensively within circles of "friends" who intended to surpass each other's news feed turning it into a self-reinforcing loop—while serious news that might have given an external and perhaps more objective perspective on the events now became deprioritized in their news feeds. It shows how Facebook's sentimental understanding of contacts as "friends" does not necessarily bring global friendliness with it, but can easily gloss over malicious, even conspiratorial groups of people. Given cases such as these, one might well dream that Facebook's increasing monitoring departments would focus their forces on serious and criminal cases, such as the spectrum ranging from personal injuries to harassment, threats, persecution of individuals, to terrorist plots or coordinated violence—rather than increasingly policing their platform with the large and vague catalog of taboos applied to everything from nudity and sex to diffuse "hate speech" and unspecified violations, to euthanasia and violent images, and to quotes, satire, irony and a wide range of other non-criminal content which is subject to wagging index fingers, moralism, removal and sanctions.

Maybe Facebook is slowly taking its first steps in this direction. In July 2018, WhatsApp launched an experiment featuring a limit on the number of "chats" a user could participate in on the messaging service—after discovering how groups in India had knowingly spread misinformation on the service by political agents acting in 10–20 interwoven chat-groups. At the same time, Facebook announced the removal of content from the site if it is deemed on the brink of turning into violence: "There are certain forms of misinformation that have contributed to physical harm, and we are making a policy change which will enable us to take that type of content down," a Facebook spokesperson said.[18] It is certainly a step forward if—contrary to unspecified "hate speech"—the focus is on content that actually calls for imminent violence. Then we may slowly approach the American judicial system's standard interpretation of the limits to freedom of expression as "incitement to imminent lawless action". This might have been discovered much earlier, if lawyers, intellectual historians, or sociologists had been asked, instead of believing that the tech environment itself holds the answer to everything. But how to *identify* such content remains problematic in the new initiative: "To help figure out when misinformation has tipped from "just plain wrong" to "wrong and possibly contributive to violence", Facebook will partner with local civil society groups that might better understand the specific cultural context."[19] Facebook's naive belief in the good of local, cultural "communities" may become a danger. There is no information on which groups in India, Sri Lanka and Myanmar Facebook wishes to confide in, but local communities may often be part of the problem rather than the solution. Many such local groups might have widely different opinions and have their own agendas; far from all of them are necessarily democratic, and some of them may even be active parts of the conflict. Doubtlessly, publishing the names of such collaboration groups could put them in danger—but *not* doing so will contribute to even more to the opaqueness of Facebook's removal policy and will promote local rumor formation, plot speculation and conflict. Obviously, on-site notifiers need to be locally connected, but it seems important to construct a

[18] Quot. from E. Dreyfuss "Facebook's Fight Againt Fake News Keeps Raising Questions" *Wired.* 07-20-18.

[19] Ibid.

procedure for selecting such helpers, to make sure they have some level of skill, neutrality and some knowledge of universal rights, e.g. from local media or human rights organizations. Or else, basing removal policy on the preferences of local cultural groups may turn out to be yet another mistake in Facebook's "annus horribilis" which seem to go from singular to plural.

Chapter 16
Trust Busting the Tech Giants?

In light of the many problems caused by the tech giants' somewhat opaque transformation of the public sphere, it is quite necessary to ask the question of how they can be brought to show greater accountability when it comes to the public sphere. It is not just a matter of pushing a few buttons—there are elementary structural defects to the very setup. There are two ways to change this: the coercive or the voluntary. The first is often discussed in terms of the increasingly monopolistic behavior of the giants. We have already touched upon their dominant role in the market. The present situation is a far cry from the anarchist—or free-market liberalist—Internet of the 1990s, with its diversity of users and small companies all competing with each other. The dot-com bubble burst around the turn of the millennium and wiped out many of the small firms, helping to usher in the next phase, the 2000s. Here, a few companies gradually gained control of the market, only to become the world's richest during the 2010s. Scrooge McDuck's amazing career from shoeshine boy to the richest duck in the world has long been replaced by the story of Mark the Nerd who founded Facebook in his college dorm room in 2004, and long before turning 30 became one of the world's most wealthy and powerful people. Facebook and Google are approaching a duopoly in the online advertising market based on non-paying

F. Stjernfelt, A. M. Lauritzen, *Your Post has been Removed*,
https://doi.org/10.1007/978-3-030-25968-6_16

users, with Microsoft and Apple bordering on duopoly in the field of software, and finally Amazon with its near-monopoly on Internet trade. The latter is less central to freedom of expression, but still includes a relevant dimension, as the size and market dominance of Amazon has made the company's bookstore capable of putting unprecedented pressure on its suppliers—the publishing companies. The story of Jeff Bezos is well known, how he saw the enormous possibilities of Internet trading and decided to start from one corner: books. It was an industry of durable, easily transportable goods with a distribution network then dominated by small local players. It turned out to be the perfect place to launch a disruption of trade patterns through e-commerce. Amazon grew explosively and managed in but a few years to establish itself as a key player in the sales and distribution of books in many countries. Among the secrets to the company's success was placing its headquarters in Seattle, in sparsely populated and remote Washington State, which meant that mail order buyers outside of the state could avoid taxes, allowing Amazon to undercut the prices of local bookstores. In the longer run, Amazon's strength allowed the company to put pressure on the pricing policies of publishing companies.

This became clear in the case of Amazon's dispute with large French publishing group Hachette, which also owns a number of American publishing houses. In April 2014, the contract between the two was set for renewal negotiations when Amazon came up with a new demand: Hachette was to reduce the price of most of its e-books to 9.99 USD. Hachette refused—and, as a counterstrike, Amazon made it more difficult to purchase Hachette's books through its website.[1] The books could no longer be pre-ordered on Amazon, and if a buyer managed to order a Hachette book, the delivery time

---

[1]This does not, however, make Hachette a persecuted company, free of any guilt. In 2012, the US Department of Justice filed an antitrust case against Hachette and Apple, accusing the two companies of having made clandestine deals to keep e-book prices artificially high. Hachette concluded a settlement while Apple took the case which it ended up losing.

was extended to several weeks. Hachette is a major player with revenue of around 10 billion USD, making it one of the five largest publishing groups in the US—but still a dwarf as compared to Amazon's turnover in the trillions. Amazon's blackmail tactics gave rise to a protest by 900 authors, led by Malcolm Gladwell and Philip Roth who claimed that Amazon deliberately hurt both Hachette and the authors' own opportunity for income and freedom of expression. At a price of 9.99 USD, Amazon not only deflated the price of books, but indirectly manifested the company's perception of the value of books—the cost of producing a book is based exclusively on print, inventory and shipping and not on the intellectual capital, creativity and years of work going into it. The authors called for Amazon to be reported to the US Department of Justice in order to file an antitrust suit.

Clearly Amazon could only get away with its pressure policy because the company has a quasi-monopoly in the field of online book sales. As things had evolved, Hachette was in no position to simply turn away and look for another distributor. In June, Amazon wrote to a handful of selected Hachette authors and offered them 100% payments for the duration of the lawsuit—arguing publicly that publishers like Hachette should simply cease to exist entirely now that people could go ahead and publish their books online. The outcome of the conflict was a compromise: Hachette retained the right to price its own products, but a number of strong incentives to put promotional offers up on Amazon were imposed on them. Over the duration of the suit, Hachette's revenue fell by 18.5% against the previous year—illustrating the power of a company like Amazon, which controls more than half of US book sales. The case against Hachette is not the only one in which Amazon has used special methods towards its suppliers, and one might fear that Amazon, with its extraordinary economic muscle, is slowly gaining control over which books can be published and at what price—a situation with obvious problems for freedom of speech. Today, Amazon itself is already the largest publisher of books in the US, primarily of popular fiction, and is currently in the process of establishing itself in neighboring industries, as a producer of television shows, etc. Is it a good thing that the same monopoly company not only sells and distributes content, but produces it as well? Publishers today already have no alternatives to Amazon—could the next step be authors who have no real alternative channels of publishing and distribution?

The role and position of Amazon are easily to understand—it is the world's largest retailer. But how should companies like Google and Facebook be categorized? On some occasions Facebook calls itself a neutral "platform for all ideas", on others a "community" based on certain values. Others have called it a "means of communication" or a "social network", and still others have used the words "media" or a "social media", while others claim it is a piece of infrastructure—a "public utility". This battle for categorization is by no means a simple matter of semantics—it is crucial to how we can imagine a solution to the problems of tech giants discussed in this book. As stated by Senior Editor of *New York Magazine*, Max Read, there is real difficulty in describing what kind of social, cultural and economic phenomenon Facebook really is: "Over the past year I've heard Facebook compared to a dozen entities and felt like I've caught glimpses of it acting like a dozen more. I've heard government metaphors (a state, the E.U., the Catholic Church, Star Trek's United Federation of Planets) and business ones (a railroad company, a mall); physical metaphors (a town square, an interstate highway, an electrical grid) and economic ones (a Special Economic Zone, Gosplan). For every direct comparison, there was an equally elaborate one: a faceless Elder God. A conquering alien fleet. There are real consequences to our inability to understand what Facebook is."[2] Zuckerberg's May 2017 "listening tour" to all US states was reminiscent of a visit from the Pope, and led to speculation as to whether he was preparing to run for President.

Nevertheless, a categorization must take into consideration the company's monopoly-like status. In the spring of

---

[2] Read, op.cit.

2018, at the hearings in the US Congress and the European Parliament, Zuckerberg waved off critical questions about Facebook's alleged monopoly status. He claimed that the average American communicates through eight different apps—but at the same time, he was unable to name a single competitor who offered services to the user similar to those of Facebook. Zuckerberg's argument is misleading—it is a bit like if the owner of all the roads in a country were asked if he had a monopoly and the owner replied: *Everyone is moving in at least eight ways—they crawl, walk, run, ride a bike, fly, drive a car, ride the bus and ride the train.* Needless to say, Zuckerberg's contention aligns badly with his own explicitly stated ambitions on the company's behalf: to form a global community.

A growing number of observers find that market dominance of the tech giants must be fought through antitrust legislation. In a US context, antitrust legislation dates back to the decades around 1900, when many trusts had sprung up within a number of industries. Many companies from the same industry branches had joined forces, been bought up or entered into agreements, especially on price regulation. Theodore Roosevelt (US President 1901–09) stands out as the strongest anti-trust fighter. As early as 1890, the Sherman Antitrust Act was adopted, and in 1898 Roosevelt's predecessor William McKinley founded the *U.S. Industrial Commission on Trusts*, which then summoned Andrew Carnegie, John D. Rockefeller, and Charles M. Schwab to a hearing. In 1902, Roosevelt challenged railroad company Northern Securities, led by business tycoons such as J.P. Morgan and James J. Hill. The case went all the way to the Supreme Court, which in 1904 ordered Northern Securities split up into smaller companies. More than forty trusts were dissolved during the Roosevelt era. The trust-busting campaign peaked under Roosevelt's successor William H. Taft, who broke more than ninety monopolies in his Presidential term in the years around 1910. In the presidential election of 1912, trustbusting was the central theme, and Taft, who at the time had now developed a plan for state leadership of commerce and production, lost the election to Woodrow Wilson who ran on an anti-trust agenda informed by anti-trust lawyer Louis Brandeis as his advisor.[3]

One of the most famous cases was the one filed against Standard Oil, the dominant oil company of the times, owned by four families and headed by John D. Rockefeller. As early as 1890, it controlled 88% of the oil trade. In 1906, an antitrust suit was brought against Standard Oil, and it was sentenced to split up into 34 locally-rooted companies, among them later giants Mobil, Chevron and Exxon. The US Supreme Court approved the split-up in 1911. From 1916, Louis Brandeis sat on the Supreme Court, and along with Oliver Wendell Holmes he became famous for a radical interpretation of the First Amendment: that freedom of expression should be curbed by the State only in cases where a concrete situation presented a "clear and present danger". But Brandeis was also a fierce advocate of antitrust legislation, deriving from James Madison's view that power concentrations in a market were not only an economic but also a democratic and political issue: citizens should be able to control the political power of large privately-owned operators.

Brandeis' activist anti-monopoly position on the Supreme Court was later filled by Thurman Arnold, who led F.D. Roosevelt's anti-monopoly campaign around World War II. Arnold, however, increasingly endorsed efficiency-based arguments, i.e., that competition ensured a level of efficiency lost in monopoly formation. With his focus on efficiency and price formation, Arnold weakened public interest in the political role of monopolies. The legacy of Brandeis, however, was definitively broken in the 1970s and 1980s, by economists of the Chicago school, led by Richard Posner and influential Yale economist Robert Bork. In his landmark book *The Antitrust Paradox* from 1978, Bork argued that often consumers actually *benefit* from company mergers, as they can lead to better and cheaper goods, making antitrust legislation appear economically irrational in many cases. Therefore,

---

[3]Wu (2018) p. 76.

Bork's argument was that antitrust decisions should only consider the matter economically, that is, from the point of view of the consumer and of price formation—and not from the point of view of ensuring competition, preventing power concentration, securing democratic control, etc. This attitude gradually became dominant in the US Supreme Court and would turn out to play an important part in the deregulation of the economy from the 1980s and on.

In the wake of the emergence of tech giants, today a new movement of "neo-Brandeisians" is growing—a movement which argues for the resumption of antitrust legislation with a broader legal base.[4] Advocates are also called "hipster anti-trusters" and include people like Lina Kahn, Tad Lipsky, Tim Wu, and Barry Lynn.[5] This position is gaining support in parts of the Democratic Party, for instance by Senator and attorney Elizabeth Warren, who is calling for action against monopolies: "In many ways, tech monopolies are similar to the oil and sugar and railroad trusts of the 19th century. And antitrust enforcers have the tools to stop tech companies from engaging in practices that choke off competition, but only if they use them. But there's one key difference between the 19th-century trusts and today's tech companies, and that's data. Companies today gather more data on everything from where we work to where we shop, to our political views, to what we eat for breakfast. There's this belief, when it comes to tech companies, that when people don't pay up front, there's no antitrust concern. But that's a myth. Data is power. And data allows companies to push tailored advertisements to both shape and drive our preferences, and ultimately to benefit the corporation's bottom line. That's why it's critically important that antitrust enforcers focus on the ways data can be used to undermine competition."[6]

---

[4] Cf. Khan (2018).

[5] The nickname was invented by one of their opponents, Konstantin Medvedovsky 2018, "Hipster Antitrust—a Brief Fling or Something More?" *Competition Policy International*. 04-17-18.

[6] Quoted from Zornick, G. "Elizabeth Warren's 'Big Fight' Against Monopolies" *The Nation*. 02-15-18.

However, there are also many Republicans who see the danger—not least because of signs of indirect support of the tech giants for the Democrats. An example is Republican political campaign strategist Eric Wilson, who speaks on behalf of monopoly regulation of the companies due to his own experience with Facebook's acceptance of political ads based on "fake news": "Regulation should include limits on the information Facebook may gather on its users and subsequently sell to advertisers, greater oversight and transparency related to its compliance with federal election laws and more cooperation with researchers about the adverse effects of its various platforms on individuals and communities. More broadly, the government should begin looking into breaking Facebook into smaller entities to allow for greater competition and more consumer-friendly practices in the online advertising, publishing and communications spaces."[7]

A strong political voice realizing the manifold problems with the tech giants is Senator Mark R. Warner (D) whose white paper "Potential Policy Proposals for Regulation of Social Media and Technology Firms" appeared in July 2018. Here, Warner advocates a number of policies for regulating the excesses of tech giants. He sets out with emphasizing the monopoly problem: :"[...] the rise of a few dominant platforms poses key problems for long-term competition and innovation across multiple markets, including digital advertising markets (which support much of the internet economy), future markets driven by machine-learning and artificial intelligence, and communications technology markets."[8] Warner's detailed list of proposals include a GDPR-like law in order to protect the privacy of users; making tech algorithms more transparent and accessible to government audit; demanding data portability between platforms; making tech firms liable for defamation referring to existing state tort laws; requiring that automatized activity like bots is explicitly

[7]Wilson (2018).

[8]Warner, M. R. "Potential Policy Proposals for Regulation of Social Media and Technology Firms" Whitepaper, *Axios*. 07-30-18.

labeled as such; the development of educational and public policies to build media literacy among users.

It is hardly surprising that dominant Silicon Valley figures like Peter Thiel—Facebook's first major investor and still an executive board member—run counter to such views by stating that monopolies actually deserve their position in the market. By this line of argument, a monopoly is the logical result of their victory in the competitive game, a competition which is then rendered unnecessary. Thiel is a radical libertarian and by definition he considers states—even democracies—as the enemy: "I no longer believe that freedom and democracy are compatible."[9] Monopolies are, however, the very thing that allows him to create a free world protected against taxation and state intervention. By contrast, Thiel speaks directly against competition between suppliers of the same type of product, as it will only eat away profits.[10] His line of thought makes it clear that devotion to the free market is no longer the same as devotion to free competition.

A leading figure of the neo-Brandesian movement is Barry Lynn from the Open Market program at the think tank New America. After supporting antitrust legislation against the tech giants, he was fired in August 2017, shortly after the EU fined Google. According to the *New York Times,* the reason behind the firing was that Google was among the sponsors of New America, and Google CEO Eric Schmidt seems to have personally demanded Lynn's departure. President and CEO of New America Anne-Marie Slaughter shut down the entire Open Market program and emailed Lynn that the decision was "in no way based on the content of your work" but at the same time accused Lynn of "imperiling the institution as a whole".[11] The wealth of the tech giants enables them to support a very large number of think tanks, NGOs and civil

---

[9] Thiel, P. "The Education of a Libertarian" *Cato Unbound*. 04-13-18.

[10] Thiel (2014) p. 35ff.

[11] Vogel, K.P. "Google Critic Ousted from Think Tank Funded by the Tech Giant" *New York Times*. 08-30-17.

society organizations of many different political orientations—not to mention both major political parties, of course. They carry out this support based on the assurance that it will make them influential regardless of the outcome of the next elections. In this light, it is no encouragement to free speech that giant power may be used to get rid of critics representing nominally independent think tanks, which are co-sponsored by giants. One might ask: could a classic high-quality medium with a long tradition of serious investigative journalism, such as *Washington Post*, now really show critical interest in the monopoly behaviors of tech giants? Since 2013, *The Post* has been owned by Amazon CEO Jeff Bezos. An uncanny parallel is Facebook's removal of ads by Elizabeth Warren calling for Facebook break-up in March 2019. Warren said, in an ad, "Three companies have vast power over our economy and our democracy. Facebook, Amazon, and Google. We all use them. But in their rise to power, they've bulldozed competition, used our private information for profit, and tilted the playing field in their favor."[12] After public outrage, a Facebook spokesperson explained that they removed Warren's ads because they violated their policies of corporate logos. They later restored the ads.

But there are important parallels between the strong antitrust legislation in the US during large parts of the 20th century and the increasing problems with the tech giants. They have not yet been seriously subject to antitrust scrutiny, possibly due to the misunderstanding that because users get the service for free, there is nothing to get at—echoing Bork's perspective on the perspective of consumer prices. However, this ignores that in the tech giant setup, the consumer is *not* the user; rather, the paying advertisers are. The prices they negotiate when dealing with tech giants are hardly exposed to free competition, judging by the way things are now.

We have already described how the railway monopoly was trust-busted—a related case concerns freight transport by

[12] Lima, C. "Facebook backtracks after removing Warren ads calling for Facebook breakup" *Politico.* 03-11-19.

rail. It is obvious that a railway owner who also owns production companies could be inclined to give priority to transport of its own products in the freight wagons. Antitrust legislation prohibited this by adopting a principle of neutrality, so that goods must be shipped in the order they arrive, treating all customers equally and charging the same prices for the same services. This is often called a ban against "vertical integration"—that is, against allowing companies to integrate the production of goods with higher-level distribution and processing of said goods. The ban serves to block the option of giving priority to one's own products over the competitor's. The first major monopoly case in the Internet age, against Microsoft in the 1990s, in fact had exactly that characteristic. The argument was that the company combined its Windows operating system with its own browser, Internet Explorer, so customers were not free to use the browser software they wanted. It was considered so-called illegal "tie-in" in which the buyer of a product was forced to also buy another product, thus excluding other browser developers such as then-popular Netscape, from access to consumers. Microsoft claimed that the browser was not an independent product but an independent "feature" inside the operating system. In 1999, the Department of Justice won the case, obliging Microsoft to split up into two companies. In 2002, however, appeals by Microsoft led to a settlement which held that making all "tie-ins" illegal would hamper technological advances. On the other hand, the settlement obliged Microsoft to share with competitors key components of its software code, and set up a committee to make sure it happened. In the US, this was the last major antitrust case, and during the presidency of George W. Bush, not a single trust was broken. Thus, the actual gilded age of tech giants occurs in a legal vacuum where the US government seems to have forgotten its century-long antitrust legacy.

The EU, however, continues along the antitrust lines which Europe originally learned from the US. Of a similar nature as the Microsoft case is the EU Commission's recent case against Google. It made the accusation that, when users searched for a given product, Google prioritized its own price comparison feature for shopping over that of competing services. In August 2017, the EU, led by Commissioner Margrethe Vestager, fined Google 2.7 billion USD for competition abuse. A January 2017 survey by *Wall Street Journal* showed that 91% of searches on Google resulted in ads for one of Google's own products at the top of the rankings.[13] Currently, the EU Commission has ongoing cases against both Google and Apple. On several occasions, Vestager has aired classic antitrust views—simply proposing a split-up of Google into several independent companies. On July 18, 2018, the EU issued its biggest fine ever, 5 billion USD. Once again, it was Google that received the fine. The reason for this one relates closely to the Microsoft case from around the turn of the millennium. Since 2011, Google has made use of its operating system Android depend on the use of Google's own native apps. This so-called "bundling" takes away the user's freedom to choose between other apps, according to Commissioner Vestager. The verdict gave Google 90 days to change its ways, on pain of daily penalties of up to 5% of its company revenue—to no one's surprise, the company appealed the decision.[14]

These issues are also deeply tied to the entire debate on *net neutrality*. The term refers to the idea that the Internet should generally be structured so that all content is treated according to the same principles, and that no content is given priority over other content when network providers process that content. Net neutrality aims to ensure that different users, content, websites, platforms, applications, equipment or methods of communication are treated equally and are not,

[13] When entering the search "phone", up came a Google Pixel, the search "laptop" resulted in a Chromebook, "watches" an Android Smartwatch etc., cf. Nicas, J. "Google Uses Its Search Engine to Hawk Its Products" *Wall Street Journal*. 01-19-18.

[14] Anneberg, M, Nielsen, R. D. & Albrectsen, N. "Vestager straffer Google med milliardbøde" *TV2 Udland*. 07-18-18.

for example, subject to different payment or priorities during the process. This is the Internet's heir to the concept of "common carrier", which dates back to the legal basis of the transport of goods and phone conversations (Communications Act of 1934). A number of European countries have legally-based net neutrality, but in the US the concept is disputed. In 2015, the United States Federal Communications Commission (FCC) decided to allow different processing speeds, but at the same time it reclassified the web as telecommunications. This reclassification put the Internet within the scope of the principle of neutrality for common carriers. Under President Trump, however, the FCC has reclassified the web back to public infrastructure. Thus, in June 2018 the principle of net neutrality was lifted. Some observers argue that continued growth in bandwidth have, until now, made the subject less relevant in practice. Legally and politically, the issue is highly controversial, and a more detailed analysis falls outside the scope of the present work—not least because net neutrality refers to internet service providers rather than our focus here: the tech giants.

As a precedent of net neutrality, the status of telephone companies calls to mind another classic antitrust case from the US, which is even more similar to the tech giants than Northern Securities railways were. It concerned telephone company AT&T. During the 1880s, this company emerged from *Bell Telephone Company*, named after Alexander Graham Bell, inventor of the telephone. In the early years of the telephone, competing telephone companies each maintained their own cable network in such a way that a given street in US could have many telephone poles and wires from several competing companies—an example of what is often called "destructive competition". In such cases, a market can become unstable, and even in the ideal case of symmetrical competition between equal competitors of equal sizes, costs will occur that are absent in the case of monopolies (e.g. costs related to coordination and negotiations between companies).[15] Just like the network-driven Internet providers, customers back then had an obvious interest in being able to get in touch with as many other phone owners as possible—this early version of the network effect naturally concentrated customers in a few large companies. As early as 1907, AT&T had a 50% market share, a share quickly approaching a de facto monopoly. Initially, the government followed the same procedure as against Standard Oil and advocated for a split-up, but in 1913 a compromise was reached. In this deal, known as *The Kingsbury Commitment*, AT&T's natural monopoly was acknowledged. In return for the Government's promise not to split up the company, AT&T agreed to the following: give up its control of the telegraph company Western Union; stop acquiring additional companies without the permission of the authorities; commit to serve all customers, even remote ones; allow other non-competing telephone companies to connect with AT&T's attractive long-distance telephony. At the time, the company had been criticized for being able to eradicate competitors by denying them the right to connect to AT&T's long-distance service. During the 1920s and 1930s, the authorities allowed for AT&T to acquire smaller telephone companies but simultaneously, the company was subject to government price controls.

Another antitrust case, in 1949, led to a new compromise in 1956. It made the company agree to run the national telephone network only and thus not move into neighboring industries. The company's development department, the famous Bell Labs, was required to share its patents freely. The roots of Bell Labs went all the way back to Bell's very own laboratory, having been owned by AT&T and Western

---

[15] Interestingly enough, following his detailed review of the theory of natural monopolies and the American telecommunications industry, Sharkey (2008) (orig. 1982, p. 213) concludes that it is difficult to determine whether this industry is a natural monopoly, even though it has many of the features predicted by abstract theory of economics (decreasing marginal costs, many "sunk" establishment costs, lower prices of a monopoly than a duopoly, etc.).

Electric since the 1920s. It became one of the most important research labs of the 20th century, employing several Nobel Prize-winning researchers. Many important breakthroughs and inventions can be traced back to Bell Labs: radio astronomy, the transistor, some of the first American computers, the photocell, the communication satellite, the solar panel, the laser, several of the early computer languages, the quantum Hall effect, the digital mobile phone, etc. Its impact goes all the way up to today; it is now owned by Nokia. There is an irony to the fact that Bell Lab's freely available patents became central to the early development of the personal computer. As Jonathan Taplin writes, today's enormous tech monopolies rest on technologies which the giants themselves were free to access because of government antitrust action. The appearance of the first mobile phones in the 1960s was what finally led to a split-up of the Bell System in 1982. The newly arrived mobile phones did not depend on the cable network, and AT&T used its monopoly to try to prevent those phones from connecting to the company's network by increasing the price for access. As a result, calls were made in 1982 for the separation of local telephone networks—the so-called "Baby Bells"—and Bell Labs was finally sold off in 1996.

The AT&T example is prototypical for the discussion of "natural monopolies".[16] The idea is that certain products or services are naturally inclined towards monopoly. These are products where the initial costs of establishing a company's services are high, but where the marginal costs of recruiting new customers are low. This makes the marginal income increase with the number of customers. That is why earnings can explode once the company is established. Hence, new customers can be attracted at a lower price than that of new companies, who first have to pay the establishment costs (e.g. cable networks). The result is often that first movers turn into natural monopolies. At the same time, these companies are

[16] And which is chosen by Sharkey as an example to analyze.

able to provide their services at a lower price than would two competing companies (if there were two competing phone companies, all consumers would need two telephones to get the same service that one could provide, which would be more expensive for the consumer).[17] A product with the characteristics of a network may be considered a natural monopoly candidate thanks to the network effect: all customers want to belong to that company which offers the highest possible number of other customers. This effect is evident, since the very service offered is a connection between customers, and the inclusion of an additional customer is only a marginal expense once the network is established. Many natural monopolies have the traits of infrastructure like water suppliers, power providers, sewerage, road networks, railways and telephone networks.

The US Government—since 1890—developed a long antitrust tradition. Therefore, the 1913 compromise with AT&T may seem surprising—probably the decision makers realized that telephony was a natural monopoly. It would be counterproductive and artificial to insist on maintaining many competing telephone companies, each operating its own cable network (it is no coincidence that what split up AT&T 100 years after its founding was phones with no need for cables). In return for this acknowledgment of the AT&T monopoly as public infrastructure, the government regulated its acquisition of new companies, introduced price controls, prohibited the company from moving into neighboring industries and ultimately demanded the company make its research and patents public.

It is possible to view Google and Facebook as natural monopolies, except they no longer just operate in American territory, but worldwide. Thus, any possible regulation efforts in the foreseeable future must take place on a nation-state basis. These two companies have a market share similar to that of Standard Oil when it was charged as a monopoly in the 1890s (and even higher than Standard Oil's market share

---

[17] See Sharkey (2008) chs. 1 and 9.

at the time of the verdict). Also, they are similar to AT&T in a number of ways: they deal in communications infrastructure; they base their strength on the network effect; they shield themselves behind the ongoing acquisition of competitors; they continuously expand their field of activity by buying and absorbing companies from neighboring industries.

Thus, certain options for regulating the monopolies of tech companies appear on the horizon. Barry Lynn categorizes tech giants as public utility infrastructure and points to two kinds of solutions: either splitting up monopolies or regulating them.[18]

The former solution is thus splitting up the companies. Due to their character of natural monopoly, this could not follow the Standard Oil model of splitting into smaller companies of the same kind, only divided according to geographical location. It would make no sense to split up Google into local, competing search engines Giggle, Gaggle and Guggle. Pretty much the same goes for Facebook. Yet, they could be split up by being forced to sell off some of the many companies they have acquired and integrated as additional services (a pattern which could be accused of "vertical integration"), while still retaining their core service as a natural monopoly.

Another even more reasonable approach (and one which does not exclude the first) would be the recognition of a natural monopoly on information searches and on "connecting people", or however Facebook will end up being defined. As in the case of AT&T,[19] such a recognition would then come at a price, for instance some of the following: public price control (on ads prices); net neutrality and non-discrimination of customers and users; publication, public discussion and audit of algorithms; balancing off community standards at least so they are not stricter than local legislation; public control of

---

[18] Brandom, R. "The Anti-monopoly Case Against Google" *The Verge*. 09-05-17.

[19] As noted by Gillespie (2018) p. 44f, it is striking how it was agreed upon to give the tech companies comprehensive legal protection under the "Safe Harbor Act" without balancing things by giving them obligations.

and clear appeal options regarding the removal of criminal content and ditto users; a transparent procedure around copyright enforcement; transparency requirements for the publication of political ads; sharing of profits with external content providers who attract online traffic for the ad business; free access—as in the case of Bell Labs—to the results and patents of the companies' wildly expanding research departments. Companies like Google and Facebook do not produce and edit the content posted by their users—but there is one service that they actually edit and control, namely ads. Their origin, funding, content and targeting could be subject to greater control.

Obviously, as mentioned above, there are states with significantly stricter legislation on free speech than the Facebook and Google standards, and several of these states regularly push, restrict, harass or shut down these services (e.g. Turkey, Pakistan, Saudi Arabia and several other Muslim states). Others even completely disconnect the services from operating and create alternative, highly-controlled copycat services (as in China). It is not within the scope of this book to go into detail about the many different struggles and compromises that tech giants have faced when dealing with non-democratic states. In such countries, key freedom of speech issues are "classical" government and/or religious restrictions on free speech. In those cases, problems are only partly caused by tech giants. On the contrary, they have had a tendency to support freedom of speech when confronted with strict local political-religious gag laws and regulations. Here, Orwell is more relevant than Huxley. Especially in the early days, the web and tech companies actually made a whole new level of free speech possible for many groups in such countries, evidenced by Google top leaders rejoicing the Arab Spring. However, in order to also fit in to authoritarian markets, tech giants over time have tended to increasingly bow to pressure to remove content that such countries request or push to have removed—even if they were not originally covered by the company's own standards. These disputes have been around for many years and will hardly be affected by the introduction of western regulation of the services. It will primarily be a matter concerning the United States and the EU, secondarily other countries with Western models of society emphasizing liberty. At present, neo-Brandeisians supporting antitrust legislation are hardly strong enough for action in the United States even though many politicians after the congressional hearings in April 2018 are gradually beginning to speak about regulation. Furthermore, a decisive player like the European Union is now weaker than when the Google cases were launched, due to the Euro and Brexit crises.

Some may argue that given the decline in American antitrust policies, the US may have a hard case trying to split up tech giants, facing now a Supreme Court with a possible republican free-market bent. But still it can be argued that even lost antitrust cases have proven helpful because companies, during the legal process, strive to accommodate their activity in order to try to alleviate consequences in case of losing. Facebook co-founder and critic Chris Hughes cites the antitrust case lost against IBM in the 1980's which nevertheless forced the company to increased openness as well as to separate hardware and software sales.[20]

It comes as no surprise that the tech giants are not excited about growing rumblings of monopoly control. In July 2018, in a long interview with the website *recode*, Zuckerberg set up a foreign policy nightmare scenario as a warning against monopoly control: "... do we want American companies to be exporting across the world? We grew up here, I think we share a lot of values that I think people hold very dear here, and I think it's generally very good that we're doing this, both for security reasons and from a values perspective. Because I think that the alternative, frankly, is going to be the Chinese companies. If we adopt a stance which is that, 'Okay, we're gonna, as a country, decide that we wanna clip the wings of these companies and make it so

[20] Hughes, C. "It's Time to Break Up Facebook" *New York Times.* 05-09-19.

that it's harder for them to operate in different places, where they have to be smaller', then there are plenty of other companies out that are willing and able to take the place of the work that we're doing."[21] Zuckerberg's argument is that monopoly control would especially harm the opportunities of US companies to operate outside the United States. It is a rather odd remark, given the natural fact that outside the US is outside the realm of American legislation. So it is hard not to see this as straw man argument, which plays on the well-known American fear of Chinese competition—and it clearly fails to address the key arguments for monopoly control in the United States.

Anti-monopoly legislation, however, is a heavy weapon and should be used carefully. Voices against any government interference into the economy are quick to label neo-Brandeisians like Lynn as communists, supporters of planned economy, sentimental and populist protectors of small and unprofitable businesses, driven by envy of companies who have done well and grown big, and as anti-democratic paternalists who think they know better than the consumers, and so on. But anti-Brandeisians also put forward serious arguments that should be taken into account. In fact, this is a collision of two varieties of a free-market ideology. One sees competition as a *procedure* which ought to be ensured when monopolies, to a greater or lesser extent, neutralize or block competition in a given field. Such blockage implies the risk of these competition "winners" taking advantage of their strength to prevent new competition from gaining ground, to push prices up and ultimately freeze in their own inefficiency when they are no longer exposed to competition. As the market itself is unable to fight monopolies and ensure competition, the state must step in. The other emphasizes the *results* of competition—once a company has won a monopoly or duopoly in an industry, it is proof of the superiority of its business model and the high quality of the product, and thus there

---

[21] Swisher, K. "Recommended listening: Kara Swisher interviews Mark Zuckerberg" *Recode*. 07-20-18.

is no need to ensure further competition. It would only take the form of harmful government interference and abuse of the market, giving artificial support to inferior products. In this view, monopolies must be protected against the greed and ignorance of the government.

Supporters of the latter position—that of anti-antitrust—will argue that if the growth of a company is restricted in order to expose the company to competition, then immediately the companies start competing against each other in an alternative battle for political influence in order to use it against the competitors. It will cause smaller companies to seek political support against the larger ones—and perhaps consequently lead to even greater concentration, only now one that enjoys political protection. This will lead to increased lobbyism activity, where the benefit of getting along well with a small group of government officials can be greater than that of improving the business model. This argument can also be expanded to address the very real problem that introducing regulation of, for example, Facebook and Google may *secure* these companies, insofar as due to lobbyism they are better than smaller firms at influencing regulation to serve their own purposes, just as they are likely to have more resources on their hands to implement demanding regulatory procedures. A further argument goes like this: if monopoly control is also introduced for reasons other than economic ones—for instance to promote certain political, social or democratic goals—then the point could be made that special cases would support those same objectives by making *exceptions* from the regulation. Such exceptions would then be subject to further lobbyism and in turn lead to more and worse concentration.[22]

In light of the current high level of concentration, the point that regulation will lead to *worse* market concentration does not seem strong. Only on rare occasions did previous anti-

---

[22]These arguments are summarized by Manne, G. "The Illiberal Vision of neo-Brandeisian Antitrust" *Truth on the Market*. 04-16-18.

trust interventions lead to higher concentrations. The lobbyism argument, on the other hand, is stronger. It is undoubtedly true that regulation in all its forms will give companies an even stronger incentive to try to influence the political process. Taplin cites a gloomy statistic of how many top executives have switched back and forth between Google and the White House.[23] Some of them are likely to maintain a connection with or loyalty to their former employer. Anti-antitrust figures such as Law Professor Geoffrey Manne speaks as if antitrust legislation could be used indiscriminately to implement all sorts of support policies with widely different goals. This should indeed be avoided; thus monopoly suits should only be opened in case of very clear indications of destructive economic, public or political effects of the monopoly. We think that is indeed the case when looking at the tech giants, their actual management of free speech, their strong influence on democratic elections and processes, their lack of data protection, their acquisition of competitors, etc. The incentive for more lobbyism in case of antitrust intervention is undoubtedly an important factor to keep in mind—which may only be counteracted by increased transparency on and regulation of campaign support, nepotism, and corruption. In May 2019, the antitrust case received renewed impetus with an important op-ed from Facebook co-founder Chris Hughes in the *New York Times*. Here, Hughes recommended a break-up of Facebook, most easily accomplished by the forced sale of acquisitions like Messenger, Instagram and WhatsApp. Hughes refers to his old friend, attacking his unprecedented control of freedom of expression: "The most problematic aspect of Facebook's power is Mark's unilateral control over speech. There is no precedent for his ability to monitor, organize and even censor the conversations of two billion people."[24]

---

[23]Taplin (2017) p. 129f.

[24]Hughes, C. "It's Time to Break Up Facebook" *New York Times.* 05-09-19.

It is not within the framework of this book to get into details on how regulation can and should be drafted. But to us there is no doubt that the still more strong voices advocating reconsideration of antitrust trials against tech giants have a strong case going for them.

Chapter 17
The Role of Civil Society

We cannot, however, rely on government-imposed regulation to solve all the problems of the Internet. Regulation can and should set a better framework than what is currently the case, but by nature all regulation is general and framework-setting only, and nobody can expect it to solve all problems in detail. Malignant forces of many different kinds will continue to bypass, exploit and challenge even the best regulation. Therefore, actors within the public sphere and civil society must contribute to the preservation of freedom of expression on the Internet. The simplistic view of a dichotomy between state and private often seems to assume that society consists only of a number of companies and private individuals on the one hand, and on the other, a state. From that plain dichotomy, it follows that policy must then be determined by an ongoing arm-wrestle between the two. Such a polarized setup might give a rough picture of authoritarian societies. But painting the two in this oppositional way completely ignores the key role of civil society and the public sphere in modern democracies—in between the government sphere and the private sphere, so to speak. In this context, traditional media ought to adopt a leading role. It is well known that such media outlets are under pressure by tech giants, primarily because the crucial advertising income is migrating towards the tech giants and their attention economy. Print newspapers are shrinking, and people go online to find news. In this story

F. Stjernfelt, A. M. Lauritzen, *Your Post has been Removed*,
https://doi.org/10.1007/978-3-030-25968-6_17

of decay, many have been a bit too willing to see an overlapping shift, where new technology and new players replace old and outdated ones, just like cars replaced horse-drawn carriages and the drive-thru replaced roadside inns. This widely-held idea overlooks one fundamental fact: to a very large extent, the news content that people look for and find on the tech giants' platforms is still largely *produced* by the old pre-Internet media outlets, newspapers, TV-networks, publishing companies, film production companies, etc. Tech giants have indeed become great marketers of news and content, but they themselves do not produce the content they deliver. This is one of the reasons that the categorization of the giants as media is wrong. Newspapers, media outlets and publishers embody free debate and Enlightenment principles in civil society—supplemented by public-private players such as universities and other research institutions, think tanks and philanthropic foundations. Here it is crucial that such media and institutions hold on to the elementary principles of free speech and do not resort to introducing community standards. Moreover, they must keep promoting freedom, which includes also points of view considered unpopular, provocative or grotesque by the ideas of the moment and the mainstream. *One man's "hate speech" is another man's truth* may not apply to every single case but should still count as a guiding motto.

In the 2017 Spielberg film *The Post*, famous 1970s-80s editor-in-chief at *The Washington Post*, Ben Bradlee, is quoted for saying: "The only way to assert the right to publish is to publish." This ethos must be followed by strong actors in civil society. Lengthy tribute speeches in praise of freedom of expression, often heard from the tech giants, can be gripping but also entirely useless, if the companies are not willing to act on their principles. One of the inventors of virtual reality, Jaron Lanier, recently published a sharply written pamphlet encouraging people to simply delete their social media accounts. He advises people to read three independent news sites each day instead of their social media news feed—making them more well-informed faster. Tech giants are harmful for truth, for politics, and they favor people who act like assholes, to paraphrase Lanier's blunt characterization. However, he rejects the claim that the highly addictive tech giants are the tobacco industry of our day—there are also good sides to them, after all. He prefers to compare them to lead paint: it was phased out little by little—but it did not make people believe that they should stop painting their houses entirely. So, his radical proposal is not to shut down social media, but to push them to evolve in a direction away from their addictive, public-distorting traits. It seems doubtful, however, that Lanier will be able to provoke a mass movement to actually abandon the tech giants. But the threat in itself, and the rising debate in civil society, might perhaps result in a pressure to gradually guide the companies in a better direction. Lanier suggests an alternative business model where users pay for social media to be at *their* service rather than primarily serving the advertisers[1]—supplemented by the rights of users to own the data they create. That would make the companies' use of these data subject to payment, but payment in the opposite direction, to the users. Such a solution would no doubt be more bureaucratic, and relevant supporting algorithms could be written. As to whether people would really wish to pay for such services, Lanier points to the fact that they have indeed long since become used to free content but still have proved willing to pay for HBO and Netflix subscriptions to access quality television. So why should discerning consumers not also be willing to pay for a similar subscription to access high quality social media? Lanier vows a fateful oath: he will not restore his accounts with the tech giants until he is allowed to pay for them.

In general, it is important that the public sphere and civil society continuously develop new tools to face new challenges. In early 2018, a number of civil liberty organizations—some old, some new—got together to discuss a mutual interest: online freedom of expression.[2] Over two meetings in

[1] Lanier (2018) p. 104ff.

[2] The organizations are primarily American: American Civil Liberties

January and May carrying the title "Content Moderation and Removal to Scale", they articulated a possible set of principles for freedom on the major Internet platforms, given the name *Santa Clara Principles* (named after the first meeting, which took place at Santa Clara University, California). The objective was to achieve "... reasonable transparency and accountability on the Internet platforms."[3] The manifest lists three basic principles to achieve this objective, respectively 1) number of posts removed; 2) notice about removal; 3) possibility to appeal for any content removals.

About removal of content the general recommendation is: "Publish the numbers of posts removed and accounts permanently or temporarily suspended due to violations of their content guidelines." It must include the number of complaints about posts, number of posts and accounts deleted—organized by certain criteria: by the rules they are claimed to have violated; formats (text, image, video, etc.); by the type of complainant (governments, employees, users, automated); by the geographical location of the parties involved (both complaining and accused party).

Regarding notification of the affected user about removal, the general recommendation is: "The companies have to submit a notice to all users whose content has been removed or whose account has been suspended, giving the reason for the removal or suspension." Generally, the companies must provide clear guidelines with examples of both permissible and

---

Union Foundation of Northern California, the California branch of ACLU from 1920; Center for Democracy and Technology, founded in 1994 to defend free speech online; Electronic Frontier Foundation, a digital rights organization founded in 1990 by John Perry Barlow, the man behind the Cyberspace manifesto; New America's Open Technology Institute from 2009 (the technology branch of think tank New America, headed by Kevin Bankston)—plus a handful of individual researchers: Irina Raicu (Santa Clara University), Nicolas Suzor (Queensland University of Technology), Sarah T. Roberts (UCLA), and Sarah Myers West (USC)

[3]The principles can be found here "The Santa Clara Principles on Transparency and Accountability in Content Moderation" Last visited 08-04-18: https://cdt.org/files/2018/05/Santa_Clara_Principles.pdf

critical content. Any removal notice must contain: URL, content quote or other clear reference to identify the posting; what exact rule the content has allegedly violated; how the content was flagged and removed (however, individual complainants may maintain anonymity); a guideline of how to appeal the decision.

Regarding appeal, the recommendation is: "The companies have to provide reasonable opportunity to lodge an appeal for any removal of content or suspension of accounts." A proper appeal must include: a review carried out by a person or group of persons who were not involved in the first decision; an opportunity to present further arguments and have them included in the investigation; announcement of the results of the review in an understandable language.

The Santa Clara Principles address the tech giants directly, requiring them to adjust their removal procedures according to the recommendations. There is no doubt that these principles would represent a very big step forward for user freedom of expression on the tech giant platforms. They would introduce clarity, openness and a rule-governed procedure, which is not the case at present.

However, there are a number of important questions that these principles do *not* address. It appears that the Santa Clara organizations are hoping that tech giants will voluntarily adhere to their principles—government involvement in the matter is not mentioned. The problems include, for example, the nature and scope of the platforms' policies: Should tech giants be able to freely decide their own censorship policies? Should external control of their removal policies become a condition for accepting their monopolies? Are there limits to what may be prohibited? What is the relationship between the policies of the tech giants and the free speech legislations in different countries? Should governments have influence over the policies, why, and how (or why not)? Also, the principles do not state (although they may imply it) that *all* removal of content should be subject to explicit rules (based on the old doctrine *nulla poena sine lege*—no punishment without law). They also do not emphasize any conditions for *changing* the rules—tech giants are famous for continuously changing their rules, often without clearly announcing the changes or giving any clear deadline for their enforcement. And finally, the principles do not specify whether the rules are to be enforced or even controlled by a third party, which would make it difficult for tech giants to keep acting as legislative, judicial, and executive branch alike.

In June 2018, we had the opportunity to speak to one of the persons behind the Santa Clara document, Nate Cardozo from the Electronic Frontier Foundation in San Francisco. EFF was founded in 1990 by John Perry Barlow, among others, to protect people and new technological tools active on the emerging Internet from various legal threats, to monitor and criticize government interventions in the field and to organize political action in support of personal freedoms online. Cardozo says that, until now, the EFF has focused on the problem of government demanding tech companies to hand over data. But two recent developments have now put censorship by tech giants on the agenda: the election of Trump and the advance of the Alt-right movement online: "The purpose of SC manifesto is twofold—to try to make companies comply, but also, once companies accept those principles, we'll have data about removal—before that we can't even have an intelligent conversation."

– *Do you imagine the SC principles accepted voluntarily by the tech giants, or by political enforcement?*

"We have no unified view on that yet. EFF comes from a more libertarian tradition so we would never embrace political enforcement, but there should be a political pressure for transparency. We're not a fan of government regulation because the risk of error is extraordinarily high—if Congress would write a law now with the present power relations there and the present President, chances are we would not like it at all."

– *But there are mounting regulation pressures in both the US and in the EU?*

"One point where there's appetite on Capitol Hill is for data protection like in the EU—which we at EFF would be in favor of. One area of the EU GDPR which makes us nervous, however, is the "right to erasure" [the idea that people have a right to have removed claims made about them online, claims they do not like, even old statements made by themselves]. Another problem is that tech giants have way more means of affecting legislations and adapting to them—Google has thousands of lawyers on staff, a startup has none. The other possibility is that government passes something toothless which would just make matters worse because then political pressure would cease. Another area where we would welcome government intervention would be more initiative from FTC (Federal Trade Commission) on enforcing already existing rules for FIPs (Fair Information Practices) which are 20 years old, but essentially unenforced as of yet."

– *The whole complex of the criteria of removal are not addressed in the Santa Clara Principles?*

"No, that's correct. You're right, they are quite fuzzy—vague, intentionally so, because that gives a large room of manoeuvre for the companies. We talked about it but concluded: let's not let the perfect be the enemy of the good, let us first see how far we can get with transparency and then increase demands later."

– *There is tension between the broad freedom of expression granted by the First Amendment and the far more narrow removal criteria of the tech giants?*

"We are indeed hesitant to accept any criteria narrower than the First Amendment. On the other hand, platforms also have their free speech rights. If you have a dog photo site, you have your rights to delete cat photos. If you have a vegetarian site, you will delete photos of pork etc.—of course you have rights to such things—the issue is how to balance these liberties. Infrastructure companies are easy to tackle—they should not censor at all! When CloudFare and Google cut off the white supremacist site The Daily Stormer which is not illegal under US law, we took a strong line against that.[4] With things like Facebook it is different, but we're moderating our stance a bit—we don't say they should keep everything up all of the time, but they should keep up a hell of a lot more than they do today."

– *Where do you stand on the suggestions for control of monopoly?*

"We have an ongoing project in EFF to find out what we mean about that. One thing we have decided on is to back the idea of 'interoperability'—that is, the possibility to move across the big tech companies online. You should be able to leave e.g. Facebook and take all your data with you to another operator, and it should be possible to send messages across different companies. Right now, monopolies are enforced by means of NOT being interoperable, even Google turned off the possibility of interoperative chats 4 years ago, they went out of the way to turn off interoperability. Facebook has all of these privacy settings—only one of them have a default setting which *protects* your privacy, and that is about your address book. And that is in order to not letting users taking their address book with them when they leave for another company."

– *What about the AT&T example? Meeting government demands as a price in order to get accept of monopoly?*

"It makes me extremely uncomfortable to imagine what the current government might require as a price for accepting monopoly, for instance government access to personal data—I think we rather need to come up with new solutions rather than look at the AT&T example."

---

[4] Cf. Vega, N. "Internet rights group slams Google and GoDaddy's 'dangerous' decision to ban a neo-Nazi site" *nordic.businessinsider.com.* 08-18-17.

– *How is the EFF itself funded?*

"EFF lives from donations from individuals, we're only supported less than 6% from companies and 0% from the government. We had a big kick in support after the Edward Snowden affair in 2013 and another kick when Trump got elected ..."

– *Another type of censorship comes from external pressure on the companies, e.g. flagging storms by protest groups attempting to have opponents suspended from the platforms ...*

"Companies repeatedly tell us that numbers of flaggers complaining about a particular post play no role—that is obviously bullshit. They have "trusted flaggers" whose complaints are easily followed—that sort of inequality is intransparent. And postings by known people have much better chances for being preserved than postings by an unknown. Another issue is: Which elements of civil society do companies chose to engage with or ignore also has a huge influence. After Charlottesville, the tech giants have been much more willing to engage with anti-hate speech organizations like Southern Poverty Law Center (who tend to err on the side of fighting white supremacy) and Anti-Defamation League (a Jewish organization particularly focusing on antisemitism) than with free-speech organizations like us."

– *Globally, a huge issue for Free Speech is the compromises being made between the tech giants and totalitarian states?*

"If tech giants are not forced to comply with legislations in countries where they have no boots on the ground, our stance is they should NOT at all comply with the demand of those countries. We protested when Twitter opened an office in UAE [the United Arab Emirates] because now they are no longer able to ignore demands from UAE, because now they have employees there who may be pressured or threatened. We have the policy that when content is illegal in some jurisdiction but not others—e.g. insulting Erdogan in Turkey—and the companies are forced to comply with that, they should continue to make that content available in the rest of the world."

As an organization, EFF illustrates very well some of the dilemmas involved when trying to bring transparency and appropriate conditions to the technological Wild West of tech giant censorship. EFF is a strong voice in civil society hoping to help create pressure that makes the companies listen. Still, the organization refrains from supporting government intervention. The ongoing crisis after the Cambridge Analytica scandal also make this an opportune time for the public to put pressure on tech giants, because the companies might be nudged to see the advantage of taking a proactive stance—before regulation they might dislike is imposed on them.

It is crucial that civil society organizations and NGO's, such as the ones behind the Santa Clara manifesto, continuously articulate and develop demands that can inspire public and political debate on tech regulation, a debate which seems growing in both the United States and EU after the 2018 crises. The basic clarity and obvious fairness of the Santa Clara Principles ought to ensure that they have great impact. But it also seems necessary that such organizations gain public and political influence to enable them to match the tech giants' broad and well-funded lobbyism activity among Western politicians.

Another example of the abilities of civil society to interfere is a recent American NGO, *Alliance for Securing Democracy.*[5] The organization was founded in 2017 in response to the exposure of the Russian "troll factory" *Internet Research Agency* and its massive influence over the American voting public via Russian bots on the Internet. The organization is privately funded —which is very important in the United States—and bipartisan, i.e., it has no privileged affiliation with either of the two major parties. In fact, the initiative was taken by two experienced former political advisors from each party, Marco Rubio's (R) Jamie Fly and

[5] Alliance for Securing Democracy. Last visited 08-04-18: http://securing-democracy.gmfus.org.

Hillary Clinton's (D) Laura Rosenberger. The motto is: "We are not telling you what to think, but we believe you should know when someone is trying to manipulate you".

One part of the organization's activity is an ongoing mapping of Russian activities on Twitter, the main platform used for the Russian bot campaign. The project bears the title *Hamilton68*[6] after one of the American founding fathers, Alexander Hamilton, and his famous essay "The Mode of Electing the President", published in 1788 in *The Federalist Papers* vol. 68, on how to fight foreign interference in US democracy. On the project website, people can continuously keep an eye on which Russian tweets posted within the latest 24 hours rank the highest, which hashtags are used and what topics are currently addressed in Russian propaganda. The Alliance for Securing Democracy website has become a key source of information about this activity. For example, it broke the news in January 2018 that bots were now set on a mission to de-legitimize Robert Mueller III, the Special Counsel charged with investigating possible Russian collusion with key players inside the Trump campaign. The fact that it is now possible, a bit like a continuous weather report, to map out current misinformation is already a strong advance compared to the time around the 2016 Presidential elections in the US.

In a manifesto on its methods, ASD describes how the organization has identified key sources of Russian misinformation by using three methods. First, by tracking online misinformation campaigns synchronized with open and obvious Russian propaganda sources such as *RT* (Russia Today) and *Sputnik*. Next, by identifying networks of users who obviously tweeted support for Russian policy. Finally, by identifying accounts that use automatic forwarding from other accounts to multiply signals from Russian sources of influ-

[6] Alliance for Securing Democracy—Hamilton68. Last visited 08-04-18: http://dashboard.securingdemocracy.org

ence—by isolating accounts which show unusual amounts of interaction with other accounts. Such accounts may be bots which automatically forward content according to pre-defined rules, or they may be "cyborgs", partly automated but supervised by persons. Triangulation of these three data sets then enabled ASD to identify a relatively small group of accounts, around 600, as responsible for systematic Russian misinformation. The organization is especially inspired by experiences from Estonia. The tiny Baltic state was probably the first place where active Russian cyber war was felt, during a large attack in 2007 which paralyzed large parts of the state apparatus. The attack was made possible due to Estonia's high level of digitization. Former Estonian President Toomas Ilves is now on the cross-political advisory board of ASD, which also features heavy hitters with experience in international politics, security and counter-espionage such as neo-Conservative intellectual and politician Bill Kristol.

In February 2018, we had the chance to interview media analyst Bret Schaefer of the Alliance for Securing Democracy in Washington D.C.

– *How did you manage to build up your misinformation warning website?*[7]

"We were able to quickly identify about 600 accounts, who formed a network of pro-Kremlin misinformation—the most well-known is probably *RT* and *Sputnik*. The idea of making a website with automatically updated information about misinformation activities was the brainchild of security researcher Clint Watts (who has repeatedly testified on Russian interference before the Senate), who 3–4 years ago began to be interested in Russian interference in Syria and in ISIS activity. He was then helped by people such as anti-terrorism specialist J.M. Berger, social media analyst Andrew Wiseburd and

[7]The quotes from the interview with Schaefer appeared in Danish in a news article by Stjernfelt, F "Systematisk afsløring af systematisk misinformation" in Danish weekly newspaper *Weekendavisen.* 02-23-18.

Jonathan Morgan—a big data guy who founded "Data for Democracy". Those four guys are the Hamilton team with the dashboard, automatically following different activities on the 600 accounts we have identified so far."

– *How can fake news online be fought against without violating user freedom of expression?*

"Yes, that's the big question. Who should have authority and responsibility to determine what is credible and what not? We cannot be the ones doing that and you cannot leave it to the government. Facebook does not want to or cannot, and not even bipartisan NGOs can do it. It is interesting that the new flagging, which Facebook tried before Christmas proved to be counterintentional. Users would flag sketchy online content with a special flag—and it soon became apparent that this sign actually *increased* Internet traffic to the sites in question. People like the two of us might want to visit the page out of curiosity—but also people who simply do not trust common news sources and therefore actively go look for alternative, less credible sources. Facebook's idea was definitely not the right way to go. One solution right now is dealing with the automation problem, mainly on Twitter—artificial augmentation of content, taking one voice and turning it into 30,000 votes. That is what we aim to dismantle. So, our fight does not threaten freedom of expression, because users can easily turn to a conspiracy theory site, if they so wish. But we must fight the artificial inflation of this content, so it's not pushed it into people's news feeds".

– *How do you discern systematic misinformation from individual trolls and your average extreme online voices?*

"Trolls are tricky. Who is a troll? It can just be a guy with lots of time on his hands tweeting frequently. To us, it's not so important whether the source is ultimately a person or organization. We expose the artificial multiplication of the content in question—the goal is not to disclose individual URLs. It is a computerized system we use, but it also has a human element checking through the list to avoid including accounts which are not relevant, for instance American Alt-right accounts from the extreme right. They may feature bizarre content, but they are not involved in artificial dissemination of the content.

In January, the 600 accounts, which run some 10,000 bots, managed to disseminate around 80,000 messages. At the top of the list were *RT* and *Sputnik*, but many of them are indistinguishable from US accounts from the far right. A bit further down on the top-ten came more extreme pro-Kremlin sites run out of Eastern Ukraine, such as *Donbass News* and *Stalkerzone.com* calling Ukrainians fascists and calling for ethnic cleansing, and so on. Very extreme views. They link to hyperpartisan US websites to give them followers, credibility, a way of getting pro-Kremlin viewpoints in front of Americans—and to exaggerate tensions between US groups".

– *So, the Russian side is trying to use existing Alt-right websites as a kind of gateway to the US public sphere?*

"Yes, but it does not have to be extreme US websites. It may also be pro-life antiabortion websites, where maybe 80% of the traffic concerns abortion-related topics such as Catholicism—but with 20% suddenly addressing pro-Kremlin issues. For example, if I put in a link on such a website suggesting that the United States is working with IS in Syria, it gains more credibility because it appears as if it came from within the anti-abortion tribe, so to speak".

– *What is ASD's attitude to the current attempts to legislate against "fake news" and "hate speech" online—for example, the German legislation requiring social media to censor different content or the French legislation in the pipeline?*

"We're in the process of making policy recommendations also as an organization. It's a real challenge, approaching an area where governments censor content. On the other hand, not doing anything and leaving it to the tech companies is also not helpful. None of the two options is a viable one. Each month, we get more and more data and we now know that a couple of hundred million people on Facebook have seen Russian-generated content, and maybe fifty million Twitter accounts. Our claim is that automation is the low-hanging fruit here, and each further solution comes with its own problems. As I mentioned earlier, no one can or wants to be responsible for deciding what is credible and what is not. If you create rules or safeguards that are too stringent, people will just jump to other platforms—like in Germany with *Alternative für Deutschland* and *Pegida* which quickly left Facebook after the new law entered into force on January 1st, 2018. They're now jumping to *gab.ai* and other uncensored underground networks. So, the outcome of censoring Facebook is that extreme right-wing activity is forced underground where it's harder to control …"

– *That dilemma was already formulated in the eighteenth century: censorship of unwanted positions only strengthens them underground ...*

"Yes, it's new technology, but the issue is age-old. And it appears again in new ways. We may be close to having the AI technology to manipulate actual speech and video—we're still trusting what we see on tv, but in a few years it will fool some people and in ten years it is going to be very difficult ... That is the next big problem we face".

– *It never stops, does it? New technology will continuously generate new opportunities for the spread of false claims ...*

"Yes, there is no definitive solution, but one step that should be taken is for the tech giants to start working with government organizations that are able to foresee and solve the issues before they arise. Facebook and Twitter have been caught off guard, they did not see the problems coming at all".

In our view, the emergence of an organization like ASD is a healthy sign. Currently, it only unveils Russian disinformation and it is far from solving all problems, but it may act as a beacon for further public disclosure of systematic disinformation campaigns. As we have argued in this book, we agree with Schaefer that the right way forward cannot be to prohibit, censure, weed out, de-rank, flag, or otherwise remove or marginalize "fake news" or false statements online. No authorities have the divine overview of true and false required for such a procedure. Therefore, such an authority would remove statements as false which then later turn out to be true, and it would be impossible to vaccinate against political bias. Giving even more power to the tech giants would also mean going down the wrong path—it would be disastrous to hand them the right to define and determine what is true and false. Moreover, it would only make censored voices regroup and reorganize underground, on The Dark Web or in other places beyond the control of authorities and general public oversight, bestowing on them the heroic status of persecuted martyrs. As a way of dealing with the issue on a higher level, the general public and civil society can contribute with a sharpened alertness and sensitivity to systematic disinformation, which is characterized by the mass dissemination of repetitive content using bots, fake profiles, submitted by clandestine individuals, etc. All of this must be exposed and made public, on an ongoing basis and as soon as it is identified. This is by no means an easy matter, and it will involve a digital arms race because disinformers from foreign governments and other organizations are likely to further develop their tools and are probably, as we write, already on their way to figuring out how to bypass and deceive information services such as ASD and Hamilton68. ASD, on their side, is also busy developing new tools. In December 2018, they announced a new "Authoritarian Interference Tracker" covering 42 countries in North America and Europe, revealing further details of trends and tactics of Russian government interference in each of these countries. The new tool investigates the interconnection of Russian government activity in several areas:

cyberattacks, political and social subversion and economic and financial coercion.[8]

It may be a bit of a stretch to call the United Nations an NGO—but recommendations of this organization are of the same non-binding nature as those originating from civil society organizations. The UN has independent "special rapporteurs" working on a wide range of topics, especially human rights, and annual reports of these experts are not necessarily consistent. In fact, it is the rule rather than the exception that they are not. Still, we would like to point to a report published by David Kaye, Special Rapporteur on the promotion and protection of the right to freedom of opinion and expression. It was presented on April 6, 2018, and addressing the issue of freedom of expression online.[9] In concise and direct language, the report presents a number of key problems with the content control practiced by the internet companies. Section 41: "Private norms, which vary according to each company's business model and vague assertions of community interests, have created unstable, unpredictable and unsafe environments for users and intensified government scrutiny." In Section 46 of the report, the vagueness and lack of transparency of the policies are especially criticized: "Company rules routinely lack the clarity and specificity that would enable users to predict with reasonable certainty what content places them on the wrong side of the line. This is particularly evident in the context of "extremism" and "hate speech", areas of restriction easily susceptible to excessive removals in the absence of rigorous human evaluation of context." Therefore, the report recommends that the rules be based on the principles of human rights. Section 46: "Terms of service should

---

[8]"Alliance for Securing Democracy Launches New Tool to Analyze Russian Interference Operations" *Alliance for Securing Democracy.* 12-06-18.

[9]Kaye, D. "Report of the Special Rapporteur on the promotion and protection of the right to freedom of opinion and expression" *UN Human Rights Council.* 04-06-18.

move away from a discretionary approach rooted in generic and self-serving "community" needs. Companies should instead adopt high-level policy commitments to maintain platforms for users to develop opinions, express themselves freely and access information of all kinds in a manner consistent with human rights law."

Towards the end of the report, Section 64, the general recommendation is: "Opaque forces are shaping the ability of individuals worldwide to exercise their freedom of expression. This moment calls for radical transparency, meaningful accountability and a commitment to remedy in order to protect the ability of individuals to use online platforms as forums for free expression, access to information and engagement in public life." With regard to government policy, the recommendation, in Section 66, is to avoid clumsy regulation of viewpoints and instead only accept content removal carried out "by an independent and impartial judicial authority, and in accordance with due process and standards of legality, necessity and legitimacy" and also to "refrain from imposing disproportionate sanctions, whether heavy fines or imprisonment, on Internet intermediaries." States should also not activate or take part in pre-publication censorship, nor delegate legal decisions to political departments or to the companies themselves, and finally, the state should continuously publish transparency reports on all the requirements it imposes on the companies. Regarding the companies, in Section 70 the recommendation is that they should "... recognize that the authoritative global standard for ensuring freedom of expression on their platforms is human rights law, not the varying laws of States or their own private interests, and they should re-evaluate their content standards accordingly." Likewise, they should be reorganized in accordance with transparency, through greater cooperation with civil society institutions who are concerned with digital rights and avoid involvement in secret state-run content management agreements. Finally, the companies should strive to assume public responsibility, for example by developing common standards across the Internet, monitored by joint "social media councils"—a type of complaints commission for Internet companies. Of course, there are many details the report does not address, and critical issues such as the monopoly question are not mentioned, but its overall message is completely in line with our conclusions. One can only hope that the report will help guide tech companies in an era where they seem to waver about dizzy, caught between the intoxication of their own omnipotence and the growing number of severe political beatings they are taking.

The role of civil society is at risk of being underappreciated in the European debate, as we do not share the American tradition for strong private support for think tanks, NGOs and the like. Nevertheless, the Santa Clara Declaration, the Alliance for Securing Democracy, and the UN report all demonstrate that there is some possibility for different kinds of civil society efforts to put pressure on tech giants and mitigate the consequences of their sins of omission. Serious media, private funds, individual patrons, universities, government subsidizers based on the arm's length principle, etc. must find themselves in the new context and contribute to the ongoing development and refinement of such independent efforts in the public sphere.

A promising but less certain possibility is the idea of a new, decentralized Internet. It would have no central servers and be based on blockchain technology (much like the cryptocurrency Bitcoin). This would eliminate the option of any joint control efforts and ensure user freedom of expression and anonymity beyond the reach of government or tech giant control. Among the uncertainties in this idea, however, is whether such technology will in fact create an Internet with the same scope and potential as the current one. It is also uncertain whether it would attract other users beyond declared "crypto-anarchists" only, who feel they can only exist freely with encrypted protection from states and companies.[10] Another problem of this utopia is that it would probably open up new opportunities not only for civil society, but also for many types of crimes now more difficult to trace.

[10] Cf. Bartlett (2018) chap. 6.

Chapter 18
A Digital Hangover

In 1964, media theorist Marshall McLuhan noted: "The electric technology is within the gates, and we are numb, deaf, blind, and mute about its encounter with the Gutenberg technology."[1] Today, this problem is even more urgent with the rapid development of digital media. We are witnessing a radical shift of paradigms. For a long time, we have been blind to the consequences of digital intoxication. We have turned a blind eye to the fact that we are being reprogrammed by the new digital life. Slowly, sneakily and unnoticed, tech giants have been able to change our behavior, our emotions, our thoughts, our world views and our relationships with other people. The curse of our times is this blindness and dizziness. It is time to wake up.

In this book, we have attempted to expose the huge challenge of the attention economy which dominates the Information Age of today. The most valuable asset of the tech giants is also our own most valuable asset: our attention. These giants are hard at work taking advantage of that asset. They have developed a digital panopticon, where everyone is constantly being monitored and always distracted. By gathering and processing enormous amounts of data, they draw up incredibly accurate portraits of our inner drives and of our minds. They use the data to control not only mass behavior but also the behavior of individuals, and the aim is to promote

[1] McLuhan (1964) p. 3–7.

F. Stjernfelt, A. M. Lauritzen, *Your Post has been Removed*,
https://doi.org/10.1007/978-3-030-25968-6_18

their own financial interests. The tech giants preach that their real purpose is to assist their users and improve the world. But Silicon Valley is no philanthropic endeavor, but simply raw business. There seems to be still less doubt about that. Recently, more awareness has been raised about the Janus-head of tech giants. On the one hand, the massive surveillance and data harvesting make up the basic material of free, efficient and convenient platforms. But on the other hand, we have the darker side of things; it causes a fatal loss of freedom, privacy and autonomy.

The business models, global character, and clandestine procedures of the tech giants challenge and restrict freedom of expression. In this book, we have argued that this key freedom is under pressure. Tech giants capitalize freedom of expression, because commercial interests get to determine access to information and the rules of public conversation. In other words, the users are losing their fundamental right to freely seek out information and express their opinions freely without interference from a public authority—a status tech giants have misappropriated, given their emerging de facto monopoly. On the platforms, such interference happens both automatically through opaque algorithm systems and manually through vaguely worded terms of service. The giants act as legislator, police, judge and executioner. Today, with social media being accused of spreading disinformation, influencing elections and allowing—if not in fact promoting—violence, the giants have reacted by intensifying internal regulation of their content. Still growing amounts of material are subject to content regulation—material that is likely to be problematic and unpleasant in the eyes of some, but which is at the same time part of the ongoing political debate. The criteria behind content removal are extremely broad, wasting lots of time and labor on over-sensitive complaints about "hate speech", nipples and other completely harmless things, rather than directing forces at criminal content associated with immediate danger. In those cases, the internal regulation borders on censorship and counteracts freedom of speech directly. Over the same years, the giants have managed to undermine the economic value of knowledge and art. They have even used freedom of expression and freedom of information as cloaks for their lucrative business endeavors. The first digital losers are found among traditional media outlets, musicians, writers, filmmakers and other content creators, who either end up deeply dependent on the tech giants or robbed of their intellectual property, or both. Lastly the business model and automated algorithm system of the tech giants have been able to trigger serious disturbances of the public sphere. The digital echo chamber has shown that it leans towards tribalism, in the West represented by a new digital culture war and in third world countries by violent upheavals and even lynchings.

The idea that more artificial intelligence on Facebook as a miracle cure for maladies caused by Facebook itself is absurd. This is akin to saying that the solution to Facebook is even more Facebook. Politicians are currently privatizing the problem by requiring the tech giants themselves to control statements on their platforms, and moreover without a clear definition of exactly how to do it. We suggest an alternative aimed at winning back our digital autonomy. In our view, tech giants ought to be subjected to critical anti-monopoly scrutiny. Some possible models for monopoly regulation are appearing on the horizon. This is no doubt a strong weapon to be used with caution. Therefore, strong voices from the public sphere and civil society must also participate in the protection of free expression on the Internet and change the cynical business models of tech giants. It is important that organizations, news media, universities and tech companies work together to increase public resilience in the face of the new digital challenges. This cooperation must be based on a shared commitment to protect free expression and the right to express, receive and disseminate differing information or views.

Here are some proposals as to what could be done in order to guide the tech giants —with or without their consent— towards the common standards of freedom of expression of modern democracies:

- Commitment to monitoring a significantly more narrow and precisely defined set of violations, policed more efficiently;
- Approximating the terms of service towards enlightened standards, e.g. American legislation and legal practice on freedom of expression, that is, the First Amendment and the legal interpretations thereof, cf. the principle that the limits of freedom of expression are drawn at "incitement to imminent lawless action"— also aligned with the developments of the principles of freedom of expression within international human rights law;
- Better trained and better paid content moderators;
- Making publicly available and transparent all aspects and phases of the content removal process;
- Transparency of decisions made against users;
- Clear and realistic avenues to appeal;
- Alternatives to removal, such as clear indication of controversial content or explicit filtering as an option available to more sensitive users;
- Preserving controversial content could be preserved behind a barrier one has to click through, so no one runs into it spontaneously;
- Flagging should not automatically result in demands for removal, but may instead contain a menu of options such as "mark as controversial", "mark as not suited for children", and the like;[2]
- Sharing earnings with external content providers who help generate advertising activity.

---

[2] Somewhat naively, Gillespie suggests that the circumstances would improve if tech giants were to hire only "women, queer people, or people of color" (p. 202) in the coming decade. In what way gender, sexual orientation or ethnicity would be the solution to all the unrelated problems of censorship remains lost in the dark—along with the question of why the Silicon Valley libertarians should not then add social democrats and conservatives to the mix, not to mention anarchists, Nazis and communists.

Large struggles of interests are involved in the transformation of the public sphere and freedom of expression in the era of tech giants. But freedom of expression should not be determined by conflicting interests alone—but rather by elementary political principles of how democratic societies are organized. The economy of attention online has shown to be subversive to freedom, enlightenment and democracy. The democratic institutions cannot leave the massive problems to the tech giants themselves. Such a cure is likely to make things worse than the disease.

The time has come to use freedom of expression to say no to monopoly powers and to censorship resurfaced. Consider this a call for users, citizens and decision makers to take back empowerment and defend the principles of Enlightenment. Technology does not decide the future. We do.

Bibliography

Books

Bartlett, J. (2018). *The people vs tech: How the internet is killing democracy (and how we save it)*. London: Ebury Press.

Bentham, J (2002). *Rights, representation, and reform: Nonsense upon stilts and other writings on the French Revolution* (P. Schofield, C. Pease-Watkin, and C. Blamires, Eds.). Oxford: Oxford University Press ("Nonsense Upon Stilts" skrevet ca. 1795, først udgivet 1816).

Berger, J. (2013). *Contagious*. New York: Simon & Schuster.

Cassin, B. (2018). *Google me – One-click democracy*. New York: Fordham (Org. French 2007).

Davenport, T. H., & Beck, J. C. (2001). *The attention economy: Understanding the new currency of business*. Boston: Harvard Business School Press.

Ferguson, N. (2017). *The square and the tower. Networks, hierarchies and the struggle for global power*. London: Allen Lane.

Foer, F. (2017). *World without mind*. London: Vintage Publishing.

Galloway, S. (2017). *The four. The hidden DNA of Amazon, Apple, Facebook and Google*. London: Bentam Press.

Garapon, A., & Lassègue, J. (2018). *Justice digitale. Révolution graphique et rupture anthropologique*. Paris: Presses universitaires de France.

Gillespie, T. (2018). *Custodians of the internet: Platforms, content moderation, and the hidden decisions that shape social media*. New Haven, CT: Yale Univrsity Press.

Girard, R. (1978). *Des choses cachées depuis la fondation du monde*. Paris: Grasset.

F. Stjernfelt, A. M. Lauritzen, *Your Post has been Removed*,
https://doi.org/10.1007/978-3-030-25968-6

Girard, R. (1982). *Le bouc émissaire*. Paris: Grasset.

Hamerton-Kelly, R. (2007). *Politics and apocalypse*. East Lansing: MSU Press.

Han, B.-C. (2017). *Psycho-politics – Neoliberalism and new technologies of power*. London: Verso.

Hansen, P. G., & Hendricks, V. (2011). *Oplysningens blinde vinkler: En åndselitær kritik af informationssamfundet*. Copenhagen: Samfundslitteratur.

Hendricks, V. (2016). *Spræng boblen. Sådan bevarer du fornuften i en ufornuftig verden*. Copenhagen: Gyldendal.

Hendricks, V., & Vestergaard, M. (2017). *Fake News.* Copenhagen: Gyldendal.

Israel, J. (2001). *Radical enlightenment. Philosophy and the making of modernity, 1650–1750*. New York: Oxford University Press.

James, W. (1890). The principles of psychology. Chapter 11: Attention. In: C. D. Green (Ed.), *Classics in the history of psychology*, Last visited 08-05-18. http://psychclassics.yorku.ca/James/Principles/prin11.htm

Kant, I. (2017). *Oplysning, historie og fremskridt*. Aarhus: Forlaget Slagmark.

Kirkpatrick, D. (2010). *The Facebook effect. The real inside story of Mark Zuckerberg and the World's fastest-growing company*. London: Virgin Books.

Lanier, J. (2018). *Ten arguments for deleting your social media accounts right now*. London: The Bodley Head.

Lynch, M. P. (2016). *The internet of us*. New York: Liveright Publishing Corporation.

Martínez, A. G. (2016). *Chaos Monkeys: Mayhem and Mania inside the Silicon Valley Money Machine*. London: Ebury Press.

Mauss, M. *Essai sur le don. Forme et raison de l'échange dans les sociétés archaïques* (2007, org. 1925) Paris: Presses universitaires de France.

Mchangama, J., & Stjernfelt, F. (2016) MEN – Ytringsfrihedens historie i Danmark. Copenhagen: Gyldendal.

McLuhan, M. (1964). *Understanding Media – The extensions of man*. London & New York: Routledge.

Mill, J. S. (2011). *On liberty*. Canada: Batoche Books (org. 1859).

Moore, M. (2018). *Democracy hacked: Political turmoil and information warfare in the digital age*. London: One World.

Nagle, A. (2017). *Kill all normies – Online culture wars from 4chan and Tumblr to Trump and the Alt-right.* Hants, UK: John Hunt Publishing.

Negroponte, N. (1996). *Being digital*. New York: Random House.

Noble, S. U. (2018). *Algorithms of oppression: How search engines reinforce racism*. New York: University Press.

Nørretranders, T. (1997). *Stedet der ikke er – fremtidens nærvær, netværk og internet*. Copenhagen: Aschehough.

O'Neil, C. (2016). *Weapons of math destruction: How big data increases inequality and threatens democracy*. New York: Broadway Books.

Pariser, E. (2011). *The filter bubble*. New York: Penguin Books.

Pedersen, D. B., Collin, F., & Stjernfelt, F. (Eds.). (2018). *Kampen om mennesket*. Forskellige menneskebilleder og deres grænsestrid. Copenhagen: Reitzel.

Pedersen, K. K. (2016). *Phono Sapiens – Det langsomme pattedyr på speed*. Copenhagen: Loopland Press.

Postman, N. (1989). *Fagre nye TV-verden. Oversat af Tatjana Andreassen*. Copenhagen: Hekla.

Sharkey, W. W.. (2008). *The theory of natural monopoly* (2008, org. 1982). Cambridge: Cambridge University press.

Simon, H. A. (1971). Designing organisations for an information-rich world. In M. Greenberger (Ed.), *Computers, communications, and the public interest*. Baltimore: John Hopkins Press.

Stjernfelt, F. (2014). *Natural propositions: The actuality of Peirce's Doctrine of Dicisigns*. Boston: Docent Press.

Stjernfelt, F. (2017). *Syv myter om Martin Luther*. Copenhagen: Gyldendal.

Strossen, N. (2018). *HATE: Why we should resist it with free speech, not censorship*. New York: Oxford University Press.

Sunstein, C. R. (2009). *Going to extremes: How like minds unite and divide*. Oxford: Oxford University Press.

Taplin, J. (2017). *Move fast and break things*. London: Macmillan.

Thiel, P. (with B. Masters). (2014). *Zero to one: Notes on startups, or how to build the future*. London: Virgin Books.

Wu, T. (2018). *The curse of bigness: Antitrust in the New Gilded Age*. New York: Columbia Global Reports.

Zuboff, S. (2019). *The age of surveillance capitalism – The fight for a human future at the new frontier of power*. New York: Public Affairs.

Articles, Reports

Ahmed, S. Google apologizes for results of 'Michelle Obama' image search *CNN.* 11-25-09.

Alliance for Securing Democracy. Alliance for Securing Democracy Launches New Tool to Analyze Russian Interference Operations. *Alliance for Securing Democracy*. 12-06-18.

Alliance for Securing Democracy. Hamilton 68. *Alliance for Securing Democracy*. Last visited 07-30-18: http://dashboard.securingdemocracy.org.

Amnesty International. FN's verdenserklæring om menneskerettighederne (1948). *Amnesty International.* Last visited 07-30-18: https://amnesty.dk/om-amnesty/fns-verdenserklaering-om-menneskerettigheder.

Amnesty International. Myanmar: New evidence reveals Rohingya armed group massacred scores in Rakhine State. *Amnesty International.* 05-22-18.

Ananny, M. The partnership press: Lessons for platform-publisher collaborations as Facebook and news outlets team to fight misinformation. *The Tow Center for Digital Journalism.* 04-04-18.

Andersson, M. Når Facebook dræber samfundsdebatten. *Berlingske.* 07-25-18.

Angwin, J., & Grassegger, H. Facebook's secret censorship rules protect white men from hate speech but not black children. *Salon* (originally appeared on ProPublica). 06-28-17.

Angwin, J., & Tobin, A. Fair housing groups Sue Facebook for allowing discrimination in housing ads. *ProPublica.* 03-27-17.

Angwin, J. & Tobin, M. & Varner, M. Facebook (still) Letting Housing Advertisers Exclude Users by Race. *ProPublica.* 11-21-17.

Ariely, D. Apple should use the Iphone to stop distraction us. *Wired.* 04-17-18.

Associated Press. Facebook expands gender options: transgender activists hail 'big advance'. *The Guardian.* 02-14-14.

Associated Press. It's Rubens vs. Facebook in Fight over Artistic Nudity *New York Times.* 07-28-18.

Associated Press. More than 1000 Google workers protest censored China search. *Washington Post.* 08-17-18.

Barlow, J. P. A declaration of the independence of cyberspace. *Electronic Frontier Foundation*. 02-08-96.

BBC. Facebook ditches fake news warning flag. *BBC News.* 12-21-17.

BBC. Russia trolls 'spreading vaccination misinformation' to create discord. *BBC News*. 08-24-18.

Beers, B. How does Twitter Make Money? *Investopedia.* 04-25-18.

Berger, J., & Milkman, K. L. (2012). What Makes Online Content Viral? *Journal of Marketing Research, 49*, s. 192–s. 205.

Bloomberg Editorial Board. Don't Break Up Facebook. *Bloomberg Opinion*. 07-16-18.

Bloomberg Government. Transcript of Zuckerberg's appearance before House committee. *The Washington Post*. 04-11-18.

Blumenthal, P. Facebook and Google's surveillance capitalism model is In trouble. *Huffington Post.* 01-27-18.

Bokhari, A. (upload) The good censor – GOOGLE LEAK. Last visited 12-18-18: https://www.scribd.com/document/390521673/The-Good-Censor-GOOGLE-LEAK#from_embed.

Bolyard, P. 96 percent of Google search results for 'Trump' news are from liberal media outlets. *PJ Media*. 08-25-18.

Boström, H. Hatet mot Google. *GP*. 03-19-18.

Boyd, D. Streams of content, limited attention: The flow of information through social media. *Conference: Web 2.0 Expo.* 11-17-09.

Brandom, R. The anti-monopoly case against Google. *The Verge*. 09-05-17.

Brandom, R. Facebook took down a post by the Anne Frank Center for showing nude Holocaust victims. *The Verge*. 08-29-18.

Breitenbach, D. Facebook apologizes for censoring prehistoric figurine 'Venus of Willendorf'. *dw.com*. 03-01-18.

Brin, S., & Page, L. *The anatomy of large-scale hypertextual web search engine*. Last visited 04-26-18: http://infolab.stanford.edu/~backrub/google.html.

Cadwalladr, C. Google, democracy and the truth about internet search. *The Guardian*. 12-04-16.

Cadwalladr, C. Google is not 'just' a platform. It frames, shapes and distorts how we see the world. *The Guardian*. 12-11-16.

Cave, D. Australia Passes Law to Punish Social Media Companies for Violent Posts. *New York Times.* 04-03-19.

CDT. The Santa Clara Principles on Transparency and Accountability in Content Moderation. *Center for Democracy & Technology (CDT).* https://cdt.org/files/2018/05/Santa_Clara_Principles.pdf

CEMB. Facebook: stop censoring Arab Ex-Muslims and Freethinkers NOW. *Council of Ex-Muslims of Britain (CEMB)*. 02-20-16.

Cerf, V., Berners-Lee, T. m.fl. Open letter "Article 13 of the EU Copyright Directive Threatens the Internet". *Electronic Frontier Foundation.*

Chen, A. The laborers who keep dickpics and beheadings out of your Facebook feed *Wired*. 10-23-13.

Clark, N. (1996). Home alone with technology: An interview with Neil Postman. *Iowa Journal of Cultural Studies*, 151–159.

Cleland, S. Grand theft auto-mated! Online Ad-Economics Fuel Piracy &amp: SOPA Opposition. *Forbes.* 11-30-11.

Coldewey, D. UPDATE: Snopes quits and AP in talks over Facebook's factchecking partnership. *TechCrunch*. 02-01-19.

Conger, K., & Fraenkel, S. Dozens at Facebook unite to challenge its 'intolerant' liberal culture *New York Times*. 08-28-18.

Constine, J. Facebook spares humans by fighting offensive photos with AI. *TechCrunch*. 05-31-16.

Constine, J. Facebook and Instagram launch US political ad labeling and archive *TechChrunch.* 05-24-18.

Constine, J. Facebook now deletes posts that financially endanger/trick people *TechChrunch.* 08-09-18.

Corbyn, Z. Facebook experiment boosts US voter turnout: Mass social-network study shows that influence of close friends raises participation *Nature*. 09-12-12.

Dance, G., Confessore, N., & LaForgia, M. Facebook gave device makers deep access to data on users and friends. *New York Times*. 06-03-18.

DareDisrupt. Fem teknologiske temaer (Five Technological Themes). Last visited 07-30-18: http://www.kl.dk/ImageVaultFiles/id_85157/cf_202/Kommunernes_Teknologiske_Fremtid_-fuld_version-.pdf

David, J. E. Angela Merkel caught on hot mic griping to Facebook CEO over anti-immigrant posts *CNBC*. 09-27-15.

Dean, B. Google's 200 Ranking Factors: The Complete List (2018) *Backlinko*. 05-16-18.

Dewey, C. Mark Zuckerberg's Facebook censors images of the Prophet Mohamed in Turkey – two weeks after he declared 'Je Suis Charlie'. *Independent*. 01-28-15.

Döpfner, M. Why we fear Google. *Frankfurter Allgemeine*. 04-17-14.

Dreyfuss, E. Facebook's fight against fake news keeps rising questions *Wired.* 07-20-18.

Dreyfuss, E., & Lapowsky, I. Facebook is changing news feed (again) to stop fake news. *Wired.* 04-10-19.

Dwoskin, E. Facebook is the Trustworthiness of its Users on a Scale from Zero to 1. *Washington Post.* 08-21-18.

Dwoskin, E. & Romm, T. Facebook says it has uncovered a coordinated disinformation operation ahead of the 2018 midterm elections *Washington Post*. 07-31-18.

Epstein, R. The new censorship. *US News*. 06-22-16.

European Commission, Justice and Consumers, Press Release. European Commission and IT Companies announce Code of Conduct on illegal online hate speech. 05-31-16.

Facebook. Community Standards. Last visited 07-30-18: https://www.facebook.com/communitystandards/

Facebook. Community standards enforcement preliminary report. Last visited 07-30-18: https://transparency.facebook.com/community-standards-enforcement.

Facebook. *Hard questions: Where do we draw the line on free expression?* 08-09-18. Last visited 10-08-18: https://newsroom.fb.com/news/2018/08/hard-questions-free-expression/

Facebook. Elliot Schrage on Definers. *Facebook Newsroom*. 11-21-18.

Feldman, B. The only pressure Facebook understands comes from its megaplatform rivals *New York Magazine.* 08-06-18.

Fox-Brewster, T. Creepy or cool? Twitter is tracking where you've been, what you like and is telling advertisers. *Forbes*. 05-18-17.

Freedom. Forum Institute Incitement to Imminent Lawless Action. 05-12-08.

French, D. A better way to Ban Alex Jones. "Hate speech" is extraordinarily vague and subjective. Libel and slander are not. *New York Times.* 08-07-18.

Frenkel, S. The Biggest Spender of Political Ads on Facebook? President Trump. *New York Times.* 07-17-18.

Frenkel, S., Confessore, N., Kang, C., Rosenberg, M., & Nicas, J. Delay, deny and deflect: How Facebook's leader fought through crisis. *New York Times.* 11-14-18.

Gardel, U. Når Facebook censurerer. *Journalisten.* 01-11-18.

Garrahan, M. Google and Facebook dominance forecast to rise. *Financial Times*. 12-04-17.

Github. BuzzFeedNews/2017-12-fake-news-top-50 *Github*. Last visited 07-30-18: https://github.com/BuzzFeedNews/2017-12-fake-news-top-50/blob/master/data/sites_2017.csv.

Guldager, D. H. Du tjekker den 150 gange i døgnet – sådan slipper du af med afhængighed. *TV2 Nyheder.* 01-11-18.

Google. Personalized search for everyone. *Google Blog.* 12-04-09

Guess, A., Nyhan, B., & Reifler, J. Selective Exposure to Misinformation: Evidence from the consumption of fake news during the 2016 U.S. presidential campaign. 01-09-18. Last visited 07-30-18: https://www.dartmouth.edu/~nyhan/fake-news-2016.pdf.

Hansen, E. Google pulls anti-Scientology links. *Cnet*. 04-22-02.

Heer, J. (2017). Facebook's Promise of Community is a Lie. *The New Republic.* 10-07-17.

Hern, A. Google plans to 'de-rank' Russia Today and Sputnik to combat misinformation. *The Guardian*. 11-21-17.

Hern, A. Facebook protects far-right activists even after rule breaches. *The Guardian*. 07-17-18.

Heyman, S. Google books: A complex and controversial Experiment. *New York Times.* 10-28-15.

Huffington Post. 'Peace on Facebook' Tracks How Tech Promotes Peace. *Huffington Post.* 03-18-10

Hughes, C. It's time to break up Facebook. *New York Times.* 05-09-19.

Ingram, M. Here's why Facebook removing that Vietnam War photo is so important. *Fortune*. 09-09-16.

Ingram, D. Facebook begins 'fact-checking' photos and videos. *Reuters*. 03-29-18.

Jackson, J. Google: 129 million different books have been published. *PC World*. 08-06-10.

Jenkins, H. W. Jr. The weekend interview with Eric Schmidt: Google and the search for the future. *The Wall Street Journal.* 08-14-10.

Jones, J. Facebook banned Holbein's hand – but it isn't even art's sauciest. *The Guardian*. 08-31-16.

Juhler, S., & Buch, D. Facebook til Øvig: Derfor sletter vi dit nøgenfoto. *TV2 Nyheder*. 06-13-13.

Kang, C., & Conger, K. Twitter suspends Alex Jones and Infowars for seven days. *New York Times.* 08-14-18.

Kantrowitz, A. Google allowed advertisers to target people searching racist phrases. *BuzzFeed.* 09-15-17.

Karpal, A. Palantir worked with Cambridge Analytica on the Facebook data it acquired, whistleblower alleges *CNBC.com.* 03-27-18.

Kastrenakes, J. Facebook will remove the Trending topics section next week. *The Verge.* 06-01-18.

Kaye, D. Report of the Special Rapporteur on the promotion and protection of the right to freedom of opinion and expression *UN Human Rights Council*. 04-06-18.

Khan, L. The New Brandeis Movement: America's Antimonopoly Debate. *Journal of European Competition Law & Practice*, *9*,(3), s. 131–132. 03-01-18. Last visited 06-25-18: https://doi.org/10.1093/jeclap/lpy020

Kirkpatrick, M. Facebook Exec: All media will be personalized in 3 to 5 Years. *ReadWriteWeb*. 09-29-10.

Kjær, B. Facebook strammer censur-skruen over for Peter Øvig. *Politiken*. 10-03-16.

Kosinski, M., Stillwell, D., & Graepel, T. Private traits and attributes are predictable from digital records of human behavior. *PNAS.* 04-09-13.

Lafrance, A. The power of personalization. *Nieman Reports.* 10-18-17.

Lanchester, J. Googled: The end of the world as we know it by Ken Auletta. *The Guardian.* 02-21-10.

Lapowsky, I. Lawmakers don't grasp the sacred tech law they want to gut. *Wired.* 07-17-18.

Lapowsky, I. Why big tech's fight against infowars is unwinnable. *Wired.* 08-06-18.

Lapowsky, I. & Thompson, N. Facebook's pivot to privacy is missing something crucial. *Wired.* 03-06-19.

Lassen, A. På med sølvpapirshatten – Copyright-monstrene kommer!. *Jyllands-Posten.* 06-20-18.

Ledegaard, F. H., & Pedersen, R. M. Facebook har stemplet 65.000 russere som interesserede i 'landsforræderi'. *DR Udland.* 07-11-18.

Ledegaard, F. H., & Pedersen, R. M. Efter DR-afsløringer: Facebook fjerner "islam", men ikke "kristendom" *DR Indland.* 05-22-18.

Lee, N. Facebook publishes its community standards playbook. *Engadget.* 04-24-18.

Legal Information Institute. *First amendment.*

Levin, S. 'They don't care': Facebook factchecking in disarray as journalists push to cut ties. *The Guardian.* 12-13-18.

Lima, C. Facebook backtracks after removing Warren ads calling for Facebook breakup. *Politico.* 03-11-19.

Lomas, N. Palantir confirms a staff link with Cambridge Analytica. *TechCrunch.* 03-28-18.

Mac, R., Warzel, C., & Kantrowitz, A. Top Facebook executive defended data collection in 2016 memo – And warned that Facebook could get people killed. *BuzzFeed.* 03-29-18.

Maheshwari, S. How fake news goes viral: A case study. *New York Times.* 11-20-16.

Maheshwari, S., & Stevenson, A. Google and Facebook face criticism for ads targeting racist sentiments. *New York Times.* 09-15-17.

Manne, G. The illiberal vision of neo-Brandeisian Antitrust. *Truth on the Market.* 04-16-18.

Matsakis, L. Twitter releases new policy on 'Dehumanizing Speech'. *Wired.* 09-25-18.

Matsakis, L. Facebook will crack down on anti-vaccine content. *Wired.* 03-07-19.

McGirt, E. Hacker. Dropout. CEO. *Fast Company.* 01-05-07.

Medvedovsky, K. Hipster Antitrust – A brief fling or something more? *Competition Policy International.* 04-17-18.

Melnick, O. Facebook's 'hate speech' double standard. *WND*. 01-11-16.

Mitchell, A., Grieco, E., & Sumida, N. Americans favour protecting information freedoms over government steps to restrict false news online. *Pew Research Center*. 04-19-18

Moser, B. How YouTube became the worldwide leader in white supremacy. When Google promises to "curb" extremism on its lucrative video platform, it means nothing more than keeping advertisers happy *New Republic*. 08-21-17.

Moses, L. How The New York Times' Mark Thompson became the latest thorn in Facebook's side. *DigiDay*. 07-11-18

Mullins, B. & Nicas, J. Paying professors: Inside Google's Academic Influence Campaign. *The Wall Street Journal*. 07-14-17.

Murphy, P. Blasphemy law comes to Facebook. *American Thinker*. 06-27-13.

Müller, R. FDP-Politiker klagen gegen Netzwerkdurchsetzungsgesetz. *Frankfurter Allgemeine*. 06-10-18.

Nicas, J. Google uses its search engine to hawk its products *Wall Street Journal*. 01-19-17.

Nunez, M. Former Facebook workers: We routinely suppressed conservative news. *Gizmodo*. 05-09-16.

Ohlheiser, A. & Horton, A. A short investigation into Trump's claims of 'RIGGED' Google results against him *Washington Post*. 08-28-18.

Owen, L. H. News in a disintegrating reality: Tow's Jonathan Albright on what to do as things crash around us. *NiemanLab*. 02-28-18.

Pariser, E. Welcome to the Brave New World of Persuasion Profiling. *Wired*. 04-26-11.

Pedersen, J. Kendt DR-vært censureret af Facebook: Se opslaget, der fik ham blokeret. *BT*. 01-28-18.

Perez, S. Facebook, Microsoft, Twitter and YouTube collaborate to remove 'terrorist content' from their services *TechCrunch*. 12-06-16.

Phys Org. Facebook shut 583 million fake accounts. *Phys Org*. 05-15-18.

Pilkington, E. Google's book project faces growing opposition. *The Guardian*. 08-19-09.

Pinterest. *Terms of service*. Last visited 06-25-18: https://policy.pinterest.com/en/terms-of-service

Plougsgaard, H. Facebook samler også data fra personer, der ikke bruger Facebook. *Jyllands-Posten*. 04-11-18.

Pridham, D. How Google tries to buy government. *Forbes*. 07-19-17.

Read, M. Does even Mark Zuckerberg know what Facebook is? *New York Magazine.* 08-01-17.

Reporters-Without-Borders. Russian bill is copy-and-paste of Germany's hate speech law. *Reporters-Without-Borders.* 07-19-17.

Reuters. Digital News Report 2018. *Reuters Institute for the Study of Journalism*, Oxford University. Last visited 07-30-18: http://www.digitalnewsreport.org.

Ritzau Peter Øvig. Apple-censur er grotesk. *Ekstra Bladet*. 11-01-12.

Roberts, S. T. Commercial content moderation: Digital laborers' dirty work. *Scholarship@Western Media Studies Publications.* 2016.

Rogers, J. Obama 2012 campaign 'sucked' data from Facebook, former official says. *Fox News.* 03-20-18.

Romm, T. U.K. unveils sweeping plans to penalize Facebook and Google for harmful online content. *Washington Post.* 04-07-19.

Samples, J. Censorship comes to Google. *Cato Liberty*. 11-22-17.

Satariano, A., & Isaac, M. Facebook used people's data to favor certain partners and punish rivals, Documents Show. *New York Times.* 12-05-18.

Shaban, H., Timberg, C., & Stanley-Becker, I. YouTube, Apple, Facebook and Spotify escalate enforcement against Alex Jones *Washington Post.* 08-06-18.

Shapiro, B. What Tech Giants' Alex Jones Ban Got Wrong *National Review.* 08-07-18.

Sherman, E. Ex-IDF Intel Chief: 'State of Facebook' Greatest Mideast Threat to Israel. *The Algemeiner*. 01-31-16.

Shullenberger, G. Mimesis, Violence, and Facebook Part 1: Peter Thiel's French Connection. *The Society Pages.* 08-02-16.

Shullenberger, G. Mimesis and Facebook Part 2: Harnessing violence. *The Society Pages.* 08-09-16.

Silverman, C. This analysis shows how viral fake election news Stories outperformed real news on Facebook. *BuzzFeed*. 11-16-16.

Silverman, C. I helped popularize the term "Fake News" and now I Cringe every time I hear it. *Buzzfeed News.* 12-31-17.

Silverman, C., Lytvynenko, J., & Pham S. These are 50 of Fake News Hits on Facebook in 2017. *BuzzFeed.* 12-28-17.

Simonite, T. The wired guide to artificial intelligence *Wired.* 02-01-18.

Simons, D. J., & Chabris, C. F. Gorillas in our midst: sustained inattention blindness for dynamic events. *Perception*, *28*. 05-09-99.

Soave, R. Banning Alex Jones isn't about free speech – It's about the Incoherence of 'Hate Speech' *Reason.* 08-07-18.

Solon, O. In firing human editors, Facebook has lost the fight against fake news *The Guardian.* 08-29-16.

Solon, O. Ex-Facebook president Sean Parker: Site made to exploit human 'vulnerability'. *The Guardian. 11*-09-17.

Solon, O. & Levin, S. How Google's search algorithm spreads false information with a rightwing bias. *The Guardian*. 12-16-16.

Soros, G. Only the EU can break Facebook and Google's dominance. *The Guardian*. 02-15-18.

Stack, L. Facebook announces new polity to ban white nationalist content. *New York Times*. 03-27-19.

Statcounter. Search engine market share. Worldwide – May 2017 – May 2018. *Statcounter*. Last visited 06-25-18: http://gs.statcounter.com/search-engine-market-share

Statcounter Social media stats worldwide – May 2017 – May 2018. *Statcounter*. Last visited 06-*25-18:* http://gs.statcounter.com/social-media-stats

Statista. Average number of Facebook friends of users in the United States in 2016. *Statista*. Last visited 06-25-18: https://www.statista.com/statistics/398532/us-facebook-user-network-size/

Statt, N. Leaked Google research shows company grappling with censorship and free speech. *The Verge*. 10-10-18.

Sterling, G. Another court affirms Google's first amendment control of search results. *Search Engine Land*. 11-17-14.

Stjernfelt, F. Systematisk afsløring af systematisk misinformation. *Weekendavisen. 02*-23-18.

Stjernfelt, F. Monopolkontrol af techgiganterne? *Weekendavisen*. 03-30-18.

Swisher, K. Zuckerberg: The recode interview. *Recode*. 07-18-18.

Taplin, J. Is it time to break up Google?. *New York Times*. 04-22-17

Taplin, J. Why is Google spending record sums on lobbying Washington? *The Guardian*. 07-30-17.

Taub, A. & Fisher, M. Where countries are Tinderboxes and Facebook is a match. *New York Times*. 04-21-18.

Thiel, P. "The Straussian Moment" in Hamerton-Kelly (2007), pp. 189–218.

Thiel, P. The education of a Libertarian. *Cato Unbound*. 04-13-09.

Thompson, C. Your outboard brain knows all. *Wired*. 08-25-07.

Thompson, N. Our Minds have been Hijacked by Our Phones. Tristan Harris Wants to Rescue Them. *Wired*. 07-06-17.

Tiku, N. Get ready for the next big privacy backlash against Facebook. *Wired*. 05-21-17.

Tobin, A., & Varner, M., & Angwin, J. Facebook's uneven enforcement of hate speech rules allows vile posts to stay up. *ProPublica*. 12-28-17.

Topolsky, J. Hello again. *Joshua Topolsky blog*. 07-11-15.

Tsukayama, H. Facebook's Onavo app booted from Apple's App Store over privacy. *Washington Post*. 08-23-18.

Tufekci, Z. Facebook's Surveillance Machine. *New York Times*. 03-19-18

Tufekci, Z. YouTube, the Great Radicalizer. *New York Times*. 03-10-18.

Tufekci, Z. It's the (Democracy-Poising) golden age of free speech. *Wired*. 01-16-18.

Tumblr. *Community guidelines*. Modified 12-17-18. Last visited 12-20-18: https://www.tumblr.com/policy/en/community.

Twitter. *Creating new policies together*. 09-25-18. Last visited 18-12-2018: https://blog.twitter.com/official/en_us/topics/company/2018/Creating-new-policies-together.html.

Vega, N. Internet rights group slams Google and GoDaddy's 'dangerous' decision to ban a neo-Nazi site. *nordic.businessinsider.com*. 08-18-17.

Villarreal, K. Facebook-opdateringer med selvmordstanker bliver nærlæst af Facebook. *DR Indland*. 02-26-15.

Vincent, J. Facebook removes Alex Jones pages, citing repeated hate speech violations. *The Verge*. 08-06-18.

Vogel, K. P. Google critic ousted from think tank funded by the tech giant. *New York Times*. 08-30-17.

Wallaroo Media. Facebooks news feed algorithm history. *Wallaroo Media*. 06-04-18.

Warner, M. R. Potential policy proposals for regulation of social media and technology firms. Whitepaper, *Axios*. 07-30-18.

Wemple, E. Google gives Trump a look at reality. Trump doesn't like it. *Washington Post*. 08-28-18.

Westberg, A., & Englund, R. Låt inte Facebook vinna valet år Jimmie Åkesson. *Expressen*. 03-22-18.

Wieduwilt, H. Löschgesetz verlangt Facebook-Nutzern viel ab. *Frankfurter Allgemeine*. 12-30-17.

Wikipedia. Censorship by Google" *Wikipedia*. Last visited 07-30-18: https://en.wikipedia.org/wiki/Censorship_by_Google.

Wilson, E. It's time to break up Facebook. *Politico*. 03-21-18.

Wong, J. C. Facebook expects FTC fine up to $5bn in privacy investigation. *Guardian*. 04-24-19.

Worth, K. As Brazil Confronts Zika, Vaccine Rumors Shape Perceptions. *Public Broadcasting Service*. 02-16-16.

Wu, T. Attention Brokers. *NYU Law*. 10-10-15.

Ystads Allehanda's leder. Rensa nätet försiktigt. *Ystads Allehanda*. 03-12-18.

Yuan, L, & Wakabayashi D. Google, seeking a return to China, is said to be building a censored search engine. *New York Times*. 08-01-18.

Zornick, G. Elizabeth Warren's 'Big Fight' Against Monopolies. *The Nation*. 02-15-18.

Zuckerberg, M. A Blueprint for Content Governance and Enforcement. *Facebook notes*. 11-15-18.

Zuckerberg, M. A privacy-focused vision for social networking. *Facebook*. 03-06-19.

Zuckerberg, M. Mark Zuckerberg: The internet needs new rules. Let's start in these four areas. *Washington Post*. 03-30-19.

TV, Video

Channel4. Data, democracy and dirty tricks. *Channel4*. 03-19-18. Last visited 06-25-18: https://www.channel4.com/news/data-democracy-and-dirty-tricks-cambridge-analytica-uncovered-investigation-expose

Lessig, L. Laws that choke creativity. *TEDtalk 2007*. Last visited 06-25-18: https://www.ted.com/talks/larry_lessig_says_the_law_is_strangling_creativity

Riesewieck, M., & Bloch, H. (2018). *The Cleaners*.

Congressional hearings, Mark Zuckerberg, 10. & 04-11-18. Last visited 06-25-18: https://www.judiciary.senate.gov/meetings/facebook-social-media-privacy-and-the-use-and-abuse-of-data

Congressional hearing, Christopher Wylie et al., 05-16-18. Last visited 06-25-18: https://www.c-span.org/video/?445621-1/cambridge-analytica-whistleblower-christopher-wylie-testifies-data-privacy

Hearing EU parliament, Mark Zuckerberg, 05-21-18. Last visited 06-25-18: https://www.youtube.com/watch?v=A3_iZJFH9nM

Index

F. Stjernfelt, A. M. Lauritzen, *Your Post has been Removed*,
https://doi.org/10.1007/978-3-030-25968-6

www.ingramcontent.com/pod-product-compliance
Lightning Source LLC
LaVergne TN
LVHW080032210926
848481LV00011B/3169